CONSUMER BEHAVIOUR

Challenges of New Millennium Markets

CONSUMER BEHAVIOUR

Challenges of New Millennium Markets

VIPIN MATHUR

2008

CYBER TECH PUBLICATIONS

4264/3, Ansari Road, Daryaganj, New Delhi-110002 (India)
Ph.: 011-23244078. Fax: 011-23280028
E-Mail: cyberpublicationsdelhi@yahoo.com

Consumer Behaviour — Challenges of New Millennium Markets

First Edition 2008

Published by G.S. Rawat
For Cyber Tech Publications
4264/3, Ansari Road, Daryaganj, New Delhi - 110 002
E-mail : cyberpublicationsdelhi@yahoo.com
Phone : 011-23244078,
Fax : 011-23280028

PREFACE

The Increasing competition in the global markets will make the existence of the companies difficult as the consumers enjoy as the kingpin of their business. The new millennium will be the most challenging era for most of the companies delivering goods and services to the consumers directly through their network. The increasing competition in the market towards the customer value, satisfaction, and the delight chain. Hence, it becomes the prime importance to the company to analyse the consumer behaviour in right perspective and develop customer care and relationship with a view to build the long term relationship in the business. The customers are the pillars in the contemporary business environment to build and retain the brands in the market apart from the corporate strategies. In the developing economies and near monopoly markets the sellers do not pay adequate attention towards the buyers and make them in a disadvantageous position. On the contrary in the buyers markets the customers can choose the goods and services.

Marketing as a field of study is generally categorized as being part of the broader field of business administration. However, marketing also involves considerations that extend beyond these boundaries. Marketing decisions are shaped by and influence the external environments of the firm. The student of marketing must develop a facility for integrating useful contributions from many disciplines. He must also understand the functional purpose of each component in a marketing action system.

Last but not the least my publishers who appreciated this book and brought this work out in a record time.

—Editor

CONTENTS

CHAPTER 1

CONSUMER AWARENESS

Everybody is a consumer. When we pay a price for a commodity or service and use it, we become consumers. Sometimes the shopkeeper cheats us as he or she gives poor quality goods, or charges more for a commodity or service. What should we do in such cases? In this chapter, we will study about how consumers are exploited, and what the government is doing to protect their interests.

Modern age is the age of consumerism. In the modern capitalistic forms of economic system, the sovereignty of consumers prevail. With the change in preferences of the people day by day, variety of sovereignty of consumers prevail. With the change in preferences of the people day by day, variety of goods are flowing in the markets. Factors of production are getting diverted towards the commodities whose demand has been increasing. Selling costs are increasing tremendously. Through advertisements people came to know the new products availability. Hence it is obvious that modern age is the age dominated by consumers.

Meaning of Consumer Awareness

The knowledge of the consumers rights and protection of consumers is called consumer awareness. Modern age is the age of consumers. Variety of products are being produced according to the preferences of the consumers. In modern capitalistic form of economic system, markets are flooded not only with domestic goods but also with foreign commodities and consumer sovereignty has been on the top. Selling costs to attract the attentions of the consumers have been increasing. In other words, a lot of money has been spent by the producers or marketing companies on advertisements.

Consumer Exploitation

We also have a number of services including insurance, transport, electricity, finance and banking. Due to the expansion of business activities in an economy, we have a variety of goods available in the market. Consumers being not united remain indifferent about their rights and duties. Consequently, at every step, they are exploited by business community or middleman. Our demand for goods and services is influenced by the advertisements in television. Newspapers and magazines. We also find display of similar items by different companies, which makes it difficult for us to decide about a correct choice. We all know that companies spend a considerable amount on advertisements alone to attract consumers and feed information that they want us to know, but not the information that we as consumers need about the products. When we, as consumers. Do not have sufficient information about the products. We normally get exploited and are sometimes even harassed by the business community.

Common ways by which consumers are exploited by manufacturers and traders are:

Underweight ad under-measurements: The goods being sold in the market are sometimes not measured or weighted correctly.

Sub-standard Quality. The goods sold are sometimes of sub-standard quality. Selling of medicines beyond their expiry dates and supply of deficient or detective home appliances are generally the regular grievances of consumers.

High Prices. Very often the traders charge a price higher than the prescribed retail price. Duplicate Articles: In the name of genuine parts or goods, fake or duplicate items are being sold to the consumer. Adulteration and Impurity: in costly edible items, such as oil, ghee and spices. Adulteration is made in order to earn higher profits. This causes heavy loss to the customers; get spoiled suffer from monetary loss as well as get spoiled their health.

Lack of Safety Devices: Electronic goods, electrical devices or other appliances produced locally, lack the required inbuilt safeguards. This causes accidents to the consumers.

Artificial Scarcity; in order to amass illegitimate profit. Businessmen create artificial scarcity by hoarding. They sell it at the later stage at higher prices.

False or Incomplete information. Sellers easily mislead consumers by giving wrong information about a product, its price, quality, reliability, life cycle, expiry date, durability, its effect on health, environment, safety and security, maintenance costs involved, and terms and conditions of purchase. Cosmetics, drugs and electronic goods are common examples where consumers face such problems.

Unsatisfactory after-sale Service: Many of the high cost durable items, such as electrical or electronic equipments, home appliances and cars, need adequate after-sale services despite the necessary payments. Rough Behaviour and undue conditions, in matters like PLG gas connection, fixing of a new telephone line, procurement of licensed items, etc., consumers are often harassed and undue conditions are put before them.

The following factors which lead to consumer exploitation:

- The attitude of disintegration among consumers
- Lack of education
- Non-availability of systematic consumer awareness programmes
- Traditional attitude of the consumers
- Poverty
- Inferior complex in consumers
- Lack of adequate information etc.

Limited Information: In a capitalist economy, producers and sellers are free to produce any goods or services in any quantity and there is no regulation on the prices. In such cases, providing full and correct information about the product to consumers is of great importance. In the absence of information about different aspects of the products, namely, price, quality, composition, conditions of use, terms of purchase, etc., the consumers are liable to make a wrong choice and lose money. The consumers are exploited when the goods and services are not available in the required quantity or numbers. Limited supplies are a result, usually, of lower production of goods, as compared with the demand. This gives rise to a tendency of hoarding, and price-escapation. When only one producer or a group of producers controls the production and supply of a product, and is in a position to restrict the availability of supplies, there is a possibility of manipulation in prices and availability. In the production and sale of consumer durables, like houses, medicines and drugs, medical equipments. Automobiles etc., where the producers and suppliers are few, the sellers have an upper hand in fixing the price and their availability.

Law literary: Illiteracy is one of the major drawbacks that lead to exploitation of consumers. The level of consumer consciousness in our country is generally low. The level of literacy directly affects the level of awareness about products and the market.

Awareness of Consumer

The following are the main rights and duties of the consumer. (a) Right to security, to get information, right to go to consumer courts and get compensation.

In India, the concept of consumer protection is not new. References to the protection of consumers' interest against exploitation by trade and industry, underweight and measurement, adulteration and punishment for these offences, could be found in Kautilya's Arthashastra. However, organized and systematic movement to safeguard the interest of consumers is a recent phenomenon. This developed in the late 1980s and early1990s with the growing liberalisation of economy. When the government withed itself from production activities and allowed the private sector to take over, it was felt that there is a greater need to enforce discipline and regulation in the market. The consumers have to be aware not only of the commercial aspects of sale and purchase of goods, but also of the health and security aspects. Food safety has become an important element of consumer awareness these days. In case of food products, the quality depends not only on their nutritional value, but also on safety for human consumption. Contaminated or adulterated food is a major source of human illness and suffering and results in serious loss of nutrition. Ensuring the safety of food is, thus, an important aspect of creating awareness and promoting consumer welfare. This called for a strong legal measure to ensure that the manufacturers and sellers observe uniformity and transparency in prices, stops and quality of their goods.

The government also felt that promoting consumer awareness abut the possible malpractices and providing consumers the tools to combat them is the only effective way to protect the rights of the consumers. Legislations ensuring consumer rights or consumer protection means to protect the consumers against exploitation. To provide justice to consumers against exploitation on the basis of black marketing, adulteration, price discrimination etc., is the main objective of consumer protection programmes. Being influenced by worldwide consumer awareness programmes, Government of India also passed "Consumer Protection Act' in 1986. Under this legislation provisions of advisory board and judicial forums have been made. Consumer Protection councils of centre and state level shave been established. To provide timely justice to consumers National and State Commissions have been established. District Protection Forums' at the district level have been doing yeoman's service in this field. If the value of service or compensation is less than Rs. one lakh, then the complaint I registered with district protection forum. If the value of compensation is between 1 lakh to 10 lakhs; then the complaint is lodged with the State Commission on consumer Protection. If the value of compensation is more than 10 lakh then the complaint goes to National commission.

Consumer can lodge complain on a simple paper without any help of an advocate.

The consumers have the right to be protected against marketing of goods and services, which are hazardous to life and property; Right to be informed; this includes quality, quantity, potency, purity, standard and price of goods.

Assurance of access to variety of goods and services at competitive price. In case of single supplier. The consumer has the right to be assured of satisfactory quality and service at a fair price. Right to be heard; the consumer's interests should receive due consideration at appropriate forums relating to consumer welfare; right to seek redressal seek redressal against unfair trade practices or exploitation of consumers and right to fair settlement of the genuine grievances and right to consumer Education this includes knowledge about goods and issues relating to consumer welfare.

In order to secure the rights, consumers have to fulfil the following duties: (i) While purchasing the goods, consumers should look at the quality of the products as well as on the guarantee of the products and services. Wherever possible, they also have to insist for the warrantee card. They should preferably purchase quality marked products, such as ISI, Agmark, etc. (ii) wherever possible, consumers should ask for cash memo for the items purchased. (iii) consumers should form consumer awareness organizations, which can be given representation in various committees formed by the government and other bodies in matters relating to consumers, (iv) Consumers must make complaint for their genuine grievances. Even if the value of goods involved in their complaint is small, its impact on the society a whole will be large. The consumers can also take the help of consumer organisations in seeking redressal of their grievances.

Consumer Protection Measures

Government of India has been taking strongest efforts to popularize the consumer awareness programmes through seminars, advertisements etc. Topics of consumer awareness in the syllabus of schools, colleges and university classes have been incorporated. Thus we can say that consumer awareness is essential only then the interest of this community can be made secure.

Real protection of consumers can e successfully achieved only with active involvement of consumes. These duties are required to compel the manufacturers and traders to perform in a transparent manner and prevent the exploitation of the consumers. In order to protect the interests of the consumers, the government adopted three strategies; legislative, administrative and technical, Legislative measure includes enactment of the Consumer Protection Act. The government also amended certain provisions in other Acts. Distributing essential commodities through Public distribution System is an administrative measure, while the technical measure consists of standerdisation of the products. These measures are discussed in detail below: (a) Legislation concerning consumer Rights: the government enacted a specific law called the consumer protection Act in 1986. this Ac provides for the establishment of Consumer disputes Redressal Agencies at District, State and National levels for the protection and promotion of consumer interests and to redress their grievances in a speedy, simple and inexpensive manner. These agencies are required to dispose off each complaint within three months. The Act has ed to setting up of separate Departments of Consumer Affairs in central and state governments, which focus exclusively on the rights of the consumers s enshrined in the Act.

Most important feature of the Act is the provision for setting up a three tier system, popularly known as Consumer Courts at national, state and district levels. At the national level, it is called the national consumer Commission, which is the apex court under the Act, and it functions at Delhi. At the state level, it is called the State Consumer Commission. The third tier the most important court, is at the district level and is called district Forum. These courts look into the grievances and complaints of the consumers against the traders and manufacturers and provide the necessary relief and compensation. There are, at present, more than 500 district consumer courts in the country, which have handled so far, nearly 13 lakh cases of consumers grievances. Nearly 77 per cent of these case led in the consumers' courts have been disposed off. Although the consumer disputes rederessal agencies have served, to a large extent, the purpose for which they were created, it was found that the disposal of cases has not been fast enough. The government has, therefore, attempted to strengthen the Act and remove some of its bottlenecks and shortcomings through amendments of the Act carried out in 1991 and 1993.

Public Distribution System: Apart form ensuring food security to the poor as a part of certain administrative measures, public distribution system is also expected to be strengthened, measures to prevent hoarding, black-marketing and over-charging by traders need to be enforced.

Standardisation of products: another important measure taken by the government to protect the consumers from lack of quality and varying standards of goods is creation of institutions for setting up the standards for making and producing various products and enforcing them. In India, this has been achieved through Bureau of Indian Standards and Agmark. While BIS caters to the Industrial and consumer goods, the Agmark is meant for the agricultural products. The Bureau of Indian Standards earlier known as the Indian Standards institution whose headquarters is located in New Delhi. Has the responsibility of laying down the standards for industrial and consumer goods on a scientific basis and certifying the goods that met the standards and the prescribed quality. If we buy as is an assurance of conformity to the specifications. Conformity is ensured by regular surveillance of the licensee's performance by surprise inspection sand testing of samples. Drawn both from the factory and the market. In case of dissatisfaction with the quality of a certified product, a consumer can complain to the nearest regional office of the BIS. Agmark is implemented under the Agricultural Produce Act, 1937, as amended in 1986. This scheme is run by the Directorate of MARKETIGNAND Intelligence in the Ministry of Agriculture. Government of India. Products such as honey, masala and spices, carry such marks.

Just as we have standardization of products in India, at the International level also, an institution called international Organisation for Standardisation (ISO), located in Geneva, serves to provide such a common reference standard. It is a non-governemental organisation established in 1947. ISO's work results in international agreements, which are published as International standard, if you find companies, goods, institutions certified as ISO 6000, ISO 14000 and the like, they indicate specific levels of standards for a particular industry or group of products or institutions.

CHAPTER 2

CONSUMER BEHAVIOUR AND DEVELOPING RELATIONSHIP

The Increasing competition in the global markets will make the existence of the companies difficult as the consumers enjoy as the kingpin of their business. The new millennium will be the most challenging era for most of the companies delivering goods and services to the consumers directly through their network. The increasing competition in the market towards the customer value, satisfaction, and the delight chain. Hence, it becomes the prime importance to the company to analyse the consumer behaviour in right perspective and develop customer care and relationship with a view to build the long term relationship in the business. The customers are the pillars in the contemporary business environment to build and retain the brands in the market apart from the corporate strategies. In the developing economies and near monopoly markets the sellers do not pay adequate attention towards the buyers and make them in a disadvantageous position. On the contrary in the buyers markets the customers can choose the goods and services. This phenomemon can be explained in reference to the Indian markets also. Let us take an examinated by the Ambassador brand of Hindustan Motors for mass market and the Premier Automobiles Ltd. had Flat for the class market. During this period the car market had sellers' dominance and enjoyed near monopolistic conditions. The car market scenario was in transition since mid-eighties after the market intervention of Maruti Udyog Ltd. and has become highly competitive after the introduction of the new economic policy in early 90's. The current market for cars in India is a buyers market, which is very competitive in terms of quality, price, services, comforts and value for the money. It is in fact the buyers market where the consumer exercises his franchise to choose the brand and hence he plays key role in making the brand sustain in the market. The consumer behaviour is therefore a basic diagnostic tool for the companies to assess their entry into the market and sustain therein. It can be strongly stated that in the coming days only customer-centered companies will win. Those companies who can deliver superior value to the targeted customers will emerge as market leaders.

The companies which are actively engaged in marketing function should know that the consumer is sovereign. The consumer behaviour as a rule, is purposeful and gal oriented. The goods and services of the companies are accepted and rejected by the consumers on the basis of the extent they are perceived as relevant to the needs and lifestyle. It is observed that the consumerism responds to the goods and services offered by any company as long as they are backed with enough selling firepower. The National Dairy Development Board of India, the producer of *Dhara Health* brand of edible oils is one of the major corporate players which banks on the consumerism principles for promoting its product. Instances of coronary heart diseases, in urban high-income consumer segment have more occurrences and this trend has been the concern of the urban households to a large extent. Te promotion of the product is designed to build the confidence of the consumers on the single advantage of health, which is the most felt concern of the buyers of edible oils. The health factor after the product promotion motivates the consumer to get associated with the brand and generate demand pull for the product. The company claims the lowest trade margins and retails margins. The prices of the Dhara brand products are rarely changed in a year and this gives the confidence of price stability among the buyers.

The consumer behaviour therefore, can be influenced by understanding the need of the consumer. Consumer sovereignty presents a formidable challenge, but skillful marketing can affect both motivation and behaviour, provided the goods or services offered is signed to meet the basic consumer needs. The company must know that if the consumer benefits of the goods and services offered to him, the economic system is energized. The company must understand that it is the consumer who sets the agenda for the whole process of business, but not the marker. The consumer influence is socially legitimate as long as it is manifested in serving benefits to him.

Process of Consumer Decisions

The consumer makes the decision on buying of any product of the company by problem solving carefully weighing and evaluating the perceived use values and product attributes. This process is commonly defined as Rational decision making while the emotional responses; sensory pleasures or aesthetic influences in the buying decisions deliver the hedonic benefits. The consumer decision process is followed through the stages listed below:

- Need recognition
- Search for information
- Identifying alternatives
- Purchase, and
- Benefits

The consumer adjudges the buying need between the desired and actual situations and collects information about the goods and services, company, brand performance, price, quality, delivery benefits and perceived use values of the proposed product. The consumer also evaluates the alternate brands and sources and accordingly narrows his preference for the product. The purchase is an ultimate act the consumer performs and assesses his satisfaction in reference to his set anticipations. Besides this process of detail check decision making many times the consumers also make the impulse purchase due to the peer group influence, promotional drives physical attraction of the product, price and the related issues. The variables which influence the decision making process of the consumers include availability of alternatives, benefits of customer delight and self-expression, time availability, degree of involvement to engage in the decision making, perceived relevance and personal importance, social acceptance or sanctions, self actualisation, brand loyalty, peer group pressure, inertial etc. Hindustan Lever Ltd. seems to have the real talent for selling the No.1 laundry detergent Surf by showing how humilitating is dirty clothes in social occasions. Largely because of the dirt-fighting claim. Surf rose into prominence and reached 23 percent of the total market share among the detergents. It appeals to the unique sales proposition (USP) of removing the totally absorbed stains and dirt from the cloth from its visible areas without damaging the texture and tampering its life. The success of Surf has not come merely because of advertisements but the consumer behaviour built in favour of the brand helped the product to sustain in the market. The free samples of the improved Surf because branded as Surf Excel helped the product take off fast in the market. This promotional package has generated the benefit oriented decisions making process towards their commitments to buy. The decision making process needs an initiator, influencing agent, decider, buyer and the user. Since the consumers live a complex environment their decision making process is largely influenced by various factors.

Factors Influencing the Consumer Behaviour

Environmental Factors

- Culture
- Social class
- Personal Influence
- Family and Situation

Individual Factors

- Consumer resources
- Motivation and involvement

- Knowledge
- Attitudes
- Personality, lifestyle segments, demography

Psychological Factors

- Information
- Processing
- Learning
- Attitude
- Behaviour change

Culture refers to set of values; ideas, traditions and other facts that help individuals communicate, interpret and evaluate as the members of the society. The sense of identity is gained by the culture in which people inhabit. It is inherited by the people and practiced. The culture includes dress and appearance, food and feeding habits, time and value, relationship, social norms, beliefs and attitudes, thinking and learning process and working habits. The consumerism needs to be developed around these factors considering the significance of the name in decision making. The culture develops socialization and markets bring the social values. The Social class refers to grouping of people who are similar in their behaviour based upon their economicposition and cultural habits. Such groups may be identified as the status groups and the marketing promotional strategies of the company must be worked out accordingly. The personal influence is largely governed by the opinion of the reference groups that are acceptable due to inter-personal relationships. Among various types of reference groups, the highest influence and impact is usually exerted by the primary groups formed by the personas of common interest. These groups are small in strength and may also be defined as focus groups. These groups also disseminate the word of moth and play dominant role in the influencing personal choice of decision making. The excellent example may be cited of the promotional strategy of Hindustan Lever Ltd. for the fairness cream Fair and

Lovely. The commercials of the company are aimed at building the peer group/focus group pressure on the process of individual decision making. This product is targeted for the teenage girls of the age group 16-15 and it is felt that at this age one requires guidance in making decisions and hence the primary group influence plays a dominant role in motivating the buyers. The reference groups can also perform value expressive function to influence the buyer. The psychological association wit such group webs the norms, values, behaviour or response to motivate the member. Such attitude maybe seen among the members of the business or prestigious social clubs who compare their lifestyles with each other and get influenced to make buying decisions. The small reference groups may also be formed within the family for motivating buying behaviour. The motivational drive may be observed in the following actions:

- Product involvement
- Self-enhancement
- Concern for others
- Message intrigue and
- Dissonance reduction.

However, in the family purchase behaviour the role of gatekeeper is more significant. This identity holds the information about the market, product, values, user benefits, price, quality, comparative advantages and other evaluation indicators. Most of the buyers make impulsive buying decisions. And such process is largely influenced by the retail environment. The major factors that influence retail-buying decisions are:

- Music
- Layout and in-store location
- Colours
- Point of purchase displays and information

- Sales personnel
- Influence of time, and
- Need for the product.

Consumer decisions concerning products and brands are heavily influenced by the available and anticipated economic resources. The availability of liquid money and access to the credit pose greater governance economic resources of the consumers, the cognitive resources representing the mental capacity of storing and analyzing various information processing activities also play an important role in decision making process. Capacity is a limited resource. Knowledge plays an important role in developing the consumer behaviour. Comprehensive knowledge about the goods and services, image of the company, promotional packages etc. develops conviction among buyers towards the purchase. The various other factors discussed in the pre-text help the consumer to make decision on the purchase of the identified goods and services. The communication is the source of knowledge that builds the process of decision making among the consumers. The threshold of knowledge should help the consumer in identifying the needs and activating the same. A need must be activated before it is recognized. The changed circumstances may help the consumer in product acquisition, consumption and identifying the generic and derived needs. Apart form the knowledge, the involvement of the consumer in the process of decision making, analyzing the beliefs and attitudes and demographic characteristics would also determine the information search required for appropriate decision making.

The identification of the segments should be made by the company on the basis of the buyer needs and a reasonably unique buyer should be first identified. The other groups of the buyers having similar needs similar needs may be segmented wit the representative buyer of the unique segment. The other segments may be formulated on the same lines. The segment demarcation need to be done carefully to avoid duplication of need bases.

Such segment demarcation should be on the congruity of the buyers' needs or perceived use value attributes. This segment formation should needs or perceived use value attributes. This segment formation should be based on the data analysis of primary survey by asking the consumer as which product attributes they prefer to value the product. On under standing the basic needs of the consumers the dimensions of the value perceived by the consumers may be established. The survey should also rank the major dimensions of the perceived use value of consumers by allocating proper weights. The performance of the company need to be assessed in reference to its product line existing in the markets, potential products and the competition products.

It is essential that company should conduct brainstorming exercise for understanding the basic and secondary needs for the product, listing the product attributes, identifying the forced relationship of other goods and services with the new product. Idea generation in the process of new product development is a major exercise. This technique calls for a listing of all major attributes of the existing product and the needed attributes in order to improve the same product. The forced relationship of the new product with the existing accessories need also to be studied like developing a new television set may be related wit the consumer need of clock, multi-channel viewing on one screen, microphone attachment and a built-in video game. Such forced relationship has to be identified by the company before launching the product. The morphological analysis calls for identifying the structural dimensions of a pro problem and examining the relationships among them. The need identification can be done by interacting with the potential and existing customs in a focus group meet. The industrial marketers can identify new product ideas working in association wit the lead users of the product. However, the brainstorming exercise is also an important tool, which stimulates the group creativity. In brainstorming exercise the following process is prescribed:

- Negative comments in the process may be withheld till the synthesis is over.

- Welcome freewheeling and wilder ideas for better steering.
- Encourage more number of ideas and categories its utility, and
- Establish inter-relation of the ideas for an overall synergy approach.

The basic purpose of this exercise generation is to generate a large number of ideas. These ideas need to be carefully screened in the interest of the consumer satisfaction as well as the company's profit. In this process the company should avoid the Drop and Go errors. The former attempts to dismiss the good idea while the latter allows the poor ideas to more into the process of commercialization. Hence the purpose of screening the idea need to be understood carefully. It is advised that company should develop an idea-rating matrix on the basis of the emerging ideas and their usefulness. The product ideas have to be turnined into concept and the product concept can be turned later in to the brand concept. The concept testing calls for testing for these competing concepts with an appropriate group of target consumers. The concepts can be presented physically or symbolically. The consumers' response may be summerised and the strength of the concept may be judged. The need gap and product gap levels ma be checked and modified thereafter. The concept testing and product development methodology applies to any product or service. The business analysis includes the estimating sales as it would be of one-time purchase, frequently purchasing product or at regular interval purchase product. The estimates should also be made in relation to its tendency of first purchase, replacement purchase or repeat sales.

The Customer Value

The customer behaviour largely reflects in the customer value he perceives before buying the goods and services and the value he realizes after he buys the same. Le us take an example of customer behaviour towards buying of tractor where he has an option of two Indian brands—HMT (Hindustan Machine Tools

Ltd.) and Mahindra. He would like the tractor to deliver certain levels of reliability, durability, load capacity, fuel efficiency, price and services. He gives equal weightage to all the parameters and judges that the HMT provides him better services in terms of delivery, training and maintenance. Besides he also perceives the relationship marketing of the HMT personnel is better than the other brand and finally he place's a higher value for the HMT Tractor. He arrives at the values form the sources – product, services, personnel and brand image and perceives higher total customer value for this brand as compared to the closest band option. The maximization of delivered value to the customers is useful imperative framework that can be commonly applied to many business companies. The seller must assess the total customer cost and value associated with the offer of each competing company and position his strategies of adding values to the customer delight chain.

On the contrary the seller who is at the delivered cause disadvantage may look for strengthening the product, price, services and performance front or decease the cost to customer. The cost to customer comprises convenience to get the goods or services of the company, comprehensive knowledge about the product, cot incurred for getting the product which includes value of money and time and the extent of care that is given to the customer in delivering the goods and services. The customer value may be augmented by the company by providing easy accessibility to get information and demonstrations about the goods and services for making purchase decisions. The companies necessarily have to develop competitively advantageous approaches for getting the customers.

The most important dimension of the customer behaviour is the adaptability to the innovations. The new goods and services introduced by the company may be advantageous to the customers by way of economizing their cost, time and energy but many times it is difficult for the customers to overcome the set habit of getting those things. For example the real value company had introduced the vaccum containers for keeping the coked food fresh and crisp over a day. This product could not perform in the market, as the deeply entrenced consumer behaviour of consuming fresh cooked food could not be waved off the minds of users. The perceived use value of the product was also very limited. The same company had introduced handy fire extinguisher for domestic use and mainly in the kitchen to manage the fire accidents. This product also could not make a dent in the market as most of the housewives believed that their kitchen is safe and there is no need to go for any security measures. Hence, companies should assess the adaptability of the goods and services while assessing the consumer behaviour before launching the product in the market. Over the above, the goods and services should be within the affordable range of the customers. The cost of the goods and services need to be determined by the company relatively low as compared to their counter parts in the market.

The individual attention to customers makes significant difference in building customer interest towards the goods and services. It boosts up the self-esteem of the customer and he could self actualize the need for the proposed goods and services. The Eureka Forbes Company in India has experimented this strategy and switched over to total direct marketing strategy for its home-durable products like vaccum cleaners and water purifiers The sales force of the company move around the households and carries out demonstration, offers purchase schemes and post sales services. The company attends on individual customers and bears the overheads of the personnel selling costs. The individuals attention helps to enrich the customer the perceived use value of the goods and services, price parities, need, to build conviction and get associated with the product. The promotional strategies of the company also help in building the customer interest in its activities, goods and services. The customers are largely driven by the product line of the company and its appeal in the market. The companies, which have a range of goods and services easily, drive the customers to their victinity of business. The Hindustan Level Ltd., a multi-product company has been one of the top brands among the Indian companies dealing with detergents, toiletries, food products, cosmetics and other FMCG products. The new goods and services offered by this company certainly have brand advantage over the others in the market to mobilize the customers. The two-way information flow from the marketer to the customers and vice-virsa helps a lot of customers to decide over their purchase behaviour as such information flow generates the confidence among the customers that they are being served to their needs.

The need based planning for the customer care and patronage of the popular brands makes the goods and services offered by the company more attractive to the customers. The new companies some times tie-up their promotional packages with the established brands and the existing brands some times tied up with the MNC products for augmenting its sales. The example may be cited form the Indian companies like the Bajaj Scooters being associated with Titan wrist watches and Godrej refrigerators tied up with the Sony audio system for the promotion of their goods. Such promotional packages may e considered as the business patronage to generate customer drive. The customer participation in promotional programmes like quizzes, contest etc. would service customer conviction for goods and services and help in building attitude towards buying the goods and services and the company. Besides the overall performance of the brand also helps in nurturing the positive behaviour of the customers towards buying the goods and services of the company.

Customer Satisfaction

Buyers satisfaction plays an important role in sustaining his behaviour towards the repeat purchase or further association with the brand. Satisfaction is the level perception of the buyer resulting from comparing the perceived performance of the goods and services in reference to the anticipations of the buyer. There may be two levels of satisfaction, which a buyer may feel. It the buyer feels that the performance of the goods and services matches his expectations he may be considered as satisfied and if the performance exceeds the expectation of the buyer he may be considered as highly satisfied or delighted. Most of the buyers form their expectation on the basis of their previous experience or strong reliance on the word of mouth. Thus some of the companies make provocative statements of total satisfaction to t attract more customers. The Indian document company Modi Xerox claims total satisfaction of the goods and services by providing adequate warranty on the equipment and efficient services.

The model that a company should have for offering the customer delight. The companies should have direct customer relationship by involving the functional management in the process. The management should understand the Parato Principle that explains that 20 per cent of the customers contributors to the 80 per cent of the sales and shoulder the brand image of the company. Accordingly company should perform to please the customers of this category. The complaint profiles, service record and customer oriented policies need to be developed by the company along with the periodical feedback analysis. The interaction with the staff should be regular with the customers and they should be able to exercise skills, presentable styles and shared briefs among the customers. The challenge is to create a company culture so that every employee within the company works with an objective of delighting the customer. The company should feel more responsive towards the customers' needs, perceptions and reactions in order to track their expectations, perceived performance of the goods and services and customer satisfaction. The companies should carry customer satisfaction surveys, lost customer analysis and dissatisfied customers diagnosis to develop better customer orientation. There should be continuous efforts from the company personnel to deliver the goods and services to the best of the customer value. Kaizen is one of the processes, which inducts regular improvement in the delivery system. Kaizenis a Japanese term and is formed of two words Kai that means continuous and zen indicates improvement. The giant marketing company of the dairy products-Gujarat Milk Marketing cooperative Federation having a turnover of Rs. 1400 crores has a unique system of reward in its marketing personal for introducing the Kaizenin their area of work. The GCMMF has succeeded in winning the customer satisfaction for most of its products and being the brand leader in India for the dairy products. Customer satisfaction will be lower in the industry where the homogeneous goods and services that are offered to the heterogeneous market and in vice-versa situation the satisfaction to the customer may be found higher. The customer satisfaction would be lower if the switching costs are higher for the repeat purchasers however, the industries which promotes repeat purchases and retain buyers generally create a higher level of customer satisfaction. The expansion of marketing boundaries, market share of a company may cause lowering the customer satisfaction.

Customer Care

It is essential the company look into the value chain not only among its own marketing personnel but also among the distributors, retailers, promoters and patrons. In the present competitive market conditions the companies look for the effective customer value delivery system while choosing the business partners. Simultaneously the companies should also assess the customer defection rate due to frequent brand switching and should attempt to reduce the rate of brand defection. There are four steps in this process. Firstly the companies should measure the rate of customer retention for their brand. The retention rte may be the repeat buyers in FMCG products, renewal of readership for newspapers and magazines and may be the repeat selection of the same airline for travel. Secondly the company must list all the causes of customer attrition and thirdly the loss due to customer attrition need to be estimated by the company.

The customer retention should be the first imperatives, which need to be attempted by two ways—setting tall switching barriers and follow the relationship marketing. The company must build relationship with customer by redeveloping the four basic practices—(1) the sales person of the company should be accountable to the customer. He should check periodically from the customer to known the performance of the goods and services delivered to him as to what extent it is meeting the requirement of the customer

(ii) the sales person should be reactive to the customer by encouraging him to call on the services office for any problems he faces with the delivered goods and services (iii) the sales person should be proactive to the customers needs and should suggest him periodically the use value of the goods and services delivered to him and the improvements in the new versions of the same brought in the market by the company and (iv) the company should continuously work in partnership with the customer to discover the ways to effect the cost effective delivery of he goods and services and higher perceived use values of the same. The excellent Indian example on relationship marketing can be cited of Maruti Udyog Limited (MUL) which attempt to retain its buyers through the dealer network who get to follow all the four commandments in order to provide the high customer satisfaction. However, the weakness of the network of dealers of MUL is that it takes cares of customers in a quality way till he warranty period. A few examples may be quoted where the companies try to developing term relationship wit the customer. Among them the popular magazine Reader's Digist in India may be rightly mentioned as it attempts to rebuild the relationship even of the defected customers by sending term regular mails and promotional offers. The high customer value for a company helps in developing quality concepts in marketing of goods and services. The following functions need to be considered by the company attempting to achieve total quality marketing:

- Quality of goods and services
- Strong employee commitment
- High quality partners
- Cost effective goods and services
- Strong customer care and relationship.

The new companies looking for building the customer value chain should start working from the grassroots of the market. The companies goal should be not only to get the customers but more towards retaining them in the business. The companies must decide that how much relationship marketing should be invested in the different market segments. In this process the company must assess the following parameters for developing suitable strategies for the relationship marketing.

Customer Behaviour Developing Positive Interface

- ***Management—Customer:*** Parato principle, feedback system, complaint profiles, service record, customer orientation.
- ***Staff-Customer***: Effective front line, managing brand image, growth, loyalty, patronage, customer guidance
- ***Customer—System***: Sustainable, customer friendly, proactive to the customer needs, adaptable strategies at all levels
- ***Management—Staff***: Staffing, performance, evaluavation, welfare policy, feedback, shared beliefs and myths or traditions, trainign, incentives and management bywalking around.

Environment Mapping markets, competitions, attributes of goods and Services, Buying Behaviour, Marketing Patterns, Satisfaction Analysis.

Relationship Building Understanding customer, patterns of buyer relations, critical Inputs for Relationship building, categorical relations in Marketing. Attributes of Marketing Relationship, Client Account Services, Monitoring and Reviewing the Marketing Relationship. Effective Communication.

Serving marketing relations. Focus group relations, Solo Relationship, Competitive Relationship, Client Communication Networking, Problem Solving, Team building, Social and Cultural Aspects of Marketing relationship.

Analysing Relationship marketing Promoting Sales of Goods and Services, Generating Consumer Pull, Anchor Relationship in marketing. Navigating Relationship in Marketing, Futurology—Client Groups, Environment, Goods and Services, pace in Marketing,

Global Philosophy of Sales and Marketing Relationships.

Strategic marketing relationship Inter and intra-organisation, Client Groups and Service Groups, Specific Marketing relationships, sales Point Promotion Relationships, diplomatic Marketing Relationship, Goal oriented Relationship Marketing. International Relationships Marketing, monitoring and Evaluation.

Relationship marketing may be considered as an important tool for knowing the consumer, retaining his loyalty towards the brand and navigating the business on his confidence on the integrated services offered by the company. It is essential to organize frequent focus group discussions with the consumers to know their needs and problems in access to the goods and services of the company. Such association with the consumers will also nurture the elf-esteem of the consumers. The relationship marketing also develops social ties with the consumer segments and it is therefore must for the companies to develop pro-active behaviour in the wholesale dealers and carrying and forwarding agents of the products of the company.

CHAPTER 3

MANAGING THE MARKETING MIX

This deals with the consumer, the focal point of marketing effort. The consumer, by his decision to buy or not buy a product, holds veto power over the firm's entire marketing and business effort. Many of the elements that influence consumer behaviour and satisfaction are considered in this chapter The structure and organization of the book, the major topics covered in managerial marketing, and the nature of interrelationships among diverse aspects of marketing management. Among the areas discussed are: the systems approach to marketing, marketing management, the role of consumers and consumer behaviour, the managerial functions of marketing, decision strategies and techniques, and the marketing mix. Some new broader dimensions influencing the marketing manager's job are also presented, including recent developments in international marketing and management's increasing concern with the social responsibility of the firm.

These marketing developments are receiving increased consideration because their effect on marketing success is now more widely recognized. Marketing as a field of study is generally categorized as being part of the broader field of business administration. However, marketing also involves considerations that extend beyond these boundaries. Marketing decisions are shaped by and influence the external environments of the firm. Marketing, therefore, has social, economic, legal, international, and political dimensions in addition to its managerial focus. Profitable solutions to marketing problems can only be realized if the significance of environmental change on the firm and its customers is recognized. These external forces which affect consumer behaviour and business action must be reflected in marketing policies, plans, programmes, and decisions.

The student of marketing must develop a facility for integrating useful contributions from many disciplines. He must also understand the functional purpose of each component in a marketing action system. Illustration I depicts a total marketing system and services as a model for the study of marketing management. The conceptual relationships portrayed are developed in subsequent illustrations and readings. This marketing systems model is presented in the spirit of the following passage from Konrad Lorenz:[1]

I am aware that the task I have set myself makes excessive demands upon my pen. It is almost impossible to portray in words the functioning of a system in which every part is related to every other in such a way that each has a causal influence on the others. Even if one is only trying to explain a gasoline engine it is hard to know where to begin, because the person to whom one seeks to explain it can only understand the nature of the crankshaft if he has first grasped that of the connecting rods, the pistons, the valves, the camshaft, and so on. Unless one understands the elements of a complete system as a whole, one cannot understand them at all. The more complex the structure of a system is, the greater this difficulty becomes—and it must be surmounted both in one's research and in one's teaching. Unfortunately the working structure of the instinctive and culturally acquired patterns of behaviour which make up the social life of man seems to be one of the most complicated systems we know on this earth.

The Environments of Marketing

Marketing managers, by the nature of their problems, are environmentalists. They give attention to the implications of environmental changes for marketing policies and practices.

Illustration I shows the external environment in which the systemic functions of marketing are managed. These environments and interactions affect marketing opportunities, customer behaviour and satisfaction, and the degree of success achieved by the business.

In this model, the major external environmental influences on business actions are categorized as: scientific and technological forces; life style and life space forces; ethical, legal, and social forces; and both domestic and international economic and political forces. Each of these forces interacts with the corporate system. Their impact on marketing management is investigated in further chapters.

The marketing manager needs to appreciate the pervasive influence of these forces on consumer attitudes and behaviour. While the activities of any single business cannot appreciably alter any of the external forces, the converse relationship exists—any one force can affect business outcome. Customers react to and help shape their environments, and market opportunities or problems result from changed customer attitudes toward products and services.

Three linkage levels involved in the analysis of marketing systems are shown in the model.

1. Marketing activities are linked through the corporate enterprise system to the various public and private agencies external to the firm. Examples of these agencies, which are not depicted in the model, include: suppliers; advertising firms and media; financial institutions; governmental and private research organisations; federal, state, and local governmental commissions; transportation companies; and the various publics.

2. Linkages exist between marketing and the other business functions that comprise the corporate enterprise system. These other areas are represented by the firm's human, physical, and financial resources, its competitive structure, and its goals. Because the purpose of this model is depiction

of a marketing action system, other functional areas of the business have not been explicitly differentiated. Similar models could be constructed for production, finance, and other functions of an enterprise.

3. The systemic functions of marketing are linked to produce an effective marketing-customer satisfactions mix. Three sub-mixes—product-services, communications, and distribution—are combined to achieve marketing objectives. The objective of the marketing mix is to balance marketing objectives. The objective of the marketing mix is to balance marketing effort with marketing opportunity in order to provide optimal marketing support of stated corporate goals.

The nature of marketing operations within the corporate enterprise system, and emphasizes that corporate goals are achieved by concentrating on defined areas of market opportunity or, more precisely, on customers in particular market segments. Corporate goal setting is recognized today as a complex process for conglomerate, multinational, multi-plant firms.

The Consumer.

Like the others, Chapter three is future-oriented. One purpose of analyzing the articles in the book is to enable the reader to better understand and ultimately meet the problems consumers will have in the future. For example, understanding of consumer behaviour is increased by studying trends in life style and life space forces. In Chapter three, some of these trends are identified, and their impact on marketing programmes are treated in detail.

Market segmentation provides one way of identifying marketing opportunities that have arisen because of changing life styles. Broad potential markets are broken down into many smaller segments, each with its own tastes, preferences, values, and needs.

The market segmentation concept is the basis of a marketing strategy directed toward consumers with particular life styles and needs. While demographic methods are basic, other criteria for market segmentation are also useful. Examples of newer methods of segmentation analysis include the determination of differences in buyer attitudes, motivations, values, patterns of usage, and aesthetic preferences.

Consumer motivation is a function of the extent to which human needs are satisfied. One theory of human motivation holds that needs are satisfied. One theory of human motivation holds that needs are arranged on a continuum that ranges from basic physiological needs to those of self-actualisation.[2] An appreciable measure of satisfaction of lower needs is a precondition for emergence of higher ones. The marketing manager's task to is to assemble a market offer that promises gratification of at least one level in this hierarchy of needs.

Consumer behaviour is influenced by the life style ad life space force discussed in this book. Many marketing efforts of American business and many of the changes taking place in consumption cannot be understood unless life style trends are considered.

There seems to be an increasing worldwide interest in personal achievement, social goals, and a better way of life. This has been described as the "revolution of rising expectations" and seems to be worldwide. For example, throughout the world there is an upward mobility thrust toward more education and more real income. The above trends are especially evident in the United States. Trends toward home entertainment and family-centered enjoyment are related to increasing discretionary time and mobility. Changes in the geographic distribution of the population are reflected in a redistribution of the labour force and purchasing power.

Tomorrow's customers may have problems that are quite unlike the buying and consumption problems prevalent today. Future consumers will generally be better educated, have greater mobility, possess more discretionary income, and have more time to spend that income. Hopefully, new communication and distribution patterns will lead to increasingly informed decisions and prompt satisfaction of consumer wants.

Decision Making in Marketing

The articles in Chapter four deal with marketing as a prime focus of managerial decision making. Marketing management is becoming increasingly analytical as models and techniques for information gathering and problem solving are developed, and as new marketing applications of existing scientific methods are discovered. Scientific and technological developments are having a continuing impact on the advancement of science in marketing. For example, the computer is exerting a significant influence on such areas as marketing planning, the evaluation of promotional alternatives, and distribution systems. Some authorities see marketing as the great growth area of computer applications in business. The rapid accumulation of new knowledge is resulting in widespread application of mathematical, statistical, economic, psychological, and sociological techniques to marketing problems. These interdisciplinary contributions to marketing promise better understanding of complex consumer needs and of other marketing problems.

Marketing Management Functions

The functions of marketing management identified in the upper center discussed in further chapters. The functions are marketing opportunity assessment, marketing planning and programming, marketing organization and leadership, and evaluating and adjusting marketing effort. The marketing management team must perform these four entrepreneurial functions if the firm is to develop an efficient corporate marketing system in a changing environment.

Marketing opportunity assessment centers on the delineation of actual and potential customers and their wants and needs. Market opportunity exists when a business either possesses or can develop capabilities that enable it to profitably satisfy the wants of potential customers. The business must continually develop marketing strategies that will enable I to cultivate these market opportunities.

Research and development activities of business, government, and educational institutions are resulting in increasing numbers of new consumer and industrial products. Similarly, increased productivity resulting from automation and other forces has resulted in production capacity that enables most manufacturing firms to produce more than they can sell. The mass production capability of American industry is predicated on the discovery of new markets and the expansion of existing ones. This is one of the factors underlying the marketing orientation of American business.

Planning is essential to the organization, operation, and control of a business. Planning also provides a basis for an integrated systems orientation and a coordinated marketing strategy. The development of new products and new markets raises organizational and leadership problems for marketing management. The interaction that occurs between an organisation and its environment illustrates the dynamics of the systems approach and reflects the demands being placed on the marketing organization and its leadership.

Evaluating and adjusting the marketing effort enables the firm to react to changes occurring in the environment. The process of change—and the ability to cope with it –is a major challenge to marketing management. Financial and integrative controls are used to keep the marketing effort keyed to areas of profitable market opportunity.

Managing the Marketing Mix

The lower central section provide an overview of the dimensions and complexities of developing and managing a marketing mix. Preparing an effective marketing mix that furthers attainment of corporate objectives is the marketing manager's responsibility.

A marketing mix consists of three sub mixes—the product and service mix, the communications mix, and the distribution mix. The product and services mix is composed of elements that form the set of utilities a customer buys. Examples of utility set contents include the product, price, services, container, brand, label information, conditions of sale, and warranty. A communications mix consists of the firm's efforts to disseminate information about its market offer to the potential byrs. The elements of a communications mix are advertising, sales promotion, personal selling, merchandising, and special sales aids. The distribution mix I formed of two major components—channels of distribution through which goods and titles to goods flow from the firm to the ultimate purchasers, and physical distribution, which is concerned with loading, transporting, storing, and delivering the product.

The marketing manager's responsibility for formulating an effective mix and for putting it into practice does not culminate with the sale of the product or service. He must not neglect the post-transactional ingredients of his marketing mix if the firm's long-range marketing strategy is to be successful.

International Marketing

The external environmental areas of domestic and international economic and political forces. The evolution of international markets is one of the most significant trends in contemporary marketing. Further chapters presents an international view of marketing and the development of the multinational firm.

Many of the forces described in the book are related to the United States market. However, their impact in the United States Portends changes of a similar nature in many countries throughout the world. For example, the knowledge explosion, particularly in science and technology, is influencing nearly all cultures. New marketing opportunities are presented by widespread rising consumption expectations and increased interest in personal achievement and social gains. Political unrest in newly formed nations around the world reflects, at lest in part, dissatisfaction with present living standards. These people want, and intend to obtain for themselves, those goods now enjoyed by consumers in more advanced economies. Similarly, some nations with controlled economies seem to be moving from a production to a partial consumer orientation. The marketing knowledge and ability possessed by multinational firms can aid immensely in the development of balanced economies in both new and changing political-economic systems. Marketing managers must recognize, analyze, and adjust to the marketing systems of each international market. Attempts to improve the efficiency of these marketing systems must be based on a thorough evaluation of the system's socio-political environment.

Marketing plays a key role in the economic growth of developing countries. To the extent that the socioeconomic growth of a nation is related to the marketing process, marketing can be a critical element in the development process. Marketing is not only an economic tool, but a political and social tool as well. Ultimately, marketing's most important social role may lie in its contribution to the stimulation and facilitation of world peace.

Dimensions of Marketing

Marketing practitioners and academicians realize that various ethical, legal, social, economic, and political forces are becoming increasingly important for marketing Illustration I identifies these forces as major influences on markets. Their effects on marketing thought and action are discussed in this book.

The socioeconomic dimensions of marketing account, in part, for the growing concern of business and marketing leaders with public and private views of social responsibility in business. Te continuing emphasis on the need for businesses to increase their efforts to fulfill their assigned citizenship roles reflects an expanding concept of business' social responsibility.

In order to fully understand marketing's dynamics and the changes in marketing described in this book, students and managers must not only understand problem-solving techniques, they must also understand the theory underlying these techniques and practices. Some developments that influence marketing as a discipline, the interdisciplinary approach to marketing, and the contributions of theory to marketing management are explored in this book.

The articles included in the book were chosen for their contribution to an understanding of managerial marketing. The perspective throughout is that marketing managers must equip themselves to better understand the problems of potential customers and, ultimately, to help customers satisfy their requirements in a manner that meets the needs not only of customer and firm but also of society.

The Marketing Systems

Marketing managers must be environmentalists, for external and internal environmental change is often the dominant factor in marketing decisions. The rate and magnitude of change and its effect on the firm in the form of innovations, flow of new products, and new competitive pressure are fundamental influences on marketing managers who are attempting to match customer needs and wants with corporate capabilities and resources. The external environmental system surrounding the firm; it indicates the basic environmental forces that influence marketing strategy and performance. These forces are classified as: (1) scientific and technological, (2) life style and life space, (3) economic and political, and (4) ethical, legal, and social. Management's skill in meeting and adjusting to these forces is a significant determinant of the firm's profitability and growth. The articles in this chapter discuss the impact of these environmental forces on such important marketing variables as the consumer, corporate planning, and marketing strategy.

As technology and value systems change, new business problems and opportunities are created by a "society in motion." Consumption patterns, for example, are continually modified and altered by life style forces. These changing patterns are exemplified in the higher aspiration levels and goals of consumers. Constantly evolving consumer attitudes toward products and services create a need for new marketing tactics. The study of life style forces contributes to the marketing manager's awareness and understanding of the complexity of consumer behaviour, and ultimately to more efficient marketing by the firm.

Technological change may be the major environmental force for many firms. We live in a period when 90 per cent of all the scientists in the world's history are alive, and the majority of man's store of scientific literature has been published in the last decade. Thus, it is not difficult to appreciate why marketing management must become increasingly aware of technological developments if they are to focus the firm's resources on the needs of to days dynamic markets. Environmental force interact, as indicated to create marketing problems and opportunities. For example, technology and changing life styles can interact to create a major force for change, as Marshall McLuhan has noted in his evaluation of the impact of television and other communications media on society. Developments in communications technology are shrinking distances and time scales, and the scope of marketing and market concepts must be adjusted accordingly.

Marketing problems should be solved and marketing opportunities developed in light of existing political, economic, and institutional forces. Consideration of these forces is contributing to a broader view of the firm's responsibility to society. Public policy decisions have significant effects on marketing decisions. Marketing decisions, in turn, influence public policy. Marketing managers and public policymakers can make a significant contribution to the process of constructive innovation and to society through the integration of private and public objectives. An effective marketing system is essential to economic growth, not only for a developing nation, but also for a mature economy.

Ethical considerations constitute another environmental force acting on the marketing decision maker. Because marketing is a logical focal pint for ethical evaluations of business, marketing managers should integrate ethical values and scientific marketing procedures. Present-day marketing cannot be understood without recognition of both domestic and international economic and political forces. The emergence of multinational enterprises is none development arising from and contributing to such forces. Competitive pressures in the American economy, together wit other environmental forces, create the necessity for a market orientation in which the consumer becomes the focal point of all corporate activity.

Formulation of a marketing strategy requires determination of an optimal customer-satisfactions mix. Marketing resources and procedures are combined with market segmentation factors and focused on customer needs and satisfactions. The degree of success in blending these elements into a workable strategy is determined by management's skills in planning and establishing corporate goals and in the coordinating of marketing management's systemic functions. These functions and their relationships are depicted. Achievement of the fir's goal and marketing objectives depends on customer response to its marketing mix.

Marketing Action and the External Environments

Life style is an important concept for marketers, because marketing is both a product and a determinant of life style. Life style facilitates the understanding, explanation and prediction of consumer behaviour. It also influences economic activity.

Life Style Concepts and Marketing

A general concept, referred to vaguely as "life style," is being used by behavioural scientists, especially sociologists. The precise nature and scope of the concept is not clear. However, in interviews about life style, several behavioural scientists revealed that they understood its general meaning and its significance for research purposes. They were also willing to discuss relevant life-style research projects and to recommend a body of literature that reflected a life-style orientation. They did not, however, define the concept specifically, and none of the recommended literature contained a definition.

The Life Style Concept

What is life style? Life style is a systems concept. It refers to the distinctive or characteristic mode of living, in its aggregative and broadest sense, of a whole society or segment thereof. It is concerned with those unique ingredients or qualities which describe the style of life of some culture or group, and distinguish it from others. It embodies the patterns that develop and emerge from the dynamics of living in a society.

Life style, therefore, is the result of such forces as culture, values, resources, symbols, license, and sanction. From one perspective, the aggregate of consumer purchases, and the manner in which they are consumed, reflect a society's life style.

Following this defining it is logical to speak of the American life style, our family life styles, consumer life styles, the life style of various social strata, and the life style of specific groups in different stages of the life cycle.

In marketing we have been particularly interested in consumer life styles in terms of the way people individualize, and identify themselves as members of various groups, and the resulting patterns of living. For example, we have gathered and analyzed data on consumer incomes, age groups, and expenditure patterns for decades. The goal is not one of assembling statistics for the sake of statistical information. Rather it is one of translating statistical findings about consumers into models of consumer life styles that will permit us to understand and predict various dimensions of consumer behaviour, particularly purchase behaviour.

A life style hierarchy may be charted consisting of:

Culture and Society

Group and Individual

expectations and Values

Life Style Pattern and Values

Purchase Decisions

Market reaction of Consumers

Life style, therefore, is major behavioural concept for understanding, explaining, and predicting consumer and business behaviour. It is a more generalized concept than existing concepts of consumer behaviour that have been advanced in marketing. Such topics as mobility, leisure, social class, life cycle, status, conformity, mass, and the family as a consuming unit are all part of the life-style fabric. As a result, life-style studies could foster the unification of findings and theories related to consumer behaviour. In fact, life style is a point of interdisciplinary convergence among marketing and such subject-matter areas as sociology, social and cultural anthropology, psychology, demography, and social psychology.

Economists and marketing people seem to have a different perspective on the value of life style concepts and findings. In most economic studies the life style of a society is usually assumed or ignored. It is part of the "state of the art" and "other things being equal," statements. (One striking exception is Veblen who developed such concepts as vicarious consumption and vicarious leisure.)

By contrast, in marketing, life-style of actors are viewed as among the most important forces influencing and shaping economic activity. They are the very focus of a major part of marketing. Foote, for instance, has suggested that in essence marketers are becoming taste counselors. If this is the case, marketing and life style are surely intertwined.

Since ours is a materialistic, acquisitive, thing-minded, abundant economy, marketing becomes one of the cores for understanding life styles. Therefore, marketing is in a position to make significant contribution to a number of life-style oriented disciplines. Moreover, since our life style is being emulated in other parts of the world, such as Europe, Japan and Latin America, a better understanding of our life style may also enhance economic development theory.

Marketing and the Life Style of Abundance

When we think of abundance, we usually perceive of the physical capabilities and potentialities of a society. Abundance, however, is also a result of the culture itself since it stems partly from physical factors and partly from cultural forces. In large measure, our economic abundance results from certain institutions in our society which affect our pattern of living.

Potter maintains that advertising is the institution identified with abundance, particularly American abundance.[2] However, the institution that is brought into being by abundance without previous emphasis or existence in the same form is the institution of marketing. It is marketing expressed not only in advertising forms, but in such forms as the emphasis upon consumption in our society, marketing research, marketing planning, the marketing concept, new approaches to product development, credit, the management of innovation, the utilization of effective merchandising techniques, and the cultivation of mass markets; that is the institution of abundance.

Ours is a business-dominated society. Hence, business influences our life styles as profoundly as any other force. One of the unique characteristics of American business, however, is the distinctive approach it adopts to marketing. Marketing has reached its most mature form and has had its greatest impact on life styles in the American economy.

Other cultures have made significant contributions to business thought and practice in such areas as business law, ethics, accounting, finance, production systems, and organisation theory. By contrast, marketing progress to date is uniquely attributable to the American life style, and it is being studied and emulated in other parts of the world. Such institutions and techniques as self service, supermarkets, discount houses, marketing research, credit plans, and packaging are spreading part of the American life style in many parts of the world.

In a life-style sense, marketing is an institution of social control. It is an institution of social control in the same sense the school and the home are. It exerts an extensive influence on our life style which I maintain is for the betterment of our social and economic life. Moreover, since marketing is responsible to a very large extent for our standard of living it is impossible to understand our culture fully, and hence our life style, without some comprehension of marketing.

The impact of marketing on our patterns of living, particularly advertising, has not been ignored. Advertising has been criticized pointedly, Toynbee, for example, writes that if t ere demonstrated to be true "that personal consumption stimulated by advertising is essential for growth and full employment in an economy of abundance...it would also demonstrate to my mind that an economy of abundance is a spiritually unhealthy way of life, and that the sooner we reform it the better... The moral that I draw is that a way of life based on personal consumption, stimulated by advertising, needs change."[2] These are strong indictments of unfavorable marketing influences on our life style and are reinforced by the writings of such people s Warne, Galbraith, and Schlesinger.

When abundance prevails, however, the limitations and constraints upon business and other parts of our life style shift. Potter writes: "The most critical point in the functioning of society shifts from production to consumption...the culture must be reoriented to convert the producer's into a consumer's culture...and the society must be adjusted to a new set of drives and values of which consumption is paramount."[3] this becomes the challenge of marketing in altering life styles in an abundant economy. Marketing becomes an instrument for changing production-oriented value into consumption-oriented norms.

Marketing and Values

Our basic value system determines the nature and significance of various social institutions. These fundamental values, moreover, are not merely the result of the whims of marketers. It is true that we live in a sensate culture, one which stresses sensory enjoyment, materialism and utilitarianism.[4] Consumers desire and can own those items and symbols that are associated wit status, achievement, and accomplishment. Material values have become important. Marketing responds to, and reinforces, such values in our abundant culture, and in so doing appeals to the senses and emphasizes materialism.

The life-style question still to be answered, however, is one concerning the relative desirability of our life style with such emphases as contrasted with other life styles. Great materialistic stress and accomplishment is not inherently sinful and bad. Moral values are not vitiated as many critics seem to think by substantial material acquisitions. In reality the improvement of material situations can lead to a greater recognition of intrinsic values, the lifting of general tastes, the enhancement of a moral climate and the direction of more attention to the appreciation of art and esthetics.

This I would suggest is occurring today. It has also been the pattern of the past. In history great artistic and cultural advancements are at least accompanied, if not shaped, by periods of flourishing trade and commerce.

The next marketing frontier may well be an inner one—the market of the mind and the personal development of consumers.[5] Marketing in the future may be geared to filling the needs of this inner frontier. One of its roles may be that of encouraging increasing expenditures by consumers, of both dollars and time, to develop themselves intellectually, socially, and morally. This has already been accomplished to a limited degree: witness the increasing demand for classical records, good books, the attendance at symphony concerts, the purchase of good oil paintings through mail order catalogues, and the support for the arts in general. Social critics, while prone to point out the undesirable impact of marketing on our life styles, have neglected to indicate the progress and contributions that have been made.

Life Style and Consumer Expectations

Part of the American life style may be referred to as the American Dream. A big difference exists between the American Dream with its expectations and the dreams and expectations of other countries. The gap, however, is narrowing.

The American Dream as a life style concept includes a belief in equality of opportunity to obtain a good standard of living, to acquire status and success in a community through individual initiative, determination, sacrifice and skill. It involves the contradictory concept of equality for all and the rank and status orderings that result in the social ladders so characteristic of the functioning of our complex society. It requires the maintenance of an open society with opportunity for upward economic and social movement and the availability of education which is a root for social achievement, occupational advancement, and higher incomes on a widespread basis. These aspects of the Dream are reflected in our life style.

In general, American consumers, especially younger consumers, in living out the Dream exude optimism for the future. They feel sure that tomorrow will be better than today. American consumers believe that they can continue to expand their consumption and increase their relative amount of pleasure rather than merely limit desires. They feel sure they can continue increasing the are of purchasing power under their control.

One result of this optimistic outlook is that American consumers see virtue not so much in curbing desires, but rather in realizing oneself by acquiring the necessary goods and symbols. This optimistic life style has a historical root, for a Kraus has pointed out, unlike the European who only hoped that tomorrow would be no worse than today, Americans felt cheated if tomorrow were not better than today.[6] This orientation is supported and reflected in such marketing concepts and techniques as programmed innovation and product development, install-ment credit, advertising, sales promotion and merchandising activities.

Life Style and Change

In our life style we do not accept institutions, techniques, and products as permanent. Our society contains a rich tradition of expecting and anticipating change. This anticipation results from a conscious belief that change are normal, useful, helpful, and good. We seem to accept what appears to be good today and anticipate that it will be superseded by items that are superior tomorrow. The rather trite expression "innovate or perish" has rich meaning for businesses trying to meet the demands of our pattern of life.

Such an attitude is one of the foundations of aggressive marketing. Girod has written that in our culture, "Innovation, change, mobility, and movement are permanent traits," and that, "In stressing the need for innovation, Americans are fighting for the maintenance of this aspect of their way of life for permanency of the one thing to which they are attached."[7]

By contract, some other cultures which are more restrictive in their anticipations do not expect, hope for, or plan for any great change in their environment. They strive to maintain the status quo. In these cultures which are resolute against the suggestion of new ideas, new products, and new processes, marketing tends to play but a minor role.

To date, technological changes have had the greatest effect on our life styles. Changing methods of marketing are, however, very significant. Consider the effect on our life style, and the life style of other cultures, of supermarkets, self-service, discount houses, shopping centers, automatic vending machines, credit plans, new products, packages, and new communications techniques. Such process and service innovations will have an even greater effect in the future.

Consumers, Consumption, and Life Style

In the scheme of our life style, because of a previous production orientation, the relative significance of consumers and consumption as economic determinants has been under-emphasized. The importance of maintaining physical production is, of course, widely recognized. Only limited reference, however, is made to the corresponding necessity of maintaining consumption. The critical nature of consumption in an abundant economy demands that consumption should not be considered as a happenstance activity. We must establish the necessary conditions for consumption to proceed on an adequate and orderly basis.

Until recently, even the relative significance of consumer investment in our economy was greatly under-emphasized. Business investment, which is certainly a most significant factor in influencing business conditions, received almost all the attention. Katona points out, however, that "growth and expansion of the American economy are dependent on consumer investment as well as business investment...business investment and consumer investment are equally important forces which either stimulate or retard the economy."[8]

What must also be recognized is the important fact that consumer investments are not merely the function of increased income. They stem from and reflect life styles.

A distorted picture has been presented of consumers and the purchase and consumption process. Consumers have been portrayed in much of the non-marketing literature as emotional, irrational, union formed beings, manipulated at will through marketing devices. It is held that conformity, followership, waste, ostentation, and meaningless style changes have been foisted upon consumers by marketers. Rokeach points out, however, that marketers have been using the wrong psychological theory. He emphasizes that the theory that consumers are irrational creatures who must be appealed to only on an emotional level is outmoded. Modern psychological theories view man as "not only a rationalizing creature but also a rational creature curious, exploratory and receptive to new ideas."[9]

Competition as Part of Our Life Style

Essentially, competition is directly related to and can be defined only in terms of the culture and nature of the environment that surrounds it. Competition has its fullest meaning in the marketing environment of a consumeristic economy rather than in a controlled, planned, or cooperative environment such as exists in many other countries.

In thinking about competition, however, we tend to be retrospective and do not relate it to current life styles. In interpreting laws and in our economic analysis we often cling to past or previous models of competition and competitive situations. For example, we often conceptualize competition in terms of an emerging industrial society rather than a maturing industrial society, in terms of price competition neglecting convenience and service competition, in terms of an economy of scarcity with relatively low consumer purchasing power rather than an economy of abundance with widespread discretionary purchasing power; in terms of manufacturers and distributors controlling and dominating the market place rather than an economy governed (or at least influenced to a large extent) by customer sovereignty: and in terms of intra-industry competition rather than inter-industry competition.

In particular, there is a misplaced emphasis, stemming from past economic models, on *price* as the key competitive weapon. This does not mean that price competition is no longer important in our mode of living. Certainly it is. It does mean, however, that ours is a competitive situation in which *price obscurity* and not price clarity seems to be the rule and in which other variables including convenience and service are very important.[10]

We seem to take competition for granted as one of the inherent aspects of our life style. J.M. Clark points out, however, that 'There can be no certainly that competition will remain vigorous in American business," and that "The necessary conditions are a fascinating subject for speculation." The necessary and sufficient condition for the existence of keen, vigorous competition, however, is clear.

It is aggressive marketing. Changes in price, advertising, products, and channels of distribution tend to keep things stirred up and prevent competition from lapsing into routine passivity. To a large extend our marketing technology sets us apart from other cultures. It is a motivating force behind our competitive system and characterizes our life style. Marketing in the future must be recognized as a major institution in our way of life as well as a force that can contribute greatly to the influence of international life styles.

Yet analysts of our culture and life styles have virtually ignored marketing. It is often regarded as but a minor type of activity which is not important enough to be investigated. It has been neglected by psychologists, sociologists, social and cultural anthropologists, economists, and historians. It is treated as though it were a side issue in our economic activity, when in essence, it is one of the core or focal points.

REFERENCES

1. David M. Potter, People of Plenty, The University of Chicago Press, Chicago, 1954, p. 167.

2. Toynbee vs. Bernbach: As Advertising Morally Defensible?" *Yale Daily News*, Special Issue, 1963, p. 2.

3. Potter, op. cit., p. 173.

4. See Pitirim A. Sorokin, *The Crisis of Our Age*, New York, E.P. Dutton & Co., Inc., 1946, especially Chapter III.

5. For a discussion of this point see William Lazer & Eugene . Kelley, "Editorial Postscript," *Managerial Marketing: Perspectives & Viewpoints* (rev. ed.; Hotnewood, III.: Richard D. Irwin, Inc., 1963), p. 683.

6. See Michael Kraus, "The United States to 1865," The University of Michigan Press, Ann Harbor, Michigan, 1959.

7. Roger Girod, "Comment on Consumer Reaction to Innovation," In Lincoln H, Clark, ed. *Consumer Behavior, Research on Consumer Reactions*, Harper & Brothers, New York, 1958, p. 10.

8. George Katona, *Michigan Business Review*, July 161, pp. 17-20.

9. *New York Times*, November 7, 1963, p. 60, "Advertising: A Wrong Psychological Limb?"

10. See Eugene J. Kelley, "The Importance of Convenience in Consumer Purchasing," *Journal of Marketing*, July 1958. (Also reprinted in this book, pp. 155-62).

CHAPTER 4

MARKETING ORGANIZATION OF INDIVIDUAL ENTERPRISES

Individual enterprises enjoy a great deal of freedom for choice among organizational alternatives to achieve marketing objectives, ranging from ownership and operation through vertical integration, through partial vertical integration, to a variety of exclusive and selective contractual and franshising arrangements. None of these forms of organization are illegal per se, but some are very nearly so. Thus, the acquisition of a competitor by a large firm raises legal risks so serious that most firms, especially large ones, would not wish to assume them. Thus, also, exclusive dealer or exclusive territorial arrangements are almost *per se* illegal for large enterprises with substantial volumes of sales. Similarly, franchise agreements by powerful manufacturers must be drawn carefully in relation to a strong presumption of unilateral control comparable to vertical integration with out all of its risks.

The recent and current boom in franchise arrangements raises a host of unsettled legal issues. A competitive general market system in a country such as the United States should not be conceptualized in terms of the economics of perfect competition. Hence, the market system is not synonomous with the functioning of the economy. Similarly, it is a mistake to conceptualize the market system or even market economy as synonomous with capitalism. Instead, the character and capacities of the market system must be conceptualized in terms of the historical background and drift, traditions, legal system and social and political goals and values of a nation or society.

If a nation or society wishes to (a) maintain a strong, widespread, and varied private enterprise base along with (b) free consumer-buyer choices among genuine alternatives and (c) "the rule of competition" in some acceptable degree, then the general market system must have the following interrelated capacities:

— To respond to and aid the free choices of buyers at all levels, especially the choices of consumer-buyers, as mechanism of communication, coordination and organization.

— To respond to and interact with general and specific external environmental influences, forces and conditions (i.e., the system must be open ended).

— To interact among the elements of the system internally, as an input-output system, including particularly the adjustment and shifting of resources from lesser advantaged uses to products, services, or geographical areas of greater advantage.

— To allocate acceptably that portion of economic resources not allocated by government outside the market system.

— To "regulate" in the sense of placing the participants under strong competitive compulsions for both (a) the efficient use of resources in production and in marketing, and (b) the effective fulfilment of the economic wants and desires of the members of the society....

Dual Impacts of Governmental Policies and Competition Upon Marketing and Growth Decisions of Private enterprise

We turn now to a brief interpretive appraisal of the dual impacts of competition under the market system and of governmental policies and regulations upon the basic market decisions and actions of private enterprise.

It is of high importance at this point to distinguish between two broad types of competition, which may be labeled "commodity" and "enterprise" competition. Always, of course, business enterprises are the producing ad marketing entities. But in the case of so-called "commodity competition," prices are definitely established for the enterprise's homogenous products by the impersonal supply and demand forces of the market. The problem of the enterprise is to collect, combine and use productive resources so efficiently as to a make profits and allow survival under the prices registered by a great macro-supply and demand cash register.

But in the case of "enterprise competition" the enterprise is in an environment, or creates one, in which profits and survival are not so clearly related to and determined by a simple price factor. The enterprise competes not only in the use of resources in production, but also in marketing and in "selling," In sense in this situation, the enterprise has its own micro-cash register which is still linked, however, with those of other enterprises (the macro-cash register) in a series of processes similar to those of modern computers linked together and also interacting with multiple remote control operators.

One test of the economic drift or trend of an economic society is the extent to which enterprises may be classified as under "commodity" or 'enterprise type" competition. Clearly, this distinction, too, has significance of or both the nature and functioning of the market system and appropriate public policy.

The discussion to follow is oriented primarily in terms of marketing decision s under the conditions of "enterprise competition" as now the more characteristic one in the United States.

Product Policies

On the whole product innovation, development and diversification are the bright spots under "enterprise competition" in the United States. The combined effects of governmental and private research and development and encouragement in a general environment of rapid scientific and technological change have given private enterprise an enormous dynamic, innovative thrust. On the whole, governmental policies and programmes are favourable, although there are unsettled issues concerning patent rights under governmentally sponsored Research and Development in some industries and of the new products in the food and drug industries.

Promotion Policies

In the main too, the environment in the United States is favorable to the use of personal and impersonal instruments and media for selling and promotion. This observation is of high importance because product innovation and development and promotion are parts of integrated processes. Time and again, we would not obtain the benefits of invention and innovation at all or as rapidly without effective promotion.

Product differentiation and promotion are supported by strong legal trademark and copyright protections. The chief thrust of public regulation is towards he protection of buyers, especially consumer-buyers, from deceit, falsehood and misrepresentation and to maintain conditions of fair competition among enterprises. On the whole, there is a relatively little public oversight of the use of personal selling, except through some local licensing. The focus of public regulation is upon impersonal selling or advertising in its various guises. Although such conjoined federal, state and local regulation often is onerous, the net effects on the whole usually are to support and channelize the competitive compulsion of the market system.

The chief burden of the public regulation of advertising is the protection of buyers, especially consumers, both with respect to quantity (weights and measures) and quality, and safety in use. Current public issues involve packaging (Hart Bill and consumer credit sales (Douglas Bill), and additional safeguards for uses in fields in which health and safety bulk high, as food and drugs and motor vehicles. In these and other instances, the problem of public regulation is to provide the requisite protection to buyers without encumbering business enterprises with unduly, detailed positive requirements.

Public issues in the field of promotion, important thought

they may be, appear to be much less important and much more likely of reasonable mutual solution than in some other areas of business decision making. The chief ultimate risks could arise out of unnecessarily detailed prescriptions over business promotional behaviour. Promotional policies and practices should be, and for the most part are, amenable to reasonable regulation under a combination of private, individual and cooperative efforts and public oversight. In addition, legally recognized "puffing" provides some latitude and flexibility in sales promotion even in the face of stringent, positive regulations.

Pricing Policies and Practices

Public policy and regulation, like economic analysis, focuses strongly upon prices and pricing. Pricing is the holy of holies of antitrust enforcement with its per se prohibition of price conspiracies and strong suspicion of the conscious parallelism and price leadership of oligopolistic competition and of so-called administered pricing.

Public policies affecting pricing bring into shaper contrast the differences in market circumstances and compulsions affecting "commodity" and "enterprise" competition. On the one hand, there is a strong tendency to support prices artificially when under the pressures of sever commodity competition. On the other, aggressive price cutting by enterprises is under suspicion as "price chiselling' and unfair competition. There tends to be a contradictory interaction as between the efforts of antitrust to break down price conspiracies and to enhance competition and special federal and state legislation directed at the aggressive use of price cutting by individual enterprises.

Much of the controversy and issues in public regulation is centered about so-called "administered pricing," and what to do about it. In all of this there tends to be an inherent and basic contradition between public policies and regulations conceptualized in terms of traditional commodity competition and the complex, totality of business-getting variables, of which "net price" is but one, in enterprise competition.

The conflicts and issues affecting pricing are focused on three broad bodies of special regulation (1) under the Robinson-patman Act addressed to price discrimination, (2) geographical, delivered pricing and (3) the resale price maintenance of branded goods. In not one of these broad, important areas of pricing has pubic policy achieved a reasonable, balanced relationship with the forces and compulsions of competition in and the market. In all three areas, there tends to be a general impact towards uniformity in pricing quite contrary to the accepted, *per se* prohibition of price agreements. The so-called "Fair Trade" laws allow manufacturers of trade-marked goods to impose uniform price structures upon the distributive trades when such action would be unlawful by their dealers themselves. Authorities agree that the net impacts of the enforcement of the Robinson-Patman Act probably have been towards restraint in pricing and a form of direct regulation country to the purposes of antitrust.

Oversight over geographical pricing has established clearly that organized, disciplined geographical, delivered price structures are unlawful in accordance with the general per se prohibition of price agreements. But there is a large zone of uncertainty and difference of attitudes and, in fact, a basic dilemma in enforcement under the conditions of "enterprise competition." On the one hand, systematic enforced delivered pricing structures on the part of business could subvert or even stifle the normal competitive forces and surplus and deficit adjustments of geographical competition in our great internal free trade market. On the other, simple enforcement solutions of the per se species on the part of enforcement agencies, if they run counter to basic market structural factors, could either be meaningless, or could produce a type of artificial, geographical price uniformity.

Marketing Organization of Individual Enterprises

Individual enterprises enjoy a great deal of freedom for choice among organizational alternatives to achieve marketing objectives, ranging from ownership and operation through vertical integration, through partial vertical integration, to a variety of exclusive and selective contractual and franshising arrangements. None of these forms of organization are illegal per se, but some are very nearly so. Thus, the acquisition of a competitor by a large firm raises legal risks so serious that most firms, especially large ones, would not wish to assume them. Thus, also, exclusive dealer or exclusive territorial arrangements are almost *per se* illegal for large enterprises with substantial volumes of sales. Similarly, franchise agreements by powerful manufacturers must be drawn carefully in relation to a strong presumption of unilateral control comparable to vertical integration with out all of its risks. The recent and current boom in franchise arrangements raises a host of unsettled legal issues.

In most public policy issues concerning organizational arrangements, legal determination requires the analysis and appraisal of the special circumstances of the case in terms of the actual and probable effects upon competition. The spectrum of legal risks ranges from horizontal acquisition to vertical downstream integration, to vertical upstream integration, to the variety of exclusive and selective contractual arrangements. In general small and local enterprises enjoy grater elative freedom than large established national firms. The doctrine seems to be emerging that arrangements that would be restrictive of competition by large firms may aid and strengthen competition when employed by smaller firms.

Conclusion Concerning Conjoined Impacts of Governmental Polices and Competition upon Private Decision Making

It appears that private enterprise decisions and practices in product innovation, development and promotion, on the whole are in both a favourable competitive and public policy environment (with notable exceptions, of course). Public policy affecting pricing starts out bravely with its *per se* prohibition of price agreement but falters and to some extent reverses itself under the Robinson-Patman and Fair Trade Laws and shows signs of internal contradiction in geographical pricing. The broad drift of public policy affecting organizational arrangements seems increasingly to be oriented against restrictions and in opposition to growth in size, market share and vertical ownership and control, especially downstream and less so upstream. On the whole, the total net impact of governmental policies affecting private decision making, except in some strategic aspects of pricing, tend to support the internal competitive compulsions of the market system. The debits on the side of pricing may be more than offset by the credits on the side of product development and promotion.

Growth Policies and Market Structure

In recent years there has been an enormous interest in problems of economic growth in this country and even more so in the so-called undeveloped or underdeveloped countries. In the United States the discussion of National policies affecting economic growth have often been interlinked with discussions of the control of inflation and the maintenance of prices stability. Obviously, in a society with a private enterprise base, therefore, the impact of total national economic policies and of law and regulation upon growth incentives, opportunities and the patterns of growth of business firms is of highest importance. We shall omit from our discussion at this point national policies aimed at influencing aggregate demand by spending programmes, tax reduction and the like. Clearly, of course, these affect the marketing opportunities of private business. Insofar as such programmes can be timed appropriately and not used to weaken normal competitive forces, they can improve the environment of private opportunity. Our concern is more definitely with the effects of governmental regulations, including antitrust, upon incentives and policies for expansion and growth by individual firms.

First, in general, the intent of our national economic policies and regulations is not to inhibit growth of individual enterprises, except in one major respect to be discussed below, but to channelize it within the rules of the game. These rules comprise the great body of the law and regulations of unfair competition, abusive and predatory practices and behaviour and endeavours to monopolize. Such laws and regulations govern relations with competitors and suppliers and customers, i.e., all aspects of production and marketing.

Second, growth by internal expansion within the rules of the game is now looked upon much more favourably than growth by acquisitions and mergers, especially in antitrust enforcement. In general, it is believed that growth through ploughing back learnings and through gradual increase in the patronage of satisfied customers is more solid and substantial than by the acquisition of or merger wit established firms. From the point of view of antitrust it is held that growth internally expands investment and production and hence increases competition, while growth by merger and acquisition in some sense removes a competitor or a supplier or a customer from the market. In any event, there is no necessary increase in net investment or of production.

This view, when stated so simply, of course, disregards the new investments and expansion of output that might be and often are made following a merger. Even so, it cannot be defined that if this same investment had been made in developing entirely new facilities in addition to the existing ones, total investment and hence competition could most likely be greater. Much will depend upon the special circumstances and especially upon the longer run trends, including the likelihood that the acquired firm would have failed in any event.

Third, the most critical issue affecting the growth of corporations in the United States is the trend of enforcement under the 1950 revision of Sec. 7 of the Clayton Act. As of the time of writing, the number and character of cases adjudicated and in process, and the weight of opinions by the Supreme Court of the United States in the small number of cases adjudicated, indicate that almost any merger or acquisition can be questioned, and a large proportion most likely negated. There is almost no large American corporation that does no now face one of the following problems: (1) the possibility that acquisitions made earlier may be questioned under "the backward bite" of antitrust, (2) whether to invest heavily in the improvement of recent acquisitions that might be questioned, or (3) whether to move forward with acquisitions under consideration.

American business now finds itself in a new environment

so far as growth by mergers and acquisition is concerned. Under the present portents, it may well turn out that we have witnessed the last great merger movement n American history. If this be true, it could be of tremendous importance because many great American corporations were built to a considerable extent through the processes merger. To state this is not to deny the tremendous force of internal expansion separately or together with mergers.

Perhaps the most significant factor of all in terms of the maintenance and promotion of competition is that the entire force of action under Section 7 is to change market structure. But if existing and new firms are denied growth by acquisition, then powerful established corporations to some extent receive protection in growth through internal expansion. The successful, established forms whose growth by acquisition is most likely to be questioned are also the firms best equipped in terms of resources for growth through building new facilities. It would seem almost inevitable, therefore, that strong enforcement under revised Section 7 would at some stage involve an increasing interest in Big Cases under Section 2 of the Scherman Act. In other words, bigness and giantism, and concentration of market and economic power, would come to the front in antitrust policy both with respect to growth by internal expansion and growth by acquisition.

Very likely, the issues and drift on this score will be clarified somewhat when further cases involving conglomerate acquisitions are adjudicated, for these, in a very direct sense, focus upon *Bigness, per se,* or economic concentration as opposed to market concentration. But the cases adjudicated or now moving forward to the Supreme Court most likely will touch only upon peripheral issues. The determination of public policy on this issue probably will be in the political arena and not through the application of economic and marketing analysis in antitrust cases. Hopefully economics and marketing will not be disregarded entirely, however, in the political moves. The character of the testimony at recent hearings is an optimistic omen.

In public policy it was widely believed (with some dissident views) that investment diversification and growth by conglomerate acquisitions were relatively acceptable in contrast with horizontal and vertical integration and acquisitions. Horizontal expansion, especially by acquisitions, reduced competition on the same level. Vertical expansion, and especially acquisition, reduced competition presumably by removing or weakening a supplier or customer. But conglomerate diversification, broadly conceived, was held to increase competition by the entrance of established firms into new areas. In such moves, broad, inter-industry forces of competition could be promoted and presumably competition increased. But in recent years, a view has been arising that broad nonfunctional diversification, especially by the acquisition of established firms, is one of the greatest threats to competition through the exercise of "conglomerate power," allegedly a new, insidious type of monopoly power. As of new, it is impossible to reconcile these two views either in economic and managerial theory or in law and regulation. Again, we are forced to revert to the legal processes of case by case analysis and determination. Undoubtedly, conglomerate diversification at times strengthens the competitive compulsions of the market systems, and sometimes such overlapping of large corporations may be the only feasible means of doing so. Undoubtedly, too, the reverse does, or could occur, especially then large, powerful firms enter areas occupied by small local and regional enterprises. Undoubtedly, too, in public policy, some bounds must be provided to protect the market system from large indigestible globs that could become almost global in competitive outreach.

Very likely, too, in many situations, the character of the use of whatever "conglomerate power' may have been achieved, could be subject to control under either (1) Section 5 of the Federal Trade Commission Act governing unfair methods and practices of or (2) Sec. 1 of the Sherman Act governing the restraint of trade, without structural change. In this manner, the enhanced competitive impacts might be preserved but within the rules of the competitive game. Both persons and business enterprises can be expected to show restraint in the exercise of abilities and capacities. To made the mere possession of power to act the basis of action pushes regulation towards structural adjustments intended to enhance the impersonal compulsions of the market system. Whether this makes sense depends upon the actual and potential market structural and behavioural circumstances of each situation and cannot be answered in general terms.

Above all, it is a mistake to assume that the character and effectiveness of competition bear a simple, direct relationship to the number of competitors alone. Consequently, it could be a grievous error to take action based upon the mere presence of ability to act when (1) market structure adjustments would not in fact negate such power and (2) the beneficial aspects of enhanced competition could be preserved without abuse...

Appraisal in Terms of the Required Capacities of an Acceptable Market System. We are in a position now to generalize concerning the extent to which the general market system in the United States is able to exercise the five types of capacities suggested as essential for the maintenance of an acceptable, viable market system.

Response to and facilitation of buyer choices, especially of consumer buyers; In the main, the conclusion here is favourable, although many, including some top professional economists, will disagree. There is a widespread view that consumer sovereignty is a wasting, perhaps already wasted asset—that consumer choices are determined largely by a conjoined group behaviourism and Madison Avenue. No one, of course, is able to prove or disprove a generalization so sweeping and so subjective, and running so counter to the marketing experience of even the most powerful corporations. It would seem much more sensible for purposes of public policy in a democracy to accept the fact of consumer choice among genuine alternatives as given and then to continue to try to guarantee that the choices can be made from among genuine, honest, competitive alternates. The same conclusion would seem even more reasonable and easier to enforce at the other levels of buying choice The lack of opportunity for choice among independent alternatives might well be a major criterion in the selection of antitrust cases. Such opportunity, for choice, if at all possible, should be available at all levels and for all offerings in the market system.

Interaction to external environmental influences: Out market system is not a mechanical closed system but is open-ended and is responding to innumerable external pressures and influences including governmental regulations and intervention. There is not guarantee, however, that the net results of the interventions are beneficial in terms of maintaining a viable effective market system adequate for a society wit a private enterprise base. It would be an enormous contribution to make an objective considered estimate of the net effects and the general drift and tendencies.

Internal Interaction within the system: The interactions within the market system are focused most sharply on product (Out Put) markets instead of at the level of factor inputs. Increasingly, the prices of factor inputs are being removed from determination by the market system or placed under the shared rule of governmental regulations and the market. This observation applies for example to labour, energy, freight, some raw materials, some services, and some communication inputs which are outside the market bargain, more or less. The Robinson-Patman Act tends also to place restraints over the input price level. A consequence of the to accentuate rendencies towards upstream vertical integration.

So far as the shifting of resources within the system from lesser continuing processes of innovative and of imitative competition. On the whole, the American marketing system displays enormous internal vitality in terms of the innovative, adaptive and imitative use of resources in "enterprise competition." When this does to occur, because of barriers to entry or agreement among competitors, then antitrust authorities should be interested and take the appropriate steps. The largest such areas in terms of economic analysis, of course, is allegedly the short term or long term strength of market position engendered by he successful product differentiation and brand promotion as noted earlier.

In this area, however, public policy must tread softly and deftly, because much of the high strategy and dynamism of American enterprise competition is found here, and must be so in the presence of a strong anticartel policy, let alone the magnitude of the potential gains of success in our rich national market amplified by multi-national opportunities. Furthermore, opportunity for differential gain along these lines must be held out to enterprises, in order to encourage and support the cots and risks of product innovation and development.

Ability to act as an allocating medium for resources not allocated by government outside the market system: To some extent, the allocating responsibility was discussed in the preceding section in terms of the internal interactions of the system. It remains to be noted, however, that in all societies, governments talks some direct responsibility for the allocation of much or all of the land, raw material and capital resources. In some underdeveloped countries the allocations of the market system are either not trusted or are considered too slow for the purposes of economic development, and, in communist and socialist societies, the primary means of control under the Central Plan is through the allocation of basic resources.

But evening the United States, a large portion of resources allocation is outside the market system, through public ownership and employment, the public services, defense and military programmes, and tax collections and disbursements. It would be enormously help to have a solid estimate of the extent to which resource allocation occurs through the market mechanism in the United States, or is under a planned sharing of governmental regulation and the market.

In this connection there is a well publicized view that the market can or should have a decreasing role in a society of abundance, as in the Untied States. N other words, we should look forward to a broad expansion of the public services outside and in lieu of the market system. This view reflects to some extent (1) the belief that consumer sovereignty through the market has wasted away and (2) a higher degree of confidence in voting through the ballot box than through cash registers.

5. To regulate; i.e., to enforce the discipline of the "rule of competition": In the United States, the "rule of competition" is relief upon chiefly in the final, manufactured product markets and in the distributive trades. Insofar as market discipline has been removed from factor-input markets, its remaining impact is chiefly towards the efficient use of resources in production and in marketing in final product markets and in the effective fulfillment of given buyer choices or in market innovation. Obviously, this is a large important and strategic responsibility for the market system, especially because it is the medium for serving and influencing the ultimate consumers. This is also the accepted area of active antitrust enforcement, although recent indications suggest that antitrust, under new interpretations of areas of primary jurisdiction, may tend to become more effective in some of the factor-input markets than has been assumed traditionally, unless restrained by new specially legislation. It is in this area, too, that the chips as they fall, indicate the type of society or position on the spectrum between a full command society or a full market society. And finally, it is here and in the trend of the allocation of basic resources, including capital resources, that the broad economic, political drift of a society can bet be observed.

Hear the Message of the Market Place

For the past several years, the "marketing point of view" has probably been the most popular recurring topic at professional, trade association and company meetings. As a result, many companies and their managers have accepted a superficial commitment to market-mined thinking. They often lack, however, a clear understanding of what is involved for their organisations. In time, they are likely to become discouraged with results, and they may even abandon what could be the most profitable administrative change their firms could introduce.

It is important, therefore, to ask what is meant by the term "marketing viewpoint. What is its proper role in management planning and action? How can it be introduced and put to work effectively? What benefits should be anticipated?

The place to start answering these questions is not the office of the marketing vice president. Rather, it is the office of the president, the man responsible for formulating and executing a the general management function in his business.

The general management function is the brain of a business—the guiding control. It determines principal goals and organizes there sources to achieve them. It designs the policies that define a firm's character and the strategies and tactics that follow. Inevitably, therefore, the way a general manager view his business must have a strong influence on how that business is run and how it performs.

The significance of this point has not been clearly grasped in many proposals to give the marketing function greater attention. To say that marketing needs more emphasis is superficial. What managers really need is a new way of looking at their organisation, an ability to see in the familiar business a wholly different character than they formerly observed and perhaps took for granted.

This is the kind of fresh viewpoint that in the 1920's saw the opportunity to launch the Sears, Roebuck and the Montgomery ward mail-order firms into general merchandise retailing on a national scale. It is the viewpoint that in the 1930's grasped the potential of self-service grocery stores and proceeded to revolutionize the retailing of food. Te same innovative outlook is now beginning to use the grocery supermarket for distributing a variety of non-food items. Another example is offered by the successful attack of the discount house in the 1950's on the traditional high markup, full-service retailing of household appliances.

This is the kind of management imagination that sees in the computer not simply a high-powered clerical machine but an information processing tool that can change techniques of decision-making and help to displace management art and hunch with a rational, quantitative approach to the solution of complete problems.

We can best see the significance of this revolution in management thinking if we contrast two basic ways of looking at a business.

The first—which dominated management thinking through the initial phase of the industrial revolution—sees the firm primarily as a producing organism.

Management attention is focused on engineering and manufacturing problems. The drive for efficiency identifies production as the place to reduce costs. It presses to simplify product design, substitute cheaper materials, mechanize work operations, replace batch with continuous-flow processes. Most recently, the thrust is to automate manufacturing activities. In this setting, efforts to innovate are directed principally toward improving existing products and processes. In short, management sees direct relation between cost cutting and profits, and acts accordingly. Marketing is not, of course, ignored in this management view. But the sales function is treated largely as an effort to find customers for the output of the plant. Marketing costs are regarded as a necessary evil—as expenses rather than investment. The are dealt with as if they were passive influences in the total array of business activities. One common result of this attitudes is that marketing budgets tend to be established in relation to revenue, usually as a predetermined percentage of present or forecast sales.

A contrasting way of looking at a business sees the firm primarily as a marketing organism.

Question to Answer

Here, management's view looks outward toward the customer. The important questions to be answered before making policy or investment decisions are: who are the present and potential customers? Where do they live and buy? What are their purchase habits and preferences, and why? What needs are served by the company's products and services? What important needs are not adequately served? What is the state of competition? The market share? The trends? The prospects? What sales potentials are suggested by evolving economic and social developments? Out of the answers to these questions come the data for investment, research, engineering and production decisions, as well as the design of marketing programmes.

Production and engineering are not ignored in this management view. But it treats the manufacturing function and everything related to it as resources to be used in designing and delivering the most profitable responses to the challenges and opportunities of the market. Expenditures for marketing activities are seen as investments. They are determined flexibly in relation to profit potentials, rather than rigidly as ratios of costs to sales.

The history of the introduction of scientific management techniques clearly reveals the dominance of the production-centered view in management thinking throughout the first half of this century. What we call scientific management was designed for the control of manufacturing. Time and motion study, cost analysis, budgeting, mathematical rules for decision-making, in fact every advance from art to science in administration occurred initially in production. Scientific management in marketing has lagged by at least one generation. It is only since about 1950 that any lively interest has appeared in applying the new management techniques to marketing.

A Pervasive influence

The Marketimg-centered view of a businessinfluences every aspect of management. Consider, for example, the policies that govern decisions about variety in a product line. In contrast to the simplicity urged by the production view, the marketing view recommends diversity to meet the full range of customers' wants and needs. The production manager's concept of an ideal world is one in which a single product--one design, one size, one colour--moves uninterruptedly down the manufacturing line. This minimize all product costs; tooling, setup, instruction and supervision of workers, scheduling of work flow, ordering of raw materials, investment in inventories. The marketing manager's contrasting concept is one in which no customer ever has to be told he cannot have what he wants.

The historical dominance of the production view has been assisted by solid evidence (in accounting records) of costs attributable to product variety. Marketing HAS BEEN Weakened by the inability to trace an identifiable cost to an order unfilled shipment delayed because of a narrow product line or a thin inventory.

The production view presses for retaining old products for which tooling, materials and knowledge are established. The marketing view presses for discarding old products in favour of improved models, or designing new products to serve customers' needs more precisely, or gaining an advance on competitors.

> The production view, in short, is cost-oriented. The marketing view is revenue-oriented.
>
> The production view cherishes stability. The marketing view welcomes and encourages change and innovation.
>
> The production view approaches pricing decisions from the expense side. The marketing view approaches them from the revenue side. The production view asks: "
>
> How much will it cost to make this?" The marketing view asks: "How much will we make if we sell this?"
>
> The marketing view sees the present through the eyes of the future.

At the general management level the two views must, of course, be brought into balance and tested against the profit criterion. A total surrender to the marketing view could lead to a galloping case of policies growth. Nevertheless, the dynamic competitive pressures of our economy increasingly complain approach to the profit balance by way of the marketing viewpoint. This amounts to a prescription to look at a business first as a market-oriented mechanism. Production considerations can be surveyed later on the way to a summary assessment of investment, cost, risk and profit.

This changed viewpoint can be brought about even in along established industry, like railroading. The Southern Pacific, for example, has long been acclaimed for defining its business mission as the provision of transportation, not only railroad services. Another road, the Southern, has recently been applauded by observers for its creative, revenue-and-profit-conscious attack on the complex proems of fright rates.

A comparable change is being accomplished in some equipment manufacturing companies that have broadened their operations from selling individual machines to designing and marketing integrated materials handling and processing systems, under automated control.

When the marketing view takes precedence in top management thinking, the business is often seen in a new way. One of the most dramatic examples of this fresh view is the recognition that research and development can be applied in marketing as usefully and as profitably as in production. A retail chain may use one unit as an experimental laboratory for studying lay out, traffic flow, merchandise display or prices. A manufacturing company with national distribution may use one territory as a research area in which experiments are conducted on marketing methods, sales promotion techniques or customer services. New types of advertising, new copy slants or a new package are tested "guinea pig" audiences before major investment commitments are made.

In this way, the information required for a profitable approach to servicing dynamic consumer demand can become the first input to management thinking about every aspect of the business. Out of such studies come guidelines for engineering and product research. Out of these studies, too, come ideas for innovation in distribution techniques. Products maybe profitably sold in retail stores or through industrial middlemen previously not in the marketing stream. Novel packaging ideas, such as containers with secondary household uses, may be evolved. Now services or financing arrangements may be developed. Research on competitive practices and consumer demand may throw light on pricing decisions and encourage managers to break the shackles of cost-plus pricing.

More Innovation

The primacy of a marketing viewpoint is likely to be left in other areas, as well. It encourages planning and location inventories to meet customer requirements rather than production convenience. If favours scheduling a profit rather tnan a cost criterion.

Above all, leadership from the marketing viewpoint sees the future as a source of profitable opportunities ready for exploitation by imaginative management. It fears the changing circumstances that threaten investment in manufacturing facilities which may be obsolete before their useful life has been exhausted.

How can the marketing viewpoint be brought into a position of dominance in general management thinking?

There is no single, simple answer to this question. Installing an experienced marketing manager as chief executive officer will not be effective if his principal associates in research, production and finance do not change the way they look at the business. Redesigning the organisation chart to bring more marketing managers into the policy-making arena may encourage divisive factionalism and delay in planning and executing programmes.

What is required is no less than a comprehensive turn-around of the thinkihg, of the total mental set of all top-level managers. Such a transformation will do more than affect the shaping of policy at the organization's peak. It will also help to thrust the new ideas down through the layers of the line organization.

The head of one large corporation attacked the problem by hiring an our side consultant to study the company's weak market position in one part of its diversified product line and recommend a new approach He then used the consultant's radical marketing proposals as a target for interdepartmental study by working groups at several levels. From vice presidents down to middle managers in the line organization, with an assignment to examine every implication of the recommended programme for engineered, production and finance. The outcome was an amended programme to which all functions were committed. The new marketing approach was then put into operation. Its successful performance in revenues, profits and strengthened competitive position led to queries about the possibility of study other parts of the product line in the same way. In the president's view, the evolving experience, building step by step, is demonstrably encouraging an active interest in marketing potential and requirements throughout his management group.

Another company is trying a different roue toward the same objective. Outstanding divisional managers in every part of the business are begin assigned planned tours of duty in the marketing department. Here they work not as observers but as responsible line executive. Early results make the president confident that the value of a marketing viewpoint is being properly appreciated in all pars of the management team.

Whatever the approach, the job must be viewed as a comprehensive educational effort. What we know about the educational process tells to that it is slow, that it builds strength through reinforcement of theory in practice, that it needs both precept and example. No simple policy pronouncement of the "we have entered new era' variety can do more than delude the gullible and inflame the naive within a management group

CHAPTER 5

CONNECTION BETWEEN SCIENTIFIC MARKETING AND MARKET STRATEGY

The marketing area will find maximum opportunity to apply the scientific method if they consciously endeavour to formulate a concrete market strategy. Preferably, this formulation will take a written form, and be quite explicit and detailed. A market strategy combines explicit ends and the means selected to achieve them; the scientific method can be employed to a considerable degree to assess the effectiveness of alternative measures for attaining any given objective. If business management is to become more scientific, the firm's objectives must first be clearly stated. This is essential, since formulating marketing strategy involves the definition of the firm's broad objectives and the translation of these into marketing objectives. After this has been done, marketing targets must be set, and the appropriate marketing mix to achieve these targets must be selected.

Business management has been called many things: it commonly is described as an art; some describe it as a guessing game. Perhaps the height of wisdom on his subject is contained in the phrase, "business is business," for business is not like anything else. Clearly, success as a business executive requires what some people describe as "artistry" and intuition—though these probably are far less vital than just plain luck. In addition, in this paper endeavours to prove, successful business management demands careful and maximum application of the scientific method.

The scientific method obviously needs no defense; only an eccentric will maintain that guesses are more valid bases for decision than careful observation and experimentation. However, the phases of business management that are amenable to scientific methods are far from obvious.

Little is to be gained by pointing a finger at businessmen for having managerial decision-making in a relatively primitive state until recently while production men applied the fruits of science to achieve miracles in the factory. The very large number of business failures and high turnover among business executives have been punishment enough. However, the contrast between the methods by which managerial and production decisions are made deserves emphasis, for there exists an influential body of executives—and some academicians—who find the main ingredient of business success to be "good judgement and practice of the managerial art." These phrases are question begging unless one is able to define what is meant by good judgment and the managerial art. Moreover, such as view deprecates the importance of fact-gathering, rigorous reasoning, hypothesis-testing—and all elements of the scientific method that can be applied to many of the problems faced by businessmen.

It may appear pretentious to link business management with the scientific method. When one speaks of "scientific management" or "scientific marketing" he simply means that business decisions should have the maximum benefit of factual support, close rigorous reasoning, and empirical test; also, that every conclusion reached should be open to challenge and be capable of rational defense. There is no room in this concept for bowing to authority, deference to the intuitions or experience" of older men or persons associated with the business for a longer time; it requires that decisions be made on the basis of facts and logical argument rather than by appeal to authority.

No one familiar with business dreams that it will become an "exact science" which rest upon a body of proved principles analogous to what has been produced by the chemist and physicist. Everyone knows that duplicable experiments cannot be the main technique employed for arriving at generalizations applicable to business. The methods available to business executives for solving concrete problems are, at bet, relatively crude, unreliable and unproved by the standards of most physical sciences. However, the year vastly more reliable than reliance on hunch, intuitions, feel and guesses, or appeal to authority.

The scientific method, or the most scientific techniques applicable to business—however one prefers to express it—is not to be confused with the use of the conference or committee method of decision-making. All too often, these methods are applied in a manner that brings several uninformed people together to pool their thoughts and hammer out a common agreement. A "bull session," no matte by what elegant title it may be dignified, will not produce valuable results unless at least some participant are very well informed. Once maximum use is made of observation and experimentation, discussion will generally prove very valuable; however, it certainly cannot substitute for the collection and analysis of facts.

Practitioners in most fields—especially those who practice for a fee—understandably are anxious to persuade others that their fields of specialization are sciences. Only recently, however, have some person specializing are sciences. Only recently, however, have some persons specializing in business fields claimed to be "applied" scientists. To understand that they claim, one must also know what they disavow. Almost all admit their inability to remotely approach the accuracy, predictability and even objectivity of most physical sciences. But they maintain that there do exist data, methods of data collection, experimental and testing procedures, and methods of analyzing and testing findings whose application to business would greatly increase the proportion of correct managerial decisions. Rather than great accuracy in absolute terms, these people claim to be relatively accurate in a field where attempts at systematic and rigorous answers to problems remain exceptional.

How can Business Management be made more Scientific?

To make business management into an applied science, executives, must first clarify their firm's objectives. Although the selection of ultimate business objectives is necessarily unscientific, for they express the fundamental values f individuals who establish broad policy, operating objectives stated fully, clearly, and concretely are indispensable if one is to make managerial decision-making amenable to the scientific method. Once objectives are known, the selection of means becomes the task of appraising, by the best means available, the relative effectiveness of alternatives.

A Statement of a Firm's Broad Objectives. Business objectives can be stated on a variety of levels; one must begin with the ultimate—the broadest and most general—and work back to the more narrow and specific ends that they imply. The two most widely expressed ultimate objectives of corporate management these days are: first, to make maximum profits for the firm over the life of the enterprise and strictly within the limits of the law; and, second, to conduct operations in a manner that gives equal weight to the claims of; stockholders, labour, consumers and government. Bcth of these broad objectives must be translated into more specific market goals if they are to be very helpful to executives responsible for making concrete business decisions.

Statement of Market Objectives. In pursuit of maximum profits, for example, management might set its operating objectives at: a maximum of dollar or unit sales; a maximum share of total or of particular geographic markets; maximum profit figured as a percentage of net worth or of sales; it might set itself the objective of a steadily increasing return on sales or profits; or the goal of an increasing market share. Bt even if narrowed this far, the objectives are not as helpful as they can be made. It is possible to state market objectives in a form that facilitates an application of the scientific method.

Market objectives are best expressed as customer types—

narrowly defined—whose patronage the business will try especially to win. (Of course, it will not turn away others desiring to buy.) Once objectives have been refined to this on, management is in a position to formulate more specific problems in a manner that makes it readily amenable to solution by the scientific method:

A determination of the types of customers the firm should try to service in particular does not flow simply and logically from a firm's ultimate objectives. A careful consideration of alternative markets must underline the selection of those markets to be cultivated intensively.

Concept of a "Market Strategy"

Put differently, use of "scientific" methods for making marketing decisions calls for what is here termed a "market strategy," The main purpose of this paper is to explain what a market strategy consists of and how it can serve as a potent organizing tool for the decisions of business executives. It may well assist students of marketing by giving a central structure to various facets of the study of business.

A market strategy consists of two parts: (1) the definition of market targets—selecting the types of customers whose patronage will be sought; and (2) the "composition of a marketing mix"—picking a combination of sales promotion devices that will be employed. Market targets represent the operating objectives (which are subject to change of curse) of top management; the marketing mix represents a combination of instruments by which these objectives are pursued.

The scientific method finds its greatest potential application to marketing by calling for a rigorous appraisal of the relative effectiveness of alternative means of winning the patronage of particular types of potential customers. The scientific marketer must assemble the best evidence available, determine what additional evidence should be gathered, subject all information collected to rigorous analysis, formulate and test hypotheses regarding the effect on unit sales of such things as: price changes, changes in the quality of the product, advertising outlays, number of salesmen, margins offered retailers, number of retail outlets, etc.

It will be acknowledged at the outset that no generalizations about these matters can be applied to all or even to many products. Answers to specific marketing problems probably differ for each individual business—and will not even be stable for it over long periods of time. Thus, top management must reconcile itself to an unending study of the relative effectiveness of sales promotion devices. An agreement's success in achieving the market a targets it sets itself will, it is maintained here, depend upon the scientific rigor with which it conducts this endless study—rather than upon the artistry and intuition of its top executives.

The steps involved in the formulation of a market strategy will be discussed in broad general terms in this paper. First, the determination of market targets will be taken up; thereupon, the composition of a marketing mix will be discussed.

Definition of Market Targets.

No one can hope to please everybody! Person who attempt to win the friendship of everyone are likely to have few friends, for they will lack individuality and basic personality. Many will doubt their sincerity and almost everyone will get an uneasy feeling in their presence and think that there is something "fishy" about them. Businesses who try to sell to everybody risk a similar fate. If they attempt to convince their prestige conscious customers that their product represents the highest possible quality and the brand that customers buy if they do not have to worry about cost, they may repel potential customers who are extremely concerned about economy But, if they claim that the product represents both the highest possible quality and the lower price, they will be believed by almost no one.

No business needs to sell to all potential customers. A fraction of the total market is all any firm need hope for—-and the Department of Justice frowns on those wit more ambitious hopes. IT IS Almost always wise for a management to select consciously the types of customers it will try to win as their firm's main patrons; in so doing, management can mobilize the full resources of the firm to a clearly defined task. To make such a selection, management should first divide the total potential market into its "significant segments.

Potential customers must be divided into groups that have some significance from the standpoint of what management can and should do about them. The most important criteria for segmenting the market for any product are: (1) strength of their need or desire for the product: (2) channels (media, distribution outlet, etc.) through which they can be reached; (3) "appeals" (lines of argument) to which they are responsive; (4) degrees of responsiveness to particular types of sales appear (that is, their ability to be influenced by price considerations, availability of credit, sales talk of salesmen, etc.); and (5) physical location.

The most significant market segments vary widely from product to product. Customers must be classified according to the many special features of the product in question and of the circumstances under which it is sold. In almost every case, however, there are two types of criteria that should be employed: the first are the features traditionally used by market analysts. These generally can be measured and include such things as: incomes, marital status, size of family, religion age, size of community, whether or not the product is already owned, the age and condition of the product owned, etc. The second are social and psychological characteristics that almost always are unmeasurable and apply particularly to the product in question. For example, one might divide potential customers of most products into: the self-confident and those who are unsure of themselves; the adventurous and those craving the familiar; the ostentatious and the modest, etc. In addition, particular attitudes are confronted in the marketing of some products but have no being upon others. For example, it seems to have been established that the use of instant coffee is associated in the minds of many housewives with neglect of a wife's proper duties. This attitude is not likely to have any bearing upon the sale of women's hats, however.

As already indicated, the criteria by which potential customers are divided should meet two tests; (1) they should reflect differences which indicate or affect the actions that businessmen should take in trying to win their patronage; and (2) they should apply to the particular product in the specific markets in which they are being sold. In classifying potential customers, one should err, if at all, in the direction of dividing them into too many rather than too few groups. Both measurable and unmeasurable characteristics should be combined into one scheme of classification. It is likely that one will end up with many scores of market segments; as stated the more the better.

Those segments should then be scrutinized carefully to determine; (1) which ones are least adequately served at present: (2) those which the particular firm is best qualified to attract—because of its product, personnel, tradition, reputation, standing in the customer's mind, etc.; and (3) those that management would like to make the core of the business over the future, simply on grounds of personal taste.

By scrutinizing the total potential market broken down into segments possessing significance for action, a management may well find that several parts of the market had gone relatively uncovered. It so, it may profit by cultivating those particular markets, using measures especially effective in winning their patronage.

Management should also select the market segments to cultivate intensively by matching its own resources against what is needed to "sell" particular types of prospective customers. Special qualities about a firm's management, location, past performance, design of product. Company tradition, etc. may make it particularly effective in serving certain market segments. To match the firm against market segments involves a realistic appraisal of the firm's strengths and weakness and of the factors that influence the purchase of each potential customer group. Often a firm will find itself especially suited to win patronage from particular types of customers—which may also be actively cultivated by some of its competitors.

Not infrequently, there is a conflict between market targets that are an covered and those for which the firm has special talent. A choice must be made, and often it will not be an easy one.

Businessmen are people! They have likes and dislikes that do and should influence their decisions. The most profitable markets may be found in regions which require location in uncomfortable climates or uncongenial social environments. In part, a selection of market segments for intensive cultivation must be influenced by such considerations. However, management cannot long follow its inclinations if they would result in persistent losses.

To summarize what has been said upto this point, a scientific market strategy first requires that a business formulate general and broad objectives. These must then be translated into operating objectives, by specifying the particular market segments the firm will cultivate most intensively.

To make such a decision, which is among he most crucial that management must make, requires an exhaustive division of all potential customers into segments which possess marketing significance—that is, they are best cultivated in different ways. The selection of the particular segments that the firm should cultivate intensively should be made on grounds of the extent to which they are being neglected at present, the special qualifications that the firm possesses to serve them and the taste of the business owners.

Composition of the Marketing Mix. Once the firm's market targets have been specified, management faces the task of selecting measures most likely to achieve them. In modern marketing parlance, we must discuss the "marketing mix."

The "marketing mix" is composed of large battery of devices which might be employed to induce customers to buy a particular product. The same devises are involved whether one is of thinking of inducing altogether new buyers to purchase the product or of shifting customers from rival bands to one's own. These devices are here termed" sales promotion devices "and include a wide variety of instruments. It is wise to list separately those which are at the disposal of manufactures and those which may be employed by distributors and dealers.

Sales promotion devices that might be used by manufactures to induce customers to buy their products include such things as: quality of product, special product features, amount of advertising outlays, lines of advertising outlays, lines of advertising appeals employed, types of advertising media used, number of personal salesmen employed, quality f salesmen, distributive channels employed, quality of distributors used, number of distributions, location of sales effort (geographically), product guarantees, servicing arrangements, credit and accommodations supplied.

Distributors and dealers might use the following instruments to induce customers to patronize them; price inducements, advertising, number and quality of salesmen, location, air conditioning, location of merchandise departments in the store, breauth of selection offered customers, width of aisles, hours of operation, return privileges, credit accommodation, delivery service, etc.

Even though the foregoing lists of sales promotion devices are far from complete, they are long. And, what is especially significant, management must make decisions regarding almost every one of them. Either consciously or by default, a management decides whether or not to employ each device and in what form and to what degree.

Although a firm may concentrate on one particular sales promotion device, it almost invariably employs many of them to some degree. Even firms which rely primarily upon the appeal of low price must d some advertising; if they were not to do so, their low price offerings might not be noticed by many customers. Moreover, they are generally compelled to give some assurance of acceptable quality (by guarantees or return privileges). The point urged here is that each firm must employ a combination of sales promotion devices, rather than only one, and that the overriding task of marketing management consists in selecting the optimum combination. The formulation of a combination of sales promotion devices is sometimes described as the "Composition of a marketing mix" for an actual firm.

1. The selection of a marketing mix must be made very explicitly in terms of the particular market segments whose patronage is to be sought most intensively.

2. To a considerable degree, the individual sales promotion devices are substitutes for one another. One could spend more on advertising or to hire personal salesmen of higher quality, or to build more quality into the product, etc.

3. Almost every one of the possible sales promotion devices must be employed in some form ad to some degree. No single line of appeal for patronage will suffice.

4. In deciding how much to rely upon each sales promotion device, the following general rules should be applied:

   (a) Never expend sums for sales promotion unless you anticipate that they will produce enough additional revenue to cover all of the costs incurred to obtain that revenue—including the sales promotion outlay. (One must take account of the effect of a sales promotion outlay on future sales as well as their immediate impact.)

   (b) Compare alternative sales promotion devices that might be employed to obtain any specified increase in sales volume and employ that one which involves least cost.

Connection Between "Scientific Marketing" and Market Strategy

Executives with responsibility in the marketing area will find maximum opportunity to apply the scientific method if they consciously endeavour to formulate a concrete market strategy. Preferably, this formulation will take a written form, and be quite explicit and detailed. A market strategy combines explicit ends and the means selected to achieve them; the scientific method can be employed to a considerable degree to assess the effectiveness of alternative measures for attaining any given objective.

Specifically, top marketing executives will be entitled to regard themselves as 'scientific' if they carry out the following steps:

1. Formulate each problem clearly and sharply, and in a form that lends itself to maximum verification by the use of evidence.
2. Gather available evidence bearing on the problem.
3. Arrange for the collection of additional information that would contribute to a solution to the problem—within the financial means of the firm.
4. Organize and analyze the information gathered in a manner that will shed maximum light on the solution to the original problem.
5. Formulate conclusions suggested by the evidence into hypotheses, such of which implies a potential solution to the original problem.
6. Test the hypotheses to the fullest extent possible.
7. Make a list of alternative solutions to the problem that has been discarded in favour of the one selected.

Historical Antecedents of the Marketing Strategy Concept

When a new concept stands by itself, its meaning and significance often are unclear. It contrasted with other views and seen as part of a general progression of ideas, it generally can be understood and appraised rather easily. Accordingly, the notions which preceded the marketing strategy concept will be described very briefly. Historians recording the process of intellectual discovery invariably conclude that thought develops in an orderly, step-by-step method. Whether this view is valid or is the creation of the historian themselves sometimes is unclear. Consequently, the following sketch of the marketing strategy concept's development may not describe how individuals came by their idea; it does, however describe the state of thinking at successive points in time.

The marketing strategy concept attempts to organize the factors that determine the sales of individual products. We must therefore seek its antecedents among the writings of men who were interested in explaining or actually influencing the volume of sales. The earliest probably would be the merchants of ancient times and the early Green philosophers who occasionally wrote about commercial affairs. Given the modest purposes at hand, this review will pass over the early writings and will start with the "Classical" economists.

Although they doubtless knew that they were oversimplifying the matter, classical economists based their explanations of sales solely on the effect of price. (All other possible influences were held constant and left unexplored.) They offered a simple and monolithic view of the determination of sales that was later incorporated into the demand schedule. In their view, sales varied inversely with price—at any given time and with all other things remaining equal; later economists summarized the relationship between sales and price in the "law of Demand."

The second stage in the attempts of professional economists to explain the determinants of sales might be dated from the publication of Edward Chamberlin's "theory of Monopolistic Competition."[1] It was during this stage that academic economists first took explicit account of non price influences n sales. Professor Chamberlin explored the effects of advertising on sales and explained this factor in the traditional manner common to formal economics. Despite the fact that the "Theory of Monopolistic Competition" was written over a quarter of a century ago, many academic discussions of sales still proceed as if price were the overwhelmingly important determinant of sales. Little attention is devoted even now to non price influences on sales by economists, although several books have been written by academic economists on the subject of individual nonprice influences on sales.

At this stage, the development of concepts to explain product sales reached a fork in the road. One prong continued the application of traditional techniques to take account of a larger number of influences on sales. An important step in this direction was taken in 1941 when Professor Kenneth Boulding2 treated sales efforts and costs in the same way that theorists had handled production costs; this theoretical framework contained the implicit analogy between the to marketing executive and the engineer. Economists have not built on this major breakthrough, however. An article by P.J. Verdoorn in 19563 represents perhaps the high point of this line of development, which is characterized by the use of geometric tools of analysis.

Further developments along this traditional route are in the hands of persons with a mathematical orientation. The field of operations research known as "programming" handles many sales promotion activities without serious difficulty, because mathematics is vastly more powerful than geometry. Programming of sales activity is not being explored by formal economics but represents the contribution of marketing specialists in the main.

The second fork in the road reached after the writing of the "Theory of Monopolistic Competition" might be termed the checklist approach to the sales problem. It was along this road that the term "marketing mix" was introduced for the first time by Professor Neil Borden in approximately 1953.[4] Writers who have followed this route were concerned with two major factors: First, they sought to itemize the large number of influences upon sales that marketing executives must take into account; second, they were interested in facilitating practical application of the concept to concrete operating problems. Foremost among the writers who adopted this approach were Professors Neil Bordenand Albert Frey,[5] The latter attempted to relate the marketing mix concept directly to the development of marketing programmes in his publication, which carries the subtitle, "Programming for Optimum Results."

With the development of the checklist approach, the enormity of the problem confronting the top marketing executive became apparent. The task of balancing a very large umber of variables (even if one ignores their interdependence) clearly is huge. Paucity of evidence about the productivity of individual sales promotion devices, and the difference between present and future markets inevitably makes the task of the chief marketing executive overwhelming, if not impossible. The inability to see down a workable method of composing a marketing mix is not a failing of the concept itself; the concept does describe what the top marketing executive should attempt to do. It certainly represents a substantial improvement over earlier views that took explicit account of only a few factors influencing sales. The complexity of the sale function is real and not a figment of the imagination of the concept builders.

Doctrine discussing determinants of sales had reached this state when the concept of marketing strategy was first set down in 1957. This concept differs form earlier thought on the subject by relating customer targets directly to the marketing mix. (It may be regarded as another step done with road from the checklist approach to the sales problem). It emphasizes that an effective marketing mix requires top management to be explicit about the kinds of customers to whom the business is trying to sell because specific sales promotion devices that appeal to some customer will bore others and even repel some.

The addition of customer targets to the concept of the marketing mix partly overcomes the difficulties in implementing the concept caused by a lack of information. When a marketing specialist is explicit. About his target customers and informs himself thoroughly about their needs, desires, perceptions, habits, attitudes, assumptions, economic situation, etc. He can guess more confidently about the productivity of different sales promotion devices than if he thinks in terms of so unrealistic and abstraction as "the average customer."

The marketing strategy concept also directed attention to a major omission in the thinking of many business executives. When the marketing strategy concept was reduced to writing, even as today, the greatest marketing errors resulted from the failure of sellers to be explicit and selective about customer targets.

The concept of marketing strategy certainly does not represent the pinnacle of thought about the determinants of sales. It is intended primarily for businessmen who must make operating decisions—rather than is mathematicians or econometricians. Superior methods of formulating the sales problem are certain to be developed. Nevertheless, this view of sales determination may explain the sales and marketing function more clear and suggest how to deal with it more effectively than did earlier views.

The Interdisciplinary Concept

To discuss the interdisciplinary approach with clarity, several related concepts should be examined, particularly transdisciplinary, multidisciplinary, and interdisciplinary. Transdisciplinary is the broadest concept. It refers to the crossing of discipline boundaries. Both the multidisciplinary and interdisciplinary approaches, by definition, therefore, are transdisciplinary. There is, however, considerable difference between their respective approaches.

The multidisciplinary approach uses stores of knowledge and viewpoints from many disciplines. It borrows concepts and techniques. It solving capability. But it tends to leave the general discipline boundaries more or less intact.

The interdisciplinary approach integrates concepts and ideas, restructures fields, changes subject-matter boundaries, and bridges theoretical gaps. It tends to develop more coherent and logical structure, more adequate theories, and leads to new concepts, techniques, and even subjects. It synthesizes concepts, findings and ideas. Sometimes it even results in new disciplines. Often the interdisciplinary approach follows the multidisciplinary.

Since marketing problems have been studied by subject-matter specialists external to marketing—for example, psychologists and sociologists – marketing has long felt the impact of a multidisciplinary approach. Specialists, however, investigate marketing problems from the perspectives of their own particular disciplines. A useful overflow from one area to another often occurs, and disciplines are given new vitality, but they are not transmuted Yet this very transfer of knowledge can challenge old categories and strain discipline boundaries.

Marketing has borrowed from both the social and behavioural sciences. Initially, major contributions from the social sciences resulted in a heavy macroperspective. Later multidisciplinary contributions emphasized the behavioral sciences and a microemphasis. This is to be expected since "the twentieth century. Marks the coming-of-age of the behavioural sciences"

The interdisciplinary approach requires a true federation of disciplines. It is not just a matter of borrowing among disciplines. It is concerned with the combination and integration of the endeavor of several specialized fields of study for the purpose of gaining marketing knowledge and solving marketing problems. The interdisciplinary approach offers tentative concepts, findings, postulates, working hypotheses, an methodology for the direction and organization of inquiry in marketing. It abandons reified categories o disciplines and tends to unify scientific inquiry.

The interdisciplinary approach, however, is not one unified approach—rather it is many approaches. It is a loose coalition of perspectives, findings, and avenues. It can sometimes be a maze of conflicting hypotheses, findings, and ideas. This conflict, of course, can be challenging and desirable, and can lead to imaginative research.

In relating to other disciplines, marketing has drawn from four discipline groups.

1. Those that are directly allied to marketing. This includes microeconomics, management, organization theory, finance, and accounting. These disciplines investigate many marketing problems and subjects as part of their normal approach.

2. Those that study behaviour, particularly human behaviour

such as psychology, sociology, and cultural anthropology.

3. Those that focus on broader societal issues and problems such as philosophy, political science, and macroeconomics.

4. Those that concentrate on tools and techniques. This includes mathematics, statistics, systems engineering, and computer science.

It is worth noting that an intradisciplinary approach has also been felt in marketing. It leads to the integration and blending of concepts, ideas, and findings within the marketing discipline itself. It is being spurred by the acceptance of a systems approach to marketing. For example, physical distribution, the result of a systems approach, integrates transportation, storing, warehousing, distribution, handling, sorting, and moving. Marketing intelligence results from an amalgamation of various subjects dealing with gathering, analyzing, interpreting, and using data. Marketing promotion refers to the coordination of all promotional aspects—advertising, personal selling, and publicity.

Kinds of Interdisciplinary Contributions

The interdisciplinary approach to marketing results in three kinds of contributions: those that are direct and immediate, those that are direct but potential, and the indirect and potential contributions.

Direct and immediate contributions refer to those concepts, ideas, and findings that can be applied directly by marketing. Included are various techniques of measurement, concepts such as life cycle, social stratification, and data including income and demographic data. They result in an immediate infusion of knowledge. We shall consider such contributions later.

Direct but potential contributions are those that seem to have direct tarry over but require further research, development, or refinement. They constitute the bulk of the interdiscipliary contributions. For example, research on farm product innovations reveals that innovators and early adopters are more means-oriented, tend to be more secure as individuals, and have greater ability to with abstractions. Is this true for other product categories? Similarly, the following changes in values have been ascribed to our society:

1. Less emphasis on personal values and more on group standards and welfare.
2. Increased positive evaluation of psychological criteria.
3. Receding of value on future success in favour of respectable and stable security.
4. Rise in value of aesthetic considerations.
5. Greater value placed on explicit values.

These changes seem to hold implications for marketing, but further research is required before the implications are those which are somewhat tangential but contain a glimmer of an idea, a concept, or suggest hypotheses that, with considerable work, may be useful. Resemblances, analogies, and identities often fall into this category. For instance, reasoning that marketing might be analyzed as a system, or seeking what correspondence the concepts of homeostasis, transaction, and transaction have in marketing while indirect, at least initially, and requiring development, often proves useful. Hart's two laws of social change: (1) that Law of Cultural Acceleration, which states that the means for accomplishing purposes have increased at an accelerating rate; and (2) the Law of Logistic Surges, which explains that the logistics curve describes specific instances of cultural accumulation, are examples of indirect potential contributions. They are suggestive in developing and understanding product innovation and acceptance. Similarly, diagrammatic representation of ten theories of the direction of change have been offered. They seem to hold potential for developing marketing thought.

Current Status

What is the present status of the use of other disciplines in marketing. Marketing's use of other disciplines to date may best be charactrised as multidisciplinary rather than interdisciplinary.

Yet, marketing as an area of study is moving from the multidisciplinary to the interdisciplinary stage. This current multidisciplinary emphasis is the prelude to the adoption of a more integrated interdisciplinary orientation. As a result of the current stage of progress, throughout the rest of the paper I shall not distinguish the multidisciplinary from the interdisciplinary.

Cronbach's statement about the lack of integration of various psychological approaches is very appropriate for marketing. He states that if approaches are "kept independent, they can give only wrong answers or no answers at all regarding certain important problems." For example, we cannot argue that marketing will deal with market forces and consumer behaviour, while psychology will formulate the laws of motivation or change.

But the aim of the interdisciplinary approach should not be the cross-fertilization of ideas to unify the disciplines. Rather it should be the use of various tools and concepts to come to grips wit marketing problems. It should offer a joint attack on common problems in marketing, using the contributions of various disciplines, rather than promise unification of all disciplines.

The lines of disciplines are blurring, and an integration and federation of some of them is occurring. It is becoming more difficult to differentiate parts of psychology and sociology from marketing and vice versa. Will the disciplines be united into fewer and fewer subject-matter areas: Will the marketing boundaries vanish? The answer, I believe, is no. Several forces will hold the marketing discipline intact. Its problems, theories, and methods; its instructional involvement; its identification with functions that are most significant to business; and its meaning for competition and international development will insure that marketing will continue as a unit for teaching, research, and problem solving.

But the gaps among marketing and other areas will narrow. The tools will become similar. The concepts and ideas of many disciplines will continue to converge on marketing problems. More hybrid disciplines will emerge, and common concepts will evolve. Conceptual bridges between marketing and neighboring subject-matter areas will emerge. Marketing's relationship with other disciplines will change. It will become more reciprocal in nature.

Currently, there are shifts in environmental factors encouraging the convergence of the research effort from many disciplines on marketing factors. Psychology, for example, is now feeling the impact of automation and abundance, and the "area of psychological research interest tends to shift from the producer to the consumer...what is needed is an understanding of consumer behaviour." Such influences will buttress the interdisciplinary approach to marketing.

Interdisciplinary emphasis is affecting the development of marketing in yet another way. As the marketing discipline built on concepts from other disciplines, and as the field of marketing became established, specialization spread. Marketing as a discipline turned inward and became fractionalized. With the interdisciplinary approach, marketing has turned outward, and the result is more meaningful perspectives, new concepts and theories, improved techniques, and a more useful body of knowledge.

An investigation of marketing management practice and marketing thought reveals that a more rigorous and penetrating analysis of marketing and business has resulted from multidimensional approaches to the study of marketing. Consider the use of economic theory. Demand a core marketing concept, is now analyzed in terms of dimensions that extend well beyond those of the initial economic boundaries. It is viewed in terms of motivation, perception, status, imagery, symbolism, communications networks, conformity, resistance to change, levels of aspiration, life cycle, life style, mobility, search and expectations. New questions are asked and new answer sought. Realistic involvement of many disciplines results. "A vast body of material which is potentially useful to marketing management exists in other disciplines."

Kapp has noted that "the essential characteristics of society are those of structural interdependence. Social structure is primary, and from it all social inquiry must derive its basic scientific strategy." In fact, some disciplines have been referred to as integrating disciplines. "For example, both anthropology and sociology are claimed to be ;integrating sciences,' the one taking 'culture' as the basic and integrating idea, and the other, 'social group or society.' Viewed from this perspective, marketing is an integrating discipline. Markets are among the core institutions of our society. Marketing is characteristically American and exerts basic influences on our life style, culture, wealth, production, and values. Marketing provides a common conceptual framework for studying many problem that cross disciplinary lines. The very scope and dimension of marketing problems carry theorists and practitioners over discipline boundaries. Although the "point of departure and the focus of study differ among the disciplines...there are frequently great similarities between marketing and other disciplines in both methodology and content."

The interdisciplinary approach confronts the empirical findings of marketing with the conceptual an theoretical formulations of other disciplines and vice versa. The result is that all confronted disciplines benefit. Marketing's direct and significant ties with economics and sociology are examples.

It seems that the most rapid period of progressive change in marketing is associated not with discoveries within the field but wit the importation, borrowing, and diffusion of contributions outside marketing. In turn, however, these borrowed elements are changed in the assimilation process which results in new ideas and concepts.

In reality, marketing and its research are brought into existence to serve a purpose—a specific area of study. Yet as soon as marketing discovers ideas and information, it also serves other purposes and works with other subjects. As it does, it adds valuable dimensions and a wider purview to one's understanding of both marketing and relate areas. Marketing problems are seem in many dimensions.

CHAPTER 6

NEW CRITERIA FOR CONSUMER MARKETS

Economic information is essential to effective marketing management. Changes in demography not only affect the structure of market demand, but also have far-reaching implications for such marketing decisions as product design and media selection. A review of important socioeconomic characteristics at various stages of the family life cycle is presented.

Families by Age Characteristics

A striking 90 per cent of the growth in the nation's family population expected during the Sixties will be accounted for by the relatively young and the relatively old—by families under 30 and those over 55. In the preceding 10-year span these age groups represented only tow fifths of the total growth.

As these simple statistics suggest, the age composition of our population is being significantly altered. Two major demographic tremors have been working their way through the nations population structure over the past to years. The first shock wave was triggered by the sharp drop in births during the Depression Thirties, the second by the postwar birth boom.

The changing age structure of our population is, of course, of special interest to marketers. Clearly, it is not only affecting the structure of demand, but it also has far-reaching implications for such merchandising decisions as product design and media selection. This article, the first of two, reviews the most current available demographic and economic information on families by age of head. A second story will be concerned with the purchasing patterns of families at various stages of the life cycle.

Family Head Under 25

Households under 25 account for about 5 per cent of the nation's families, not only 3 per cent of all consumer demand. Last year the median earnings of these families came to roughly $4,300, or about 25 per cent below the all-country figure. Three out of every five young couples earned less than $5,000 and barely 15 per cent had over $7,000.

The birth rate at this stage of the family's life cycle is at a peak level. Thus, although they constitute only 5 per cent of the family population these households had 26 per cent of all children born last year. Two thirds of all under-25-year-old homes include children and about 30 per cent have more than one. Nevertheless, well over half of all wives work all or part of the year. A third of all young families live in the central cities of metropolitan areas, and about 20 per cent own their own homes.

Three out of every five family heads of his age have earned high school diplomas, a level of education well above the all-country average. However, fewer youngsters in this age bracket have finished college than in next-oldest grouping. Youngsters who remaining school longer generally marry later.

Family Head 25-34

A fifth of all households and about the same share of the country's spending power are to be found in this age bracket. The median annual income is about normal, and at this age a full third of all families ears more than $7,000. But indebtedness as well as income has increased: two thirds of these families owe money.

Although the birth rate has slowed appreciably at this age

level, to about one new arrival in every four homes annually, over half of all children born last year were to parents in this bracket. Close to 90 per cent of these households include children, and two thirds of them more than one.

As would be expected under these circumstances, relatively fewer wives now work; of those that do, about three in five work the year round. The proportion of families living in the suburbs is far greater than that for the under-25 group. The frequency of home ownership has increased substantially, although it is still under the all-family rate.

This age group is better educated than any other. Close to 15 per cent of the household heads have completed college, and an additional 43 per cent have high school diplomas. Roughly one quarter of all males are employed in professional-technical occupations or are managers and officials. Craftsmen as count for an additional fifth, operatives for another quarter.

Family Head 35-44

The largest proportion of total family spending power—an estimated 27 per cent –is in the hands of this age group, which accounts for a quarter of households. The median family earns well above he norm: close to hall of these homes are in the over $7,000 bracket. The frequency of indebtedness continues in the neighbourhood of two thirds, but the six of outstanding obligations appears to have declined in this bracket.

A very large proportion of these families have children living at home, but fewer households include youngsters under six. Nevertheless, over two fifths of our entire child population is accounted for the 35-44 age bracket.

The ratio of working wives in this group is near the average. The family now appears to be fully rooted, and barely 15 per cent change their residence in the course of a year. The rate of home ownership has increased sharply: two thirds of these families own their homes.

The level of educational achievement is well above average, with one out of every two household heads having completed high school. This is a slightly smaller fraction than in the 25-34 age bracket, as each upcoming generation in recent years has been staying somewhat longer in school than the one preceding.

Family Head 45-54

This the most affluent of all the age groups. Earning capacity at this stage of the life cycle is at its peak. Last year the median income of these families exceeded $7,000. More than a quarter of all homes in this age category have incomes in excess of $10,000. All in all, this group accounts for a fifth of all families but a quarter of all spending power. Only one out of every two of these households in debt.

The proportion of families with children has dipped below 60 per cent. Actually, many of the offspring of these families have by now reached 18 and hence are no longer classified as children in government statistics.

As would be expected, there is a sharp increase at this age level in the proportion of wives who work, and an even greater rise in the number working all year.

The educational level of this age category is substantially below that of the preceding. Most of the family heads in this group were of school age during the depression years of the Thirties. All in all, fewer than two fifths of them achieved a high school diploma.

The occupational mix of this category more or less parallels the factional pattern, except that there are slightly fewer professional and technical persons and some what more managers and officials.

Family Head 55-64

The income pattern in this age bracket reflects the presence of some retired and semi-retired families. There is clustering at both ends of the income scale. Nearly 40 per cent of these families—

a substantially larger proportion than found in the 45-54 group—earn below $5,000. At the end of the scale, one fifth of all households, a better than average, have annual incomes exceeding $10,000. On balance, median are still above par. Indebtedness has dropped sharply, to only about one third of these families.

Only one out of every five of these households includes children. Family size has now declined to 3.0, as compared to an all-family average of 3.7. Also, there are relatively fewer working wives in this group than among younger families. And there apparently has been some moving back into town from the suburbs.

Only slightly better than a quarter of these family heads have completed high school, vehicle a third failed to go the full course in elementary school. Some decline in the ownership of durable goods is in evidence at this stage of the life cycle, sharpest of all in cars. However, three founds of these families still operate automobiles, and one in five has two or more vehicles.

Family Head 65 and above

This is the age of the retired. Median income for this group last year was $3,200, or only slightly better than half the all-family figure. Above 70 per cent of these household shave less than $5,000 a year to spend, wile only about one in ten have over $10,000. In the neighbourhood of 10 per cent of total demand originates with this age bracket, which includes about 15 per cent of all our citizens.

Few of these families still have youngsters living at home. As a matte of fact, there has been a rather substantial change in family composition—fewer husband and wife units, more cases of a man or a woman living with a relative. Close to one fifth of all wives, however, are still working.

A relatively large proportion of families reside outside the urbanize areas, which probably explains the continued high level of home ownership.

The general educational achievement of this group is lower than that of any other: only one out of every five family heads has completed high school. More than two out of every five have failed to complete elementary school. This generation was born in an era in which less emphasis was put on formal training.

A relatively high proportion of this group (20% as compared to national average of only 8%) work on farms. This may reflect the five that while persons employed in industry tend to retire upon coming age, farmers are more likely to continue working on a reduced schedule age, farmers are more likely to continue working on a reduced scheduled. A

Also, in the recent migration away from the land, younger families left relatively large numbers.

There is a further contraction in the proportion of families owner durable goods in this age bracket. Cars are now maintained by less the half of all households.

Families by Age II: Expenditures

The changing age structure of our growing population influence many marketing decisions. Marketing strategies for consumer markets must recognize that shifts in preferences for various goods and services occur as families read successive stages of the life cycle. Families are categories by the age of the family head, and their spending patterns are reported.

Never before in the nation's history—not even during the great immigration early in the century—has the age structure of our adult population gone through as sharp a change as in the present period. We are now experiencing the combined consequences of the sharp fall in births during the depression Thirties and the spectacular baby boom of the prospectors Fifties. All this means a shift in the goods and services that are in demand and has a far-reaching effect on many aspects of merchandising strategy from packaging to the phrasing of the promotion message.

This, the second of two articles on the characteristics of

households in each stage in the life cycle, is concerned with spending patterns. The preceding story reviewed social and income traits. The observations the follow are based on the Bureau of Labour Statistics' recent study is spending habits of urban families and single consumers. The complex study covers the years 1960 and 1961; however, the only data related thus far are for the earlier year. This information was collected in metropolitan areas and in 16 small cities. Since a similar survey was conducted in 1950, it is possible to examine the changes in consumer preferences over the past decade. In comparing past and present expenditure patterns, 1950 data have been converted to 1960 dollars.

Head Under 25

The typical consumer unit in this age bracket spent $4,500 for good and services in 1960, or substantially less than the national average aggregate this group accounts for less than 5 per cent of all buying.

A large proportion of people in this bracket are single consumers, a fact reflected in the group's general expenditure profile. The percentage of income that goes for food, clothing, medical and personal care is below the all-country norm. Shelter is a significant item percentage-wise at this age level, although actual dollar outlays for this purpose are below par. Expenditure for automobiles, on the other had, are quite large, both in absolute and relative terms.

A much smaller proportion of the young household'

S budget now goes for food and clothing than did so 10 years ago. Hose furnishings and equipment, too, now make a smaller claim. Spending for housing on the other hand—shelter and particularly home operations—has grown more important than it was in 1950.

Head 25-34

Most of the spending units in this group are husband-wife families. Spending for consumption came to $5,600 in the survey year, which is fractionally above average. This group accounts for close to a fifth of total consumer buying.

Expenditures in this age bracket broadly follow the all-country pattern. The proportion of resources channeled into the home-shelter, household operations and home furnishings—is above par, while outlays food and clothing are slightly below the national average, measured in relative terms, and about equal to the all-household figure in actual dollars. The automobile also takes a somewhat smaller share of total spending, although dollar outlays are higher than they are in the average American family.

The average household in this bracket spends about a quarter more on foods and services than does the typical under-25-year-old family. However, food, alcohol, tobacco and clothing expenditures are mu^h more than 25 per cent greater. (Te consumer unit is bigger now—there are more reasons to feed and clothe.) The rise in outlays for house furnishings, and particularly for autos, is less than for all spending.

As in the case of the youngest families, a substantially smaller share of is gage group's spending now goes for food, clothing and home furnishings than did so a decade ago, while a much greater proportion is for shelter and household operations. Personal and medical care, have increased in importance in this bracket, and more is being spent automobiles.

Head 35-44

Roughly a quarter of total consumer buying is represented by this age group. In the survey year the average household spent about $6,500, more than in any other bracket.

Although more money is now being spent on cars, home furnishing and household operations than in the preceding age group, the increases for these items are less than the increment in all spending. The big rise in outlays is for food and clothing, which account for an above average portion of this age group's budget. This is because, at this stage of the this cycle, and household has reached its peak size.

As observed in connection with the other age groups, food, clothing and home furnishings are less significant percentage wise than age, but shelter, particularly household operations, and the automobile at more important.

Head 45-54

Through the family is now at its peak earning level, expenditures for current consumption have declined moderately, to $6,200. Only above 90 per cent of income after taxes finds its way to the market, as compared 95 per cent for the preceding age category. In large measure this development explained by a decline in household size. Many of the offspring of the families have reached adulthood and left home. However, this age category is of most importance to markets since it accounts for over quarter of all consumer spending.

The decrease in family size is reflected in expenditure habits. Total outlays are roughly 5 per cent below the next-youngest bracket but spending for food, shelter, and the home generally has declined by an even larger proportion. The decrease is also relatively big for automobiles. On the other hand, spending for some items is off by less than 5 per cent. These include medical and personal care. Expenditure for alcohol increases.

Changes in this age group's spending habits over the past decade are special. Food now claims a smaller share of the family's budget, housing personal car a somewhat larger share. The importance of clothing is changed.

Head 55-64

In this age bracket we find some significant changes in the composition of the family, its earnings and its spending habits. While the majority of household heads are at their peak earning capacity, many others and retired or semi-retired. The average family now spends $5,000 for goods and services, or about 85 per cent of post-tax income.

Total consumption of this group is a full fifth less than in the 45-to 54 bracket. Many items, however, are off by much more, notably house furnishings, clothing, recreation, alcohol and automobiles. On the other hand expenditures decline only moderately for medical care, shelter, and household operations. The decrease in food spending is also surprisingly small.

The share of the budget going for food has dropped from 29 per cent to 25 percent in the last 10 years, while the portion devoted to housing has increased largely because of the shelter and operation components. Autos and personal and medical care have become more important since 1950, but the weight assigned to clothing has remained the same.

65 and above

The average household in this retired age bracket spend slightly the $3,200 in the survey year for all goods and services, representing above 90 percent of its post-tax income. About 19 per cent of all consumer units are in the bracket, but they account for only a little better than 11 per cent of total spending. The average household has declined to 1.8 persons.

With the sharp reduction in spending, essentials such as food and housing take a comparatively large share of the budget. Three fifths total outlays go for these items. An additional 12 per cent are for personal and medical care.

Consumption is more than a third less than in the 55-to-64 group. More items, of course, have fallen by much more, notably tobacco and alcohols clothing, house furnishings, transportation and recreation. Among item that have decreased by less than the drop in total spending are house food and medical care.

A decade ago, older families spent a larger share of their budget is food and clothing, but a smaller proportion for housing, than they today. Outlays for medical and personal care are appreciably highly having increased form roughly a tenth of the budget to about an eight.

New Criteria for Market Segmentation Analysis

Segmentation analysis—the evaluation of all potentially useful ways of segmenting a market—may produce a more effective marketing strategy than does segmentation based solely on demographic characteristics. The strategic choice concept of segmentation broadens the scope of marketing planning to include the positioning of new as well as established products. Marketing must develop its own interpretive theory if it is to optimize the value of segmentation analysis.

The director of marketing in a large company is confronted by some of the most difficult problems in the history of U.S. industry. To assist him, the information revolution of the past decade puts at his disposal a vat array of techniques, facts and figures. But without a way to master this information, he can easily be overwhelmed by the reports that flow in to him incessantly from marketing research, economic forecasts, cost analyses, and sales breakdowns. He must have more than mere access to mountains of data. He must himself bring to bear a method of analysis that cuts through the detail to focus sharply on new opportunities.

In this article, I shall propose such as method. It is called segmentation analysis. It is base don the proposition that once you discover the most careful ways of segmenting a market, you have produced the beginnings of a sound marketing strategy.

Unique Advantages

Segmentation analysis has developed out of several key premises:

In today's economy, each brand appears to self effectively to only certain segments of any market and not to the whole market.

Sound marketing objectives depend on knowledge of how segments which produce the most customers for a company's brands differ in requirements and susceptibilities from the segments which produce the largest number of customers for competitive brands.

Traditional demographic methods of market segmentation do not usually provide this knowledge. Analyses of market segments by age, sex, geography, and income level are not likely to provide s much direction for marketing strategy as management requires.

Once the marketing director does discover the most pragmatically useful way of segmenting his market, it becomes a new standard for almost all his evaluations. He will use it to appraise competitive strengths and vulnerabilities, to plan his product line, to determine his advertising and selling strategy, and to set precise marketing objectives against which performance can later be measured, Specifically, segmentation analysis help him to—

...direct the appropriate amounts of promotional attention and money in the most potentially profitable segments of his market;

...design a product line that truly parallels the demands of the market instead of one that bulks in some areas and ignores or scants other potentially quit profitable segments;

...catch the first sign of a major trend in a swiftly changing market and thus give him time to prepare to take advantage of it;

...determine the appeals that will be most effective in his company's advertising; and, where several different appeals are significantly effective quantify the segments of he market responsive to each;

... choose advertising media more wisely and determine the proportion of budget that should be allocated to each medium in he light of anticipated impact;

... correct the timing of advertising and promotional efforts so that they are massed in the weeks, months, and seasons when selling resistance is leant and responsiveness is likely to be at its maximum;

...understand otherwise seemingly meaningless demographic market in formation and apply it in scores of new and effective ways.

These advantages hold in the case of both packaged goods and have goods, and for commercial and industrial products as well as consumer products.

Guide to Strategy

Segmentation analysis cuts through the data facing a marketing director when he tried to set targets based on markets as a whole, or when relies primarily on demographic breakdowns. It is a systematic approved that permits the marketing planner to pick the strategically most important segmentations and then to design brands, products, packages, communications, and marketing strategies around them. It infinitely simplifies the setting of objectives.

In the following sections we shall consider non demographic ways of segmenting markets. These ways dramatize the point that finding marketing opportunities by depending solely on demographic breakdowns is like trying to win a national election by relying only on the information in a census. A modern census contains useful data, but it identifies neither the crucial issues of an election, or those groups whose voting habits are still fluid, nor he needs, values, and attitudes that influence how those groups will vote. This kind of information, rather tan census-type data, is the kind that wins elections—and markets.

Consider, for example, companies like Procter & Gamble, General Motors, or American Tobacco, whose multiple brands sell against one another and must, every day, win new elections in the marketplace:

These companies sell to the whole market, not by offering one brand that appeals to all people, but by covering the different segments with multiple brands. How can they prevent these brands from cannibalizing each other? How can they avoid surrendering opportunities to competitors by failing to provide brands that appeal to all important segments? In neither automobiles, groups, nor cigarettes do demographic analyses reveal to the manufacturer what products to make or what products to sell to what segments of the market. Obviously, some modes of segmentation other than demographic are needed to explain why brands which differ so little nevertheless find their own niches in the market, each one appealing to a different segment.

The on that issue is not that demographic segmentation should be regarded, but rather that it should be regarded as only one among away possible ways of analyzing markets. In fact, the key requirement of segmentation analysis is that the marketing director should never assume is advance that anyone method of segmentation is the bet. His first job should be to must all probable segmentation and then choose the most meaningful ones to work with. This approach is analogous to that used in search in the physical sciences, where the hypothesis that best seems to explain the phenomena under investigation is the one chosen for working purposes..

Let me stress three points:

1. We should discard the old, unquestioned assumption that demographical always the best way of looking at markets. The demographic premise implies that differences in reasons for buying bran choice influences, in frequency of use, or in susceptibility to be reflected in differences in age, sex, income, and geographical region. But this is usually not true. Markets should be scrutinized for important differences in buyer attitudes, motivations, values, usage pattern, sesthetic preferences, or degree of susceptibility. These may have demographic correlatives. Above all, we must never assume in advance that we know the best way of looking at a market. This is the cardinal rule of segmentation analysis. All ways of segmentation markets must be considered, and them we must select out of the various methods available the ones that have the most important implications for action, this process of choosing the strategically most useful mode of segmentation in the essence of the marketing approach espoused in this article.

In considering cases like those described, we must understand that we are not dealing with different types of people, but with differences in people's values. A women who buys a refrigerator because it is the cheapest available may want to buy the most expensive towels. A Ford-owner Kellogg's Corn Flakes-eater may be closed off to Chevrolet but sustainable to Post Toasties; he is the same man, but he has had different experiences and holds different values toward each product he purchases segmenting markets on the basis of the values, purposes, needs, and attitudes relevant to the product being studied, we are misleading information derived from attempts to divide people into type.

2. The strategic-choice concept of segmentation broadens the scope marketing planning to include the positioning of new products as well of established products.

It also has implications for brand planning, not just for individual products but for the composition of a line of competing brands where any meaningful segment in the market can possibly support a brand. One explanation of he successful competing brand strategy of companies like Procter & Gamble is that they are base don sensitivity to the many different modes of market segmentation. The brands offered by P & G often appear very similar to the outsider, but small, marginal differences between them appeal to different market segments. It is this rather than intramural competition that supports P&G successes.

3. Marketing must develop its own interpretive theory, and not borrow a ready-made one from the social sciences.

Marketing research, as an applied science, is tempted to borrow its theoretical structures from the discipline from which it derives. The socio sciences offer an abundance of such structures, but they are not applicable to marketing in their pure academic form. While the temptation to apply them in that form is great, it should be resisted. From sociology, for example, marketing has frequently borrowed the concept of status. This is a far-reaching concept, but it is not necessarily the most important one in a marketing problem, nor even one of the important ones. Again, early psychoanalytic theory has contributed an understanding of the sexual factor. While this can sometimes be helpful in an analysis of buying behaviour in a given situation, some motivation researchers have become oversensitive to the role of sex and, as a result, have made many mistakes. Much the same might be said of the concept of social character, that is, seeing the world as being "inner-directed," "other-directed," "tradition-directed," "autonomous," and so forth.

One of the values of segmentation analysis is that, while it has drawn on the insights of social scientists, it has developed an interpretive theory within marketing. It has been homegrown in business. This may explain ability to impose patterns of meaning on the immense diversity of the market, and to provide the modern marketing director with a systematic method for evolving true marketing objectives.

Product Differentiation and Market Segmentation as Alternative Marketing Strategies

Product differentiation efforts attempt to control demand through the promotion of product differences, while market segmentation efforts seek control by discovering, and responding to different product preferences. Success in deciding a product and services mix requires the use of both product differentiation and market segmentation as components of marketing strategy. The relationship of the strategies in imperfectly competitive markets in discussed.

Product differentiation and market segmentation are both consistent with the framework of imperfect competition. In its simplest product differentiation is concerned with the depending of demand to this will of supply. It is an attempt to shift or to change the slope of the demand curve for the market offering of an individual supplier. The strategy may also be employed by a group of suppliers such as a fare cooperative, the members of which have agreed to act together. It revels from the desire to establish a kind of equilibrium in the market brining about adjustment of market demand to supply conditions favourable to the seller.

Segmentation is based upon developments on he demand side of the market and represents a rational and more precise adjustment of product and marketing effort to consumer or user requirements. In the language the economist, segmentation is disaggregative in its effects and tends to bring about recognition of several demand schedules where only one was recognized before.

Attention has been drawn to this area of analysis by the increasing number of cases in which business problems have become soluble by doing something about marketing programmes and product policies that over generalize both markets and marketing effort. These are situations where intensive promotion designed to differentiate the company's products was to accomplishing its objective—cases where failure to recognize the reality of market segments was resulting in loss f market position.

While successful product differentiation will result in giving the marketer a horizontal share of a broad and generalized market, equally successful Application of

The strategy of market segmentation tends to produce depth of market position in the segments that are effectively defined and penetrated. The differentiator seeks to secure a layer of the market cake, whereas one who employs market segmentation strives to secure one or more wedge-shaped pieces.

Many examples of market segmentation can be cited; the cigarette and automobile industries are well-known illustrations. Similar developments exist in greater or lesser degree in almost all product areas Recent introduction of a refrigerator with no storage compartment for frozen foods was in response to the distinguishable preference of the segment of the refrigerator market made up of home freezer owners who frozen food storage needs had already been met.

Strategies of segmentation and differentiation may be employed simultaneously, but more commonly they are applied in sequence in response to changing market conditions. In one sense, segmentation is a momentary of short-term phenomenon in that effective use of this strategy may lead to more formal recognition of the reality of market segments through redefinition of the segments as individual markets. Redefinition may result in a swing back to differentiation.

The literature of both economics and marketing abounds in formal definitions of product differentiation. From a strategy viewpoint, product differentiation is securing a measure of control over the demand for a product by advertising or promoting differences between a product and he products of competing sellers. It is basically the result of sellers' desires to establish firm market positions and/or to insulate their businesses against price competition. Differentiation tends to be characterized by heavy use of advertising and promotion and to result in prices that are somewhat above the equilibrium levels associated with perfectly compatible market conditions. It may be classified as a promotional strategy of approach to marketing.

Market segmentation, on the other hand, consists of viewing a heteroneous market (one characterized by divergent demand as a number of smaller homogeneous markets in response to differing product preferences among important market segments. It is attributable to the desires of consumers or users for more precise satisfaction of their varying wants. Like differentiation, segmentation often involves substantial use of advertising and promotion. This is to inform market segments of the availability of goods or services produced for or presented as meeting their needs with precision. Under these circumstances, prices tend to be somewhat closer to perfectly competitive equilibrium. Market segmentation is essentially a merchandising strategy, merchandising being used here in its technical sense as presentation the adjustment of market offerings to consumer or user requirements.

The Emergence of the Segmentation Strategy

To a certain extent, mart segmentation may be regarded as a force in the market that will not be denied. It may result from trial and error in the sense that generalized programmes of product differentiation may turnout to be effective in some segments of the market and ineffective in other. Recognition of, and intelligent response to, such as situation necessarily involves a shift in emphasis. On the other hand, it may develop that products involved in marketing programmes designed for particular market segments may achieve a broader acceptance than originally planned, that products involved in marketing programmes designed for particular market segments may achieve a broader acceptance than originally planed, thus revealing a basis for convergence of demand and a more generalized marketing approach. The challenge to planning arises from the importance of determining, preferably in advance, the level or degree of segmentation that can be exploited with profit.

There appear to be many reasons why formal recognition of market segmentation a a strategy is beginning to emerge. One of the most important of these is decrease in the size of the minimum efficient producting or manufacturing unit required in some product areas. American industry has also established the technical base for product diversity by gaining release from some of the rigidities imposed by earlier approaches to mass production. Hence, there is les need today for generalization of markets in response to the necessity for long production runs of identical items.

Present emphasis upon the minimizing of marketing costs through self-service and similar developments tends to impose a requirement for better adjustment of products to consumer demand. The retailing structure, in its efforts to achieve improved efficiency, is providing less and less sales push at point of sale. This increases the premium placed by retiles upon products that are pre sold by their producers and are readily recognized by consumers as meeting their requirements as measured by satisfactory rates of stock turnover.

It has been suggested that the present level of discretionary buying power is productive of sharper shopping comparisons, particularly for item that are above the need level. General prosperity also creates increased willingness "to pay a little more' to get "just what wanted."

Attention to market segmentation has also been enhanced by the recent ascendancy of product competition to a position of great economic importance. An expanded array of goods and services is competing for the consumer's dollar. More specially, advancing technology is creating competition between new and traditional materials with reference to metable construction materials, textile products, and in many other areas. While such competition is confusing and difficult to analyze in its early stages, it tends to achieve a kind of balance as various competing materials find their markets of maximum potential as a result of recognition of differences in the requirements of market segments.

Many companies are reaching the stage in their development where attention to market segmentation may be regarded as a condition or cost of growth. Their core markets have already been developed on a generalized basis to the point where additional advertising and selling expenditures are yielding diminishing returns. Attention to smaller or fringe market segments, which may have small potentials individually but are of crucial importance in the aggregate, may be indicated.

Finally, some business firms are beginning to regard an increasing share of their total costs of operation as being fixed in character. The higher costs of maintaining market position in the channels of distribution illustrate this change. Total reliance upon a strategy of product differentiation under such circumstances is undesirable, since market share available as a result of such a promotion-oriented approach tends to be variable over time. Much may hinge, for example, upon week-to-week audience ratings of the television shows of competitors who seek o out differentiate each other. Exploitation of market segments, which provides for greater maximization of consumer or user satisfactions, tends to build a more secure market position and to lead to greater over-all stability. While traditionally, high fixed costs (regarded primarily from the production viewpoint) have created pressures for expanded sale of standardized items through differentiation, the possible shifting of certain marketing costs into the fixed are a of the total cost structure tends to minimize this pressure.

Conclusion

Success in planning marketing activities requires precise utilization of both product differentiation and market segmentation as components of marketing strategy. It is fortunate that available techniques of marketing research make unplanned market exploration largely unnecessary. It is the obligation of those responsible for sales and marketing administration to keep the strategy mix in adjustment wit market structure at any point in time and to produce in marketing strategy at least as much dynamism as is present in the market. The ability of business to plan in this way is dependent upon the maintenance of a flow of market information that can be provided by marketing research as well as the full utilization of available techniques of cost accounting and cost analysis.

The Concept of the Marketing Mix

The marketing mix evolves from the firm's strategy and tactics, its resources, and market forces. An optimizing marketing mix must blend empirical information with an assessment of future market empirical information with an assessment of future market trends, Understanding an application of the marketing mix is a step forward in the development of scientific marketing. I have always found it interesting to observe how an apt or colourful term may catch on, gain wide usage, and help to further understanding of a concept that has already been expressed in less appealing and communicative terms Such a s been true of the phrase "marketing mix." Which I began to use in my teaching and writing some 15 years ago. In a relatively short time it has come to have wide usage. This not tells of the evolution of the marketing mix concept.

The phrase was suggested to me by a paragraph in a research bulletin on the management of marketing costs, written by my associate, Professor James Culliton (1948). In this study of manufacturers' marketing costs he described the business executive as a "decider," and "artist"—a "mixer of ingredients," who sometimes follows a recipe prepared by others, sometimes, prepares his own recipe as he goes along, sometimes adapts a recipe to the ingredients immediately available, and sometimes experiments with or invents ingredients no one else has tried.

I liked his idea of calling a marketing executive a "mixer of ingredients," one who is constantly engaged in fashioning creatively a mix of marketing procedures and policies in his efforts to produce a profitable enterprise.

For many years previous to Culliton's cost study the wide variation in the procedures and policies employed by managements of manufacturing firms in their marketing programmes and the correspondingly wide variation in the costs of these marketing functions, which Culliton aptly ascribed to the varied "mixed of ingredients," had become increasingly evident as we had gathered marketing cases at the Harard Business School. The marked differences in the patterns for formulae of the marketing programmes not only were evident through facts disclosed in case histories, but also were reflected clearly in the figures of a cost study of food manufacturers made by the Harvard bureau of Business Research in1929. The primary objective of this study was to determine common figures of expenses for various marketing functions among food manufacturing companies, similar to the common cost figures which had been determined in previous years for various kinds of retail and wholesale businesses. In this manufacturer's study we were unable, however, with the data gathered to determine common expense figures that had much significance as standards by which to guide management, such as had been possible in the studies of retail and wholesale trades, where the methods of operation tended toward uniformity. Instead, among food manufactures the ratios of sales devoted to the various functions of marketing such as advertising, personal selling, packaging, and so on, were found to be widely divergent, no matter how we grouped our respondents. Each respondent gave data that tended to uniquences.

Culliton's study of marketing costs in 1947—48 was a second effort to find out, among other objectives, whether a bigger sample and a more careful classification of companies would produce evidence of operating uniformities that would give helpful common expense figures. But the result was the same as in our early study: there was wide diversity in cost ratios among any classifications of firms which were set up, and no common figures were fond that had much value. This was true whether companies were grouped according to similarity in product lines, amount of sales, territorial extent of operations, or other bases of classification.

Relatively early in may study of advertising, it had become evident that understanding of advertising usage by manufacturers in any case had to come from an analysis of advertising's place as one element in the total marketing programme of the firm. I came to realize that it is essentiai always to ask: what overall marketing strategy has been or might e employed to bring about a profitable operation in light of the circumstances faced the management? What combination of marketing procedures and policies has been or might be adopted to bring about desired behaviour of trade and consumers at costs that will permit a profit? Specifically, how can advertising, personal selling, pricing, packaging, channels, warehouse and the other elements of a marketing programme be manipulated and fitted together in a way that will give a profitable operation? In short, I saw that every advertising management case called for a consideration of the strategy to be adopted for the total ·marketing programme, with advertising recognized as only one element whose form and extent depended on its careful adjustment to the other parts of the programme

The soundness of this viewpoint was supported by case histories throughout my volume, *The Economic Effects f Advertising* (Borden, 1942). In the chapters devoted to the utilization of advertising by business, I had pointed out the innumerable combinations of marketing methods and policies that might be adopted by a manager in arriving at a marketing plan. For instance, in the area of branding, he might elect to marketing plan. For instance, in the area of branding, he might elect to adopt an individualized brand or a family brand. Or he might decide to sell his product branded or under private label. Any decision in the area of brand policy in turn has immediate implications that bear on his selection of channels of distribution, sales force methods, packaging, promotional procedure, and advertising. Throughout the volume the case materials cited show that the way in which any marketing function is designed and the burden placed upon the unction are determined largely by the overall marketing strategy adopted by managements to meet the market conditions under which they operate. The forces met by different firms vary widely. Accordingly, the programmes fashioned differ widely. Regarding advertising, which was the function under focus in the economic effects volume.

In all the above illustrative situations it should be recognized that advertising is not an operating method to be considered as something apart, as something whose profit value is to be judged alone. An able management does set ask, "Shall we use of not use advertising," without consideration of the product and of other management procedures to be employed. Rather the question is always one of finding a management formula giving advertising is due place in the combination of manufacturing methods, product form, placing, promotion and selling methods, and distribution methods. As previously pointed out different formulate, i.e., different combinations of methods, say be profitably employed by competing manufacturers.

To portray this broadened concept in a visual presentation requires merely:

(1) a list of the important elements or ingredients that make up marketing programmes;

(2) a list of the forces that bear on the marketing operation of a firm and to which the marketing manager must adjust in his search for a mix of programme hat can be successful.

The list of elements of the marketing mix in such a visual presentation can be long or short, depending on how far one wishes to go in his classification and sub-classification of the marketing procedures and policies with which marketing managements deal when devising marketing programmes. The list of elements which I have employed in my teaching and consulting work covers the principal areas of marketing activities which call for management decisions as revealed by case histories. I realize other might build a different list. Mine is as follows:

Elements of the Marketing Mix of Manufacturers

1. Product Planning –policies and procedures relating to:
   (a) Product lines to be offered—qualities, design, etc.
   (b) Markets to sell: whom, where, when, and in what quantity,
   (c) New product policy—research and development programme.
2. Pricing—policies and procedures relating to:
   (a) Price level to adopt.
   (b) Specific prices to adopt (odd-even, etc.).
   (c) Price policy, e.g., one-price or varying price, price maintenance, list prices, etc.
3. Branding—policies and procedures relating to:
   (a) Selection of trade marks.
   (b) Brand policy—individualized or family brand.
   (c) Sale under private label or unbranded.
4. Channels of Distribution—policies and procedures relating to:
   (a) Channels to use between plant and consumer.
   (b) Degree of selectivity among wholesalers and retailers.
   (c) Efforts to gain cooperation of the trade.
5. Personal Selling—policies and procedures relating to:
   (a) Burden to be placed on personal selling and the methods

to be employed in:

(i) Manufacturer's organization.

(ii) Wholesale segment of the trade.

(iii) Retail segment of the trade.

6. Advertising—policies and procedures relating to:

   (a) Amount to spend—i.e., the burden to be placed on advertising

   (b) Copy platform to adopt:

      (i) Product image desired.

      (ii) Corporate image desired.

   (c) Mix of advertising: to the trade; through the trade; to consumers.

7. Promotions—policies and procedures relating to:

   (a) Burden to place on special selling plans or devices directed at or through the trade.

   (b) Form of these devices for consumer promotions, for trade promotions.

8. Packaging—policies and procedures relating to:

   (a) Formulation of package and label.

9. Display—polices and procedures relating to:

   (a) Burden to be put on display to help effect sale.

   (b) Methods to adopt to secure display.

10. Servicing—policies and procedures relating to:

   (a) Providing service needed.

11. Physical Handling—policies and procedures relating to:

   (a) Warehousing.

   (b) Transportation.

(c) Inventories.

12. Fact Finding and Analysis—policies and procedures relating to:

(a) securing, analysis, and use of facts in marketing operations.

Also if one were to make a list of all the forces which managements weight at one time or another when formulating their marketing mixes, it would be very long indeed, for the behaviour of individuals and groups in all spheres of life have a bearing, first, on what goods and services are produced and consumed, and, second, on the procedures that may be employed in bringing about exchange of these goods and services. However, the important forces which bear on marketers, all arising from the behaviour of individuals or groups, may readily be listed under four heads timely the behaviour of consumers, the trade, competitors, and government.

The outline below contains these four behavioural forces with notations of some of the important behavioural determinants within each force. These must be studied and understood by the marketer, if his marketing it is to be successful. The great quest of marketing management is to understand the behaviour of humans in response to the stimuli to which they are subjected. The skillful marketer is one who is a perceptive and psychologist and sociologist, who has keen insight into individual and group behaviour, who can foresee changes in behaviour that develop a dynamic world, who has creative ability for building well-knit programmes because he has the capacity to visualize the probable response of consumers, trade, and competitors to his moves. His skill in forecasting response to his marketing moves should well be supplemented by a further skill in devising and using tests and measurements to check consumer trade response to his programme or parts thereof, for no marketer has so much prescience that he can proceed without empirical check.

Below, then, is the suggested outline of forces which govern the mixing of marketing elements. This list and that of the elements taken together provide a visual presentation of the concept of the marketing mix.

Market Forces bearing on the Marketing Mix

1. Consumers' Buying Behaviour, as determined by their:
   (a) Motivation in purchasing.
   (b) Buying habits.
   (c) Living habits.
   (d) Environment (present and future, as revealed by trends, for environment influences consumer's attitudes toward products and their use of them).
   (e) Buying power.
   (f) Number (i.e., how many).
2. The Trade's Behaviour—wholesalers' and retailers' behaviour, as influences by:
   (a) Their motivations
   (b) Their structure, practices, and attitudes.
   (c) Trends in structure, practices, and attitudes.
   (d) Trends in structure and procedures that portend change.
3. Competitor's Position and Behaviour, as influenced by:
   (a) Industry structure and the firm's relation thereto.
      (i) Size and strength of competitors.
      (ii) Number of competitors and degree of industry concentration.
      (iii) Indirect competition—i.e., from other products.
   (b) Relation of supply to demand—oversupply or undersupply.
   (c) Product choices offered consumers by the industry—i.e., quality price, service.
   (d) Degree to which competitors compete on price vs. non-price bases.

(e) Competitors' motivations and attitudes—their likely response to actions of other firms.

(f) Trends, technological and social portending changes in supply and demand.

4. Governmental Behaviour—Controls over marketing:

(a) Regulations over products.

(b) Regulations over pricing.

(c) Regulations over competitive practices.

(d) Regulations over advertising and promotion.

The manager must devise a mix of procedures that fit that resources. If his firm is small, he must judge the response of consumer trade, and competition in light of his position and resources and the influence that he can exert in the market. He must look for special opportunities in product or method of operation. The small firm cannot employ the procedures of the big firm. Though he may sell the same kind of product as the big firms, his marketing strategy is likely to be widely different in many respects. Innumerable instances of this fact might be cited. For example, in the industrial goods field, small firms often seek to build sales on a limited and highly specialized line, whereas industry leaders seek patronage for full lines. Small firms often elect to go in for regional sales rather than attempt the national distribution practiced by larger companies. Again, the company of limited resource often elects to limit its production and sales to products whose potentials too small to attract the big fellows. Still again, companies with small resources in the cosmetic field not infrequently have set up introductory marketing programmes employing aggressive personal selling and a "push" strategy with distribution limited to leading department stores. Their initially small advertising funds have been directed through these selected retail outlets, with the offering of the products and their story told over the signatures of the stores. The strategy has been to borrow kudos for their products from the leading stores reputations and to gain a gradual radiation of distribution to smaller stores in all types of channels, such as often comes from the trade's follow-the leader behaviour. Only after resources have grown from mounting sales has a dense retail distribution been aggressively sought and a shift made to place the selling burden more and more on company-signed advertising.

The above strategy was employed for Toni products and Stoppette deodorant in their early marketing stages when the resources of their producers were limited (cf. case of Jules Montenier, Inc. In Borden and Marshall, 1959, pp 498-518). In contrast, cosmetic manufacturers with large resources have generally followed a "pull" strategy for the introduction of new products, relying on heavy campaigns of advertising in a rapid succession of a are introductions to induce a hoped-for, complete retail coverage from the start (cf. case of Bristol-Myers Company in Borden and Marshall, 1959, pp. 519-533). These introductory campaigns have been undertaken only after careful programmes of product development and test marketing have given assurance that product and selling plans had high promise of success.

Long Versus Short Term aspects of Marketing Mix

There are continuous tactical maneuvers: a new product, aggressive promotion, or price change initiated by a competitor must be considered and met; the failure of the trade to provide adequate market coverage or display must be remedied; a faltering sales force must be reorganized an stimulated; a decline in sales has are must be diagnosed and remedied; an advertising approach that has lost effectiveness must be replaced; a general business decline must countered. All such problems call for a management's maintaining effective channels of information relative to its own operations and to the day-to-day behaviour of consumers, competitors, and the trade. Thus, we ma observe that short range forces play a large part in the fashioning of the mix to be used at anytime and in determining the allocation of expenditures among the various functional accounts of the operating statement.

But the overall strategy employed in a marketing mix is the product of longer range plans and procedures dictated in part by past empiricism and in part, if the management is a good one, by management foresight as to what needs to be done to keep the form successful in a changing world. As the world has become more and more dynamic, blessed is that corporation which has managers who have foresight, who can study trends of all kinds—natural, economic, social, and technological—and, guided by these, devise long-range plans than give promise of keeping their corporations afloat and successful in the turbulent sea of market change. Accordingly, when we think of the marketing mix, we need to give particular heed today to devising a mix based on long-range planning that promises to fit the world of five or ten or more years hence. Provision for effective long-range planning in corporate organization and procedure has become more and more recognized as the earmark of good management in a world that has become increasing subject to rapid change.

To cite an instance among American marketing organizations which has shown foresight in adjusting the marketing mix to meet social and economic change, I look upon Sears Roebuck and Company as an outstanding example. After building an unusually successful mail order businesses to meet the needs of a rural America, sears management foresaw the need to depart from its marketing pattern as a mail order company catering Primarily to farmers. The trend from a rural to an urban United States was going on apace. The automobile and good roads promised to make town and city stores increasingly available to those who continued to be farmers. Relatively early, Sears launched a chain of stores across the land, each easily accessible by highway to both farmer and city resident and with adequate parking space for customers. In time there followed the remarkable telephone and mail order plan directed at urban resident to make buying easy for Americans when congested city streets and highways made shopping increasingly distasteful. Similarly, in the areas of planning products which would meet the desires of consumers in a fast changing world, of shapping its servicing to meet the needs of a wide variety of mechanical products, of pricing procedures to meet the challenging competition that came with the advent of discount retailers, the Sears organization has shown a foresight, adaptability, and creative ability worthy of emulation. The amazing growth and profitability of the company attest to the foresight and skill o its management. Its history shows the wisdom of careful attention to market forces and their impending change in devising marketing mixes that may assure growth.

Use of the Marketing Mix Concept

Like many concepts, the marketing mix concept seems relatively simple, once it has been expressed. I know that before they were ever tagged with the nomenclature of "concept," the ideas involved were widely understood among marketers as a result of the growing knowledge about marketing and marketing procedures that came during the preceding half century. But I have found for myself that once the ideas were reduced to a formal statement with an accompanying visual presentation, the concept of the mix has proved a helpful device in teaching, in business problem solving, and, generally, as an aid to thinking about marketing. First of all, it is helpful in giving an answer to the question often raised as to "what is marketing?" A chart which shows the elements of the mix and the forces that bear on the mix helps to bring understanding of what marketing is. It helps to explain why in our dynamic world the thinking of management in all its functional areas must be oriented to the market.

In recent years I have kept an abbreviated chart showing the elements and the forces of the marketing mix in front of my classes at all times. In case discussion it has proved a handy device by which to raise queries as to whether the student has recognized the implications of any recommendation the might have made in the areas of the several elements of the mix. Or, referring to the forces, we can question whether all the pertinent market forces have been given due consideration. Continual reference to the mix chart leads me to feel that the students' understanding of "what marketing is" is strengthened. The constant presence and use of the chart leaves a deeper understanding that marketing is the devising of programmes that successfully meet the forces of the market.

In problem solving the marketing mix chart is a constant reminder of:

(i) The fact that a problem seemingly lying in one segment of the mix must be deliberated with constant thought regarding the effect of any change is that sector on the other areas of marketing operations.

(ii) The need of careful study of the market forces as they might bear on problems in hand.

In short, the mix chart provides an ever ready checklist as to areas into which to guide thinking when considering marketing questions or dealing with marketing problems.

Marketing: Science or Art?

The quest for a "science of marketing" is hard upon us. If science is in part a systematic formulation and arrangement of facts in a way to help understanding, then the concept of the marketing mix may possibly be considered a small contribution in the search for a science of marketing. If we think of a marketing science as involving the observation and classification of facts and the establishment of verifiable laws that can be used by the marketer as a guide to action with assurance that predicted results will ensue, then we cannot be said to have gotten far toward establishing a science. The concept of the mix layout the areas in which facts should be assembled, these to serve as a guide to management judgement in building marketing mixes. In the last few decades. American marketers have made substantial progress in adopting the scientific method in assembling facts. They have sharpened the tools of fact finding—both those arising within the business and those external to it. Aided by these fact and by the skills developed through careful observation and experience, markets are better fitted to practice the art of designing marketing mixes than would be the case had not the techniques of gathering facts been advance d as they have been in recent decades. Moreover, marketers have made progress in the use of the scientific method in designing tests whereby the results from mixes or parts of mixes can be measured. Thereby marketers have been learning how to subject the hypotheses of their mix artists to empirical check.

With continued improvement in the search for and the recording of facts pertinent to marketing, with further application of the controlled experiment, and with an extension and careful recording of case histories we may hope for a gradual formulation of clearly defined and helpful marketing laws. Until then, and even then, marketing and the building of marketing mixes will largely lie in the realm of art.

Probable Future Trends and Developments in the Field

It is not difficult to predict the direction of future efforts in the field of business logistics. Among the more important of future efforts will be:

1. Increased emphasis on total profit as opposed to total cost analysis. Basically, this involves an assessment of the effect of various logistics systems,

2. The extension of logistics systems analysis to include activities carried one by suppliers and customers as well as firm in question. The goal of such forts should be to an increasing extent the maximization of the long-run profit performance of the long-run profit performance of a channel of distribution composed of more than one or profit centre.

3. The increased systematic capture of data on an inter firm basis. Typical of efforts in this regard is the recent establishment of a Standard Transportation Commodity code for identifying various commodities transported in United Sates. Additional comes to provide the framework for collecting about shipments methods, origins destinations, transit times. Commodity exponents, and weights will be designed for Governmental

and inter-firm computer storage. The authorization of the first Census of Transportation out in 1963 provided the impetus for much of this effort.

Implications for Marketing Students and Executives

In view of the trends which might be expected to take place in business one might expect marketing management to become increasingly involved and interested in physical as well as promotional capabilities of distribution systems. This should lead to a greater concern for the measurement and control of customer responses to various levels of physical service. In terms of research efforts, it should produce more interest in measuring the behaviour of customers other than ultimate consumers, for logistical considerations often out weight those of a promotional nature in the distribution effort conducted at the wholesale and retail levels of consumer product channels and in industrial marketing.

Traditional management theory dealing with organisation has imposed an unrealistic view of organization relationships on marketing and logistics management. Business relationships external to a firm's formal oganisation are perhaps more important to the firm's success than those of an effort, attempts will be made to an increasing degree on the part of "channel captain' firms to extend managerial control to include certain this is the plan by which retailers' inventory control programmes can be linked to their suppliers in a system featuring automatic inventory monitoring, ordering, order-filling, and billion by the supplier.

The increased role of logistics management in distribution should have a leaving effect on decisions formerly controlled by promotional manufacturing executives or negotiated by both. The result should be the type of logistics programme which can meet the needs of customer and supplier alike at a lower cost to the former and a higher profit to the latter.

Because of the variety of organizational arrangements by which logistics activities will be managed, it will be incumbent upon logistics and promotional managers to coordinate efforts and communicate ideas and programmes. The isolation and identification of responsibility for logistics activities and costs should make this task somewhat easier in the future.

Basic Duties of the Modern Sales Department

How should the marketing concept affect sales management and the field sales force? What should the modern sales department contribute to company's success?

Sales department responsibilities increase under the marketing concept. Sales personnel, at both the managerial and field levels, are asked to their area of interest and "raise their sights."

Under the marketing concept, salesmen are urged to look beyond achieving clearly defined objectives. The marketing concept emphasizes this interaction and interrelationship of selling and other marketing related activities.

The sales manager and *field sales force* must now perform important management functions. An increasing number of companies are insisting that their sales managers demonstrate an ability to plan and execute creative field sales strategy and to integrate sales activities with the other elements of the marketing mix.

In short, the marketing concept is resulting in a re-evaluation of the nature and scope of the sales department.

Sales Manager's Duties

Under the marketing concept, the sales manager is concerned with management of the total sales effort. His job consists of more that recruiting, selecting and training salesmen. His major responsibility is one of creating a growth atmosphere and planning and coordinating sales force strategy n order to achieve company objectives.

Sales management operating under the marketing concept recognizes innovation and experimentation as the essential ingredients of sales and marketing progress. Under this concept, sales management realizes opportunities.

The duties of sales managers operating under the marketing concept fall into two broad areas: (1) sales administration, and (2) sales force management.

Sales administration includes the planning and organizing functions such as determining sales potentials, programming sales effort, coordinate sales inputs, and controlling sales outputs. In addition, the increasingly important functions of sales innovation, sales communication and sales search are sales administration responsibilities.

Sales force management includes the important functions of recruiting, electing, training, supervising, compensating and motivating the field sales force.

Both sales administration and sales force management are of crucial importance. To date many sales managers have done a better job of recruiting, selecting, and training salesmen than the have of executing their sales administration responsibilities. In the future various pressures of competition, innovation, automation, high fixed costs and changing markets will force increased emphasis on sales administration.

Sales Strategy Emphasis

The modern sales manager is concerned with the strategy inherent in a real approach to overall sales. He still has the bread-and-butter tasks of achieving quotas and directing salesmen in the accomplishment of predetermined objectives; but he also is charged with helping to create market acceptance, establish brand or corporate images, provide research information, develop marketing man power and establish harmonious dealer relationships.

The vital role of the sales manager in achieving corporate goals is emphasized in the marketing concept approach to sales strategy.

Two Dimensions

Marketing has two dimensions. First, marketing is an increasingly significant element in the total complex of business operation. Management sales a marketing decision after consideration of it effect on the whole business system and the overall objectives.

Second, marketing is an integrated subsystem. The marketing programme comprised of a mix of communications, distribution elements and good services "inputs". The essence of an integrated marketing programme is the managerial attention is given to coordinating the interacting elements of the marketing mix to achieve predetermined goals.

It is not possible for a sales manager to understand the true dimensions marketing change if he thinks only in terms of traditional sales management functions. Thinking of marketing as a cooperative effort—as a system"—enables him to understand the place of sales in the ιotal marketing effort.

Total Sales perspective

Actually, sales operates within a framework determined by various access beyond the control of management. These include competitive, social and political forces. Sales managers will have to be more sensitive the influence on sales strategy of these forces. Non-business disciplines such as psychology and sociology can be useful in supplying information on the external business environment.

Sales manager with a total sales perspective is less likely to see particular problem as an isolated entity. For example, the problem of sales compensation is appraised in its relation to other components of sales such s manpower development, selection, training, motivation, supervision and control.

Sales managers able to think in terms of how the field sales force is affected by the flows of information, money, and manpower are needed. These men will be in a better position to execute the policies of marketing-minded corporate managements. Since sales management will be working under this "systems concept' approach, understanding it will be a prerequisite for advancement.

Salesmen's Duties

The systems concept should be important to salesmen as well as sales managers. This is particularly true if the salesman's job is seen as that of managing a market area as it is on other hand, the salesman is looked upon as an order taker, the concept is not as applicable.

An increasing number of companies are realizing that the job of the salesman has strategic and innovative dimensions, just as does sales force management. Many salesmen are faced in their own territories with problems of goal determination, planning and long-run market development. Acting in these capacities, the field man is a manager of a market area.

The distinction between a salesman and a manager of a market area important; it is the difference between viewing salesmen as employees of as members of management. More important, it affects the way the salesman sees his own job. Under the market area management concept the creative, strategic, and innovative powers of the field sales force more likely to be tapped and utilized. In short, the market area management concept of field selling can bring about a fundamental change in the character of the salesman's job.

A man's ability to maintain this subtle but fundamental perspective the management of his territory or his sales force is a basic criterion of his development potential for higher positions of managerial and administrative responsibility.

Elements of Total Sales

It is important for corporate success that sales personnel view of the protection of marketing elements as a single system. Many successful and sales managers have been aware that change in one component of sales action has an impact on the rest of the system. But organized, systematic, and intensive attention to such interaction is relatively new in marketing and selling.

The three components of the overall marketing effort which

particularly relevant to sales management are: input, communications and output.

1. Inputs. Market planners and field sales planners must recognize the such resources as manpower, money, information, products and service are the "inputs' of the sale action complex. The concept of assembling pre-determined inputs to achieve specified sales objectives is a useful notion.

2. Communications. Communications with the customer and the company are key contributions of salesmen to total sales. The complexities communications in sales are just beginning to be recognized. Salesmen must overcome the barriers of time, space and lack of knowledge in produce a sustained flow of meaningful information. Sales communicative links the customer and his needs with the salesmen's firm.

   The sales manager has the important assignment of coordinating this information flow. The sales manager links not only management to the sales force, but also the customer to higher management levels. This is one the key concepts of the marketing management philosophy.

3. Outputs. Sales managers can be appraised in terms of a variety of measurable outputs. The most common, of course, are volume and profit standards. These criteria will always be fundamental, but others are being recognized as important. Such contributions as the type and quality information provided for management planning are becoming more significant bases of evaluation.

Areas of mutual interest for all participants in the sales program can be identified and developed under the "systems" approach to sales. The salesman in the field is more likely to see how his efforts support supplement the specialist in the home office. The headquarters specials can be helped to see that it is the salesman who produces the market which insure corporate survival and growth.

The idea of teamwork is easier to establish when all component sales are recognized as contributing certain inputs which will be combines with other contributions to produçe a predetermined set of sales output.

Scope of Concept

This concept of the sales action complex is also a way of looking new areas of market opportunity. In an era when technology s developing new products and product applications at an accelerating rate, it behooves marketing sales management to investigate the possibilities of "systems selling.

In fact; many firms can view markets not only in terms of companies but as complex business "systems'. And the same cooperative attitude should also carry through into manufacturer-dealer relations.

Many manufacturers do not recognize the mutual dependency aspects their relations with suppliers and dealers. Frequently, distributors and manufacturers fail to recognize the community of interest involved in customers. How many manufacturers see their dealers as part of extended sales system? Many say they do, but often unnecessary exist where cooperation should prevail.

The specific benefits of the adoption of the systems approach to sales management are:

1. Coordination of corporate, marketing and sales efforts.
2. Integration of volume and profit targets established by the company of the operating activities of sales management.
3. Establishment of a circular and continuous relationship between corporation objectives and customer wants, needs and desires.
4. Combination of all sales inputs into an integrated marketing thrust. Through coordinated impact on the market place, effective and efficient sales will result.
5. The systems concept approach requires sales management to

achieve a perspective of marketing and corporate activities extending beyond the normal activities on such functions as production, purchasing and personnel.

6. The approach promotes teamwork. Decision makers at various corporation levels recognize the ramifications of their decisions at all levels. The human executing tactics in particular sales situations recognizes the contribution to the field sales team made by the men who devise sales strategy.

An Introduction to the Personal Selling

It is the ability to persuade people to buy goods or services at a profit to the seller and with benefit to the buyer. Stated a little differently, it is the ability induce others to accept a benefit at a fair price, the benefit being the services rendered.

The sales force is the infantry that has to visit customers and channels of distribution to impart information and knowledge (as in the case with medical representatives), actually obtain orders from specific customers or ensure that existing customers are happy with the firm and its service. A host of other objectives may be ascribed to the firm's selling effort. A sales force is one of the most effective marketing tools that can be used by a company to create and keep customers. Sales forces are found in non-profit as well as profit organisations. The people who do the selling go by many names: sales people, sales representatives, accounts executives, sales engineers, field representatives, agents and marketing representatives. Selling is one of the oldest professions in the world. Personal selling is a creative art. The salesman creates wants where there was none.

Personal salesmanship is a direct, face-to-face, seller-to-buyer influence which can communicate relevant facts about the product and the firm to the prospect so that he can take a buying decision.

Three distinctive features of personal selling are as follows:

Personal Confrontation: Personal selling involves an alive,

immediate and interactive relationship between two or more persons.

Cultivation: It permit all kinds of relationships to spring up, ranging from a matter-of-fact relationship to a deep personal friendship. The sales representative normally will keep the customer's long-run interests at heart.

Response: The buyers has a greater need to attend and respond, even if the response is a polite 'thank you'.

Delivery of Product: This group does a stereotyped job, i.e., it delivers products to customers, generally in their houses or work places, such as agents of periodicals, retailer sellers of milk to households, local suppliers of gas cylinders etc.

Counter Salesmen: In this case the buyers have already made up their minds as to what products to buy, from which shop to buy and the like. The salesmen do not leave the place of business but take such positions as to be easily accessible; their main job is to take orders from customers as they arrive receive payments and deliver the goods. It is this group that is the largest in size.

Field Representatives: This group works outside. It undertakes travel, meets customers at different places, takes orders from them and arranges for supplying them the goods. The salesmen use their individual judgment in selecting their prospective customers and exercise persuasion with them.

Technically qualified people who are well-acquanted with the products, their utility and other relevant matters. Their major function is to call on manufacturers, research institutes and explain the technicalities of products for promoting sales.

Public relationists are also called "Missionary Relationships". Their main job is to call on people to promote goodwill for their organization and educate them about its products and policies. They are not expected to solicit orders. Pharmaceutical companies generally make use of this group of salesmen.

Tangible product sellers: In this case the buyers themselves have no feeling of needs for products nor are they are how the products would satisfy the needs. Generally sales of products like books of knowledge, encyclopaedias, works of art etc. Fall in this category. The salesmen have to rouse the need and desire for products.

Intangible product sellers: The products dealt in by this class of salesmen are intangible, e.g., advertising life insurance, medical services, educational assistance etc. As they can neither be seen or touched nor tasted, it is difficult to win the confidence of buyers and induce them to buy. The promotional part reaches its climax in this type of salesmen.

Sales force objectives:

Companies set different objectives for their sales forces. Sales people perform many tasks. They find and develop new customers and communicate information about the company's products and services and sell products. In addition, sales people provide services to customers, carry out market research and fill out sales call reports.

As companies move towards a stronger market orientation, their sales forces should become more market focused and customer oriented. The old theory was that sales people should worry about profit. The new view holds that sales people should be concerned not only with sales but also with customer satisfaction and company profit. A market oriented rather than a sales oriented sales force will be more effective in the long run. It will be effective in winning new customers as well as creating long-run, profitable relationships with customers.

Every company competes wit other firms to get orders from customers. It has to formulate its strategy on an understanding of the customer buying process. A company can use its sales techniques to contact customers. An individual sales person can talk to a prospect or customer or he can make a sales presentation to a buying group. In conference selling, a sales person brings resource people from the company to meet wit buyers to discuss problems and opportunities. Thus, the sales person often acts as an "account manage" who arranges contacts between people in the buying and selling companies. Since salespeople need help from others in the company, selling calls for teamwork. Others who might assist salespeople include top management. Technical people, customer service representatives and office staff.

A company has either a direct or a contractual sales force. A direct or company sales force consist of employees who work exclusively for the company. This sales force includes inside salespeople who conduct business from their offices and field people who travel to call on customers. Sales force strategy influences the structure of the sales force. The sales force structure decision is simple if the company sells one product, here the company would use a territorial sales force structure. If the company sells many products to any customers, it would need either a product sales force structure of a customer sales force structure.

In the territorial sales force structure, each sales person is assigned to an exclusive territory in which to sell the company's products or services. This sales force structure is the simplest sales organization and has many advantages. First, it clearly defines the salesperson's job and as one person works in a territory, he is responsible for territory sales. Secondly, as each salesperson travels within a small geographical area, he can build local business ties and also travel expenses are small. Sales people must know their products and this need has led many companies to adopt a product sales force structure in which the sales force sells along product lines. Companies often use a customer sales force structure whereby they organize the sales force along customer or industry lines. Separate sales force may be set up for different industries and for different customers. Organizing its sales force around customers can help a company to become more customers focused. When a firm sells a wide variety of products to many types of customers over a broad geographical area, it often combines several types of sales force structures.

Sales people force constitute one of the company's most

productive and most expensive assets. Therefore if the number increases, both sales and costs will increase. To set sales force size, many companies use some form of work load approach.

Sales force Compensation to attract dynamic salesmen, a company should have an attractive compensation plan. These plans vary from company to company. The level of compensation must be close to the "going rate" for the type of sales job and needed skills. Compensation is made up of many elements—a fixed salary, fringe benefit sand incentive bonus. Management must decide what mix of these compensation elements would be the most appropriate.

The selection of good salespeople ensures successful sales force operation. The performance of a poor and good salesman can be quite different. Careful salesperson selection can greatly increase overall sales force performance, poor selection will result in costly turnover. Selecting salespeople would not be a problem if the company knew what traits it wants. If it knew that good salespeople should be extrovert, aggressive and energetic, it can simply check whether applicants have these traits. After management has decided on needed traits, it must recruit salespeople. It is the function of the personnel department to recruit the right man for the right place.

Some salespeople will do their best without any special urge from management. To them, selling may be the most fascinating job in the world. But it can also be frustating. Salespeople generally work alone, and they must sometimes travel away from home. They may face different customers. Sales people often need special encouragement to do their best. Management can boost up sales force morable and performance through it organizational climate, sales quotas and positive incentives.

Organizational climate describes the feeling that salespeople have about their opportunities, value and rewards for a good performance within the company. Some companies do not attach much importance to salespeople. Some companies treat their salespeople as their prime movers and allow unlimited opportunity for income and promotion. It is quite natural that a company's attitude towards its salespeople affects their behaviour. If they are held in low esteem, there is high turnover and poor performance. If they are held in high esteem, there isles turnover and high performance.

Many companies set sales quatas for their salespeople stating the amount they should sell and compensation I often related to how well salespeople meet their quotas. Sales quotas are set on a level that is reasonably achievable.

Companies use several incentives to increase sales force effort. Incentives include sales contests, honours, cash reward, trips and profit sharing. It is rightly said, salesman are not born, nor made, but they are born and made.

Principles of Selling: Effective salespeople are highly trained in methods of territory analysis and customer management. Companies spend lots of money to teach salespeople the art of selling. All the training approaches try to convert a salesperson from as passive order taker to an active order getter. Order takers assume that customers know their own needs. There are two approaches to training salespeople to be order getters—a sales-oriented approach and a customer-oriented approach. The sales-oriented approach trains the salesperson in high-pressure selling techniques such as those used in selling automobiles. This form of selling assumes that the customers will not buy except under pressure. The customer-oriented approach trains salespeople in customer problem solving. The salesperson learners how to identify customer needs and to find solutions. This approach assumes that customer needs provide sales opportunities that customers appreciate goods suggestions and that customers will be loyal to salespeople.

Most training programmes view the selling process as consisting of the following steps that the salesperson must muster.

(i) *Prospective and qualifying*: The first step in the selling process is prospecting—identifying qualified potential customers. The salesperson must approach many prospects to get jut a few sales. One survey indicates that in the insurance industry only one out of 9 prospects becomes a customer. Salespeople should know how to qualify leads i.e., how to identify the good ones and screen out the poor ones.

(ii) *Preapproach*: Before meeting a prospect, the salesperson should learn as much as possible about the organization and its buyers. This step is known as the preapproach. The salesperson can consult standard sources, acquaintenances and others to learn about the company. The salesperson should set cal objectives which may be to qualify the prospect, to gather information or to make a sale. Another task is to decide on the best approach.

(iii) *Approach*: During the approach step, the salesperson should know how to meet and greet the buyer and how to make a good start. This step involves the salesperson's appearance, opening lines and the follow-up remarks.

(iv) *Presentation and Demonstration*: During the presentation step of the selling process, the salesperson tells the product story to the buyer, showing how the product will save money.

Companies can use three styles of sales presentation—the canned approach, the formula approach or the need satisfaction approach. Te canned approach is the oldest or scripted approach and consists of a memorized or scripted talks covering the seller's main points. This approach has limited utility in industrial selling.

With the formula approach, the salesperson first identifies the buyer's needs, attitudes and buying style, the sales person then moves into formula presentation that shows how the product will satisfy that buyer's needs. The presentation follows a general plan.

The need-satisfaction approach starts with a search for the consumer's needs by getting the customer to do most of the talking. This approach demands good listening and problem-solving skills.

(v) *Handling Objectives*: Customers always have objections during the presentation. The problem can be either logical or psychological. In handling objections, the salesperson should use a positive approach, find out hidden objections, ask the buyer to clarify any objections, take objections as opportunities to provide more information and turn the objections into reasons for buying. Every salesperson should have the skills of handling objections.

(vi) *Closing*: After handling the prospect's objections, the salesperson tries to close the sale. Some salespeople do not handle it well. They may lack confidence, or fail to recognize the right moment to close the sale. Salespeople should know how to recognize closing signals from the buyer.

(vii) *Follow-up*: Follow-up is the last step in the selling process and is necessary if the salesperson wants to ensure customer satisfaction and repeat business. Right after closing, the salesperson should complete any details on delivery time, purchase terms and other matters. Then the salesperson should schedule a follow-up call when the initial order is received to make sure there is proper installation, instruction and servicing.

The principles of personal selling are transaction oriented—their aim is to help salespeople close a specific sale with a customer. More and more companies today are moving their emphasis from transaction marketing to relationship marketing. The days of the lone salesperson working a territory and being guided only by a sales quota and a compensation plan are numbered. Today's customers are vast. They prefer suppliers who can sell and deliver a coordinated set of products and services to many locations; who can quickly solve problems that arise in their different parts of the nation and who can work closely with customer teams to improve products. Most companies cannot met these requirements. They often sell their products through separate sales forces that do not work together. Companies recognize that sales teamwork will be the key to maintaining accounts. Yet they recognize the just asking their peoplc for teamwork does not product it. Companies must revise their compensation systems to give credit for work on shared accounts and they must setup better goals and measure for their salespeople. Relationship marketing is base don the promise that important accounts need continuous attention. Salespeople working with key customers must do more than call when they think a customer might be ready to place and order.

Significance of Social Stratification in Selling

Social class frequently exerts a significant influence on consumer purchasing behaviour. Differences as well as similarities exit within each social class. The concept of under-and over privileged families is introduced as an example of an intra-class difference. In some situations, social class, like income, may not be a relevant factor in explaining market behaviour.

Dating back to the late 1940's, advertisers and marketers have alternately flirted with and cooled on the notion that W. Lloyd Warner's social class concept is an important analytic tool for their profession. The Wimerian idea that six social classes constitute the basic division of American Society has offered many attractions to marktign analysts when they have grown dissatisfied with simple income categories or ceasus-type occupational categories and felt a need for more meaning full classifications, for categorizations of the citizenry which could prove more relevant to advertising and marketing problems. However, in the course of their attempts to apply the class concept, marketers have not always found it immediately and obviously relevant. Sometimes it has seemed to shed light on advertising and merchandising problems and at other times it hasn't—with the result that many analysts have gone away disenchanted, deciding that social classes are not much more useful than income categories and procedurally far more difficult to employ.

It is the thesis of this writer that the role of social class has too often been misunderstood or oversimplified, and that if the concept is applied in more sophisticated and realistic fashion, it will shed light on a great many problems to which, at first glance, it has not seemed particularly relevant. What we propose to do here, then, is discuss and illustrate a few of these more subtle, more refined and (it must be acknowledged) more complicated ways of applying social class analyses to marketing and advertising problems. In other words, the purpose of this paper is to clarify when and in what ways social class concepts are significant in selling, and to suggest when they might not be as significant as other concepts, or at least need to be used in concert with other analytic categories.

The Warnerian Social Classes

The six social classes which are referred to in this paper are those which W. Lloyd Warner and his associates have observed in their analyses of such diverse communities as Newbuyryport, Masschsetts, Natchez Mississippi, Morris, Illinois, Kansas City, Missouri, and Chicago. These social classes are groups of people who are more or less equal to out another in prestige and community status; they are people who ready and regularly interact among themselves in both formal and informal ways; they form a "class" also to the extent that they share the same goals and ways of looking at life. It is this latter fact about social classes which makes them significant to marketers and advertisers.

Briefly characterized, the six classes areas follows, starting from the highest one and going down.

1. The Upper-Upper or "Social Register" Class is composed of local prominent families, usually with at least second or third generation wealth. Almost inevitably, this is the smallest of the six classes—with probably no more than one-half of one per cent of the population able to claim membership in this

class. The basis values of these people might be summarized in these phrases: living graciously, upholding the family reputation, reflecting the excellence of one's breeding, and displaying sense of community responsibility.

2. The Lower-Upper or "Nouvau Riche" Class is made up of the more recently arrived and never-quite accepted wealthy families. Is clouded in this class are members of each city's "executive elite," as well as founders of large businesses and the newly well-to-do doctors and lawyers. At best only one and one-half per cent of Americans rank at this level—so that all told, no more than 2 per cent of the population can be counted as belonging to one layer or the other of our Upper Class. The goals of people at this particular level are a blend of the Upper-Upper pursuit or gracious living and the Upper Middle Class' drive for success.

3. In the Upper-Middle Class are moderately successful professional men and women, owners of medium-sized business and "organization men" at the managerial level; also included are those younger people in their twenties or very early thirties who are expected to arrive at this occupational status level—and possibly higher—by their idle or late thirties (that is, they are today's "junior executives" and "apprentice professionals" who grew up in such families and/or went to the "better" colleges). Ten per cent of Americans are part of this social class and the great majority of them are college educated...

4. At the top of the "Average Man world" is the Lower-Middle Class. Approximately 30 per cent or 35 per cent of our citizenry can be considered members of this social class. For the most part they are drawn from the ranks of non-managerial office workers, small business owners, and those highly-aid blue-collar families who are concerned with being accepted and respected in white-collar dominated clubs, churches, and those highly-paid blue-collar families who are concerned with being accepted and respected in white-collar dominated

clubs, churches, and neighbourhoods. They key word in understanding the motivations and goals of this class is Respectability, and a second important word is Striving. The men of this class are continually striving, within their work, and both men and women are determined to be judged "respectable" in their personal behaviour by their fellow citizens. Being "respectable" means that they live in well-maintained homes, neatly furnished, in neighbourhoods which hare more-or-less on the fright side of town." It also means that they will clothe themselves in coats, suits, and dresses form "ice stores" and save for a college education for their children.

5. At the lower half of he "Average Man World" is the Upper-Lower Class, sometimes referred to as "The Ordinary Working Class." Nearly 40 percent of all Americans are in this class, making it the biggest. The photo-typical member of this class is a semi-skilled worker on one of the section's assembly lines. Many of these "Ordinary Working Class" people take very good money, but do not bother with using it to become respectable in a middle-class way. Whether they just "get by" at work, moonlight to make extra, Upper-Lowers are oriented more toward enjoying life and living well from day to day than saving for the future or earning what the middle class world thinks of them. They try to "keep in up with the times" (indeed, one might say the "times" are more important than the "Joneses" to this class), because they want o be at least modern, if not Middle Cass. That is, the try to take advantage of congress to live more comfortably and they work hard enough to keep themselves safely away from a slum level of existence.

6. The Lower-Lower Class of unskilled workers, unassimilated thinks and the sporadically employed comprises about 15 per cent of the population, but this class has less than 7 or 8 per cent the purchasing power and will not concern us further here. Apathy, fatalism, and a point to view which justifies "getting your kicks whenever you can" character the approach

toward life, and toward spending money, found among the people of this class.

Now, we do not mean to imply by these characterizations that the members of each class are always homogeneous in behaviour. To suggest such would be to exaggerate greatly the meaning of social classes. To properly understand them, it must be recognized that there is a considerable variation in the way individual members of a class realize these class goals and express these values...

All of this is by way of indicating that the millions of individuals who compose each social class are not necessarily similar or identical in their consumption patterns, even though they are of equal status socially and share a set of goals and points of view which are class-wide. Thus far, the literature on social class in both marketing journals and sociological publications has emphasized the similarities of people within classes and rare pointed out these variations. This has been necessary, of course, in order to properly introduce the concept and educate social scientists and marketers to its utility, but it has led on occasion to naïve misuse of he concept and ultimate disillusion. In my view, it has come time for us to advances into a more sophisticated application of social class to marketing problems which involves awareness of the differences as well as similarities with each class.

Social Class Versus Income

Let us proceed now to stating the basic significance of this class concept for people in the selling field. In the first place, it explains when income categories or divisions of Americans are quite often irrelevant analyzing product markets, consumers' shopping habits and store preferences, and media consumption. For example, if you take three families earning around $8,000 a year, but each from a different social class radical difference in their ways of spending money will be observed.

An Upper-Middle Class family in this income bracket, which in the case might be a young lawyer and his wife or perhaps a college profession is apt to be found spending a relatively large share of its resources housing (in a "prestige neighbourhood), on rather expensive pieces furniture, on clothing from quality stores, and on cultural amusement club memberships. Meanwhile, the Lower-Middle Class family—head we will say, by an insurance salesman or a fairly successful grocery owner, perhaps even a Diesel engineer—probably has a better house, in not so fancy a neighbourhood; it is apt to have as full a wardrobe though not so expensive, and probably more furniture though none by name designers. These people almost certainly have a much bigger savings account in the bank.

Finally, the Working Class family—with a cross-country truck driver or a highly-paid welder s its chief wage-earner—is apt to have less house and less neighborhood than the Lower-Middle or Upper-Middle family; but it will have a bigger, later model car, plus more expensive appliances in its kitchen and a bigger TV set in its living room. This family will spend less on clothing and furniture, but more on food if the number of children is greater, as is likely. One further difference: the man of the house probably spends much more on sports, attending baseball games (for example), going hunting and bowling, and perhaps owning a boat of some description.

The wives in these here families will be quite noticeably different in the kind of department stores they patronize, in the magazines they read, and in the advertising to which they pay attention. The clothing and furniture they select for themselves and their families will differ accordingly, and also because they are seeking quite different goals. This has become very clear in studies Social Research, Inc., has done for the Chicago Tribune on the clothing tastes of Chicago land women, for the Company on t replace of furniture in American homes, and for MacFadden Publications on the purchasing patterns and motivations of their romance magazines' Working Class readers. (These have been contracted in turn with the motivations of Middle Class women who read service magazines.)...

Up to now, we've been talking about product areas—clothing, furniture, and residential neighbourhoods—where he relationship between social class and quality of goods purchased is highest. In these things the so-called "Quality Market" and the Upper-Middle (and higher) markets coincide. That is, the purchasers of highest quality clothing and highest quality furniture are more nearly from the Upper-Middle and Upper social classes than from the highest income categories, and so on it goes down the hierarchy. The correlation between price of goods purchased and social class is relatively quite high in these product areas while the relation between price paid and annual income is lower than one might.

The "Over privileged" as "Quality Market"

Within each social class group there are families and individuals whose comes are above average for their class. The Upper-Lower family with as income above $7,000 a year-sometimes a product of both husband and wife working, and sometimes not—is example of this. So, too, is the Lower-Middle Class business owner or salesman who markets more than $10,000 a year, but has no interest in either the concerts or country clubs of Upper-Middledom and hence is still Lower-Middle Class. The Upper-Middle Class couple with more than $25,000 a year at its disposal but no desire to play the "society game" of subscription balls or private schools is also in this category. These are what might be called the "over privileged' in the absolute sense, a of course; they are "over privileged," however, relative to what is required or needed by families in their class. After they have met the basic expectations and standards of their grouping the housing, food furnishing, and clothing areas, they have quite a bit of money left over which is their equivalent of "discretionary income."

In much the same way, each class has its "underprivileged" members is the Upper-Middle Class thee are the younger couples who haven't made the managerial ranks yet, the college professors, the genteel professional and few downwardly mobile people from high-status backgrounds who are trying to hand on to what fragments of status they have left-for the most part thee people are below the $12,000-a-year marks and they can barely meet some of the basic requirements of Upper-Middle life,·in the Lower-Middle Class these are the poorly paid bank tellers, the rows of bookkeepers in railroad offices, the school teachers with considerably more status aspiration that income; and in the Upper-Lower Class it is almost any family earning less than $4,500 or $5,000 a year, at today's rates of pay in metropolitan area .

In the middle of each class's income range are its "average" member families who are might underprivileged nor over-privileged by the standards of their class. You might think of this as the Upper-Middle class family between $12,000 and $20,000 a year, the Lower-Middle family the $7,000-$9,000 range and the Upper-Lower family near $6,000 per annum. However, this word of caution is necessary: a lot of people in the middle income range of their class see themselves as underprivileged be cause they are aspiring to become one of the "over-privileged" in the class or to move on up the ladder to a higher class...

In summery, today's market for quality goods and quality brands is not necessarily drawn from what has historically been described as the "Quality Market" of Upper-Middle and Upper Class people, nor even necessarily from the highest income categories. Rather, in many instances, it drawn from those people within each social level who have the more discretionary income available for enjoying life's little extras above beyond the requirements of their class. Every merchandiser and advertise ought to take a good hard look at what he is selling and ask himself it bears this particular relationship to the class and income picture. If product doe, and if his brand is one of the more expensive, then he should merchandise it not as it it were just for social climbers of for the upper classes, but rather classes, but rather as part of the Better Life, U.S.A. If, on the other hand, his brand is one of the least expensive, then he is not just selling to the poor, but rather to those in all classes who feel it is only sensible on their part to settle for a brand such as his and save the difference for other thinking which are more important in their statement of social class aspiration and identity.

Social Class Isn't Always Important

Now, to make the picture complete, it must be pointed out that Social Research, Inc., has found some products in which the income factor is all-important and the social class variable is relevant only to the extent that it is correlated with income. Perhaps the most perfect example of this is the market for air conditioners in the Southwestern cities. There, everybody—except the sickly and the extremely old-fashioned—agrees that air conditioning one's home is imperative if summer is to be survived with any degree of comfort. Consequently the expensiveness of a family's air conditioning equipment—whether centrally installed, or window units to the number of our, three, two, or one—is directly correlated with family income. It is not merely a function of discretionary income—as in our example about purchase of medium priced cars; it is instead almost completely a function of total annual income. If more Upper-Middles than Upper-Lowers are fully air-conditioned it is only because more of them can afford to be; it is not because Upper-Middles as a group are placing higher priority on the air-conditioned existence.

Undoubtedly air conditioners are not alone in being classless—so that one more thing the marketer who uses social class in a truly sophisticated way need to understand is that there can be occasions when it is an irrelevant variable. Realizing this, he will not become disenchanted with social class when he finds a marketing problem where it does not shed light or where it does not seem pertinent. Of course, he will want to make are that in advertising such a product there is indeed no need to take class into account. After all, some apparently classless products are properly sold to the market in a segmental approach, appealing first on one ground to one class, then on other grounds to another.

There are other products—and probably air conditioning is one of the and children's play clothes may be another—where this is not necessary. For such products some factor, such as physical comfort (in the one case) or simple durability (in the other), is so basic in the consumer's consideration that all other motivations place into insignificance beside it. There are even products, like beer, where the democratic approach—that is, a tone of "lets-all-be-good-fellows-together" is exactly right and segmental appeals or snob stories are all wrong.

Another aspect to the sophisticated employment of social class refers back to the point made earlier that social class groups are not always homogeneous. It must be recognized that at times a product's market is formed by "highbrows" from the Upper-Upper Class on down to the lower-Middle, or by "suburbanites" and suburban-mined people of all classes—in which case the social class variable may confuse a market analysis more than clarify it.

Particularly must merchandisers and market analysts beware of equating "Class with "Brow"; for they are not synonymous. For example, the Upper-Middle Class and those above it are mainly middlebrow in taste (veering toward an all-American lower-middlebrow level of preferences in television shown and advertising messages) even thought the majority of highbrows are found at this level. At times advertisers have made the mistake of assuming that the Upper-Middle Class should be appealed to is a highly sophisticated fashion—and though this is just fine if he product itself is likely to appeal primarily to he Manhattanized type of Upper Middle, it is not correct if it is expected to sell to the kind of doctor in Dubuque who enjoys a visit to New York every now and then but would never want to live there.

In short, not only must the sophisticated marketer abandon social class in favour of income categories on occasion in his analysis and interpretation of a market, he must recognize that at times both income and class are superseded in importance by divisions of the public into brown levels, by divisions into "high mobiles' and 'low mobiles," innovators and non-innovators, inner-directed and other-directed, urbanites, suburbanites, ex-urbanites, ruralities, and Floridians, or what have you. Usually, of course, fullest understanding of a market will require that social class b linked is with whichever sub-categorization proves pertinent from among these is the catalogue just recited, much as income and class were linked together for fullest comprehension of the car market.

As a final point, let it be noted that the way of life and the goals of people in each social class are in perpetual flux. Neither the "who" of each class nor "what motivates tem" are constants to be assumed without continual re-evaluation. Right now, particularly, it is very clear that out society is changing. Every year the collar-color line is breaking down further. More blue-collar workers are becoming Middle-Class as well as middle income and Modern, and a white-collar position is less and less a guarantee of Lower-Middle status. As a consequence of this, the Lower Middle Class is perhaps somewhat more "materialistic" in outlook and slightly less "respectability" conscious than it was 25 years ago, or even Meanwhile, for men and women to achieve Upper-Middle status without college backgrounds is becoming more and more difficult, so that this class is turning much more worldly-wise and well-read, much less conventionally bourgeois than it was in the zenith of Babbitt's day.

In short, the form o our society and its division into social classes is not fixed as of Yankee City in 1931, Jonesville in 1944, Kansas city in 1952, it St. Louis in 1960. we won't be able to say exactly the same things about either the classes themselves or their relationships to specific markets by next year at this time. This fact about the American class structure, that it is not static, that it is in the process of change, is in itself important to merchandisers, to advertisers, to any one in selling. Among other things, it means that undoubtedly they have played a part in past changes and can play a leading role in directing future changes. But of more direct concern here, to the marketing analyst it means that if he allows his stratification concept to become dated, has use of it will cease as of that moment to be sophisticated.

CHAPTER 7

CONSUMER BEHAVIOUR ANALYSIS

The business activities must be focused on the consumer. This is an essential viewpoint in forms that operate under the marketing management concept. Any business unable to provide goods and services that fulfill the needs and satisfy the wants of consumers has lost its prime reasons for existence; it will not long survive in a competitive environment. Consumers judge business performance and determine business destinies by the manner in which they, consumers, exercise their purchasing power. Thus, whether a business is rewarded or penalized in the market-place is determined to a large extent by how well the needs and wants of its customers are understood and fulfilled.

Consumer reactions to market offerings result from a myriad of influences. Marketing managers must endeavour to understand the complexities of consumer behaviour and give due weight to what they believe to be the more important forces acting on the consumer. Before marketing opportunities can be recognized and marketing strategies adapted customer traits or characteristics that permit target market identification or segmentation must be studied. Selections in this chapter were chosen for their potential contribution to an understanding and appreciation of consumer behaviour and the forces underlying that behaviour.

Changing life styles for consumption and spending units have introduced important consideration for managers who must evaluate marketing opportunities. Discretionary time, mobility, and purchasing power helped to create a more discerning customer who in purchase decision may assign greater significance to convenience costs than to commodity cost. Similarly, social class and demographic methods of market segmentation , although still important, need to be combined with newer tools of marketing analysis. The satisfaction of customers and the attainment of marketing objectives results from successful integration of these elements.

Governmental agencies and other distinctive groups constitute specious markets that present unique marketing problems and opportunities. These markets must be analyzed in dept if their potentials are to be capitalized.

Sound marketing decisions are based on a knowledge of consumer motivations. Man is characterized as a wanting animal with a hierarchy of needs. Behaviour should be looked at a channel through which multiple needs are expressed and satisfied.

A Theory of Human Motivation

In a previous chapters various propositions were presented which would have to be included in any theory of human motivation that could lay claim to being definitive. These conclusions may be briefly summarized as follows:

1. The integrated wholeness of the organism must be one of the foundation stones of motivation theory.
2. The hunger drive (or any other physiological drive) was rejected as a centering point or model for a definitive theory of motivation. Any drive that is somatically based and localizable was shown to be atypical rather than typical in human motivation.
3. Such a theory should stress and center itself upon ultimate or basic goals rather than partial or superficial ones, upon

ends rather than means to these ends. Such a stress would imply a more central place for unconscious than for conscious motivations.

4. There are usually available various cultural paths to the same goal. Therefore, conscious, specific, local-cultural desires are not as fundamental in motivation theory as the more basic, unconscious goals.

5. Any motivated behavior, either preparatory or consummatory, must be understood to be a channel through which many basic needs may be simultaneously expressed or satisfied. Typically an act has more than one motivation.

6. Practically all organismic states are to be understood as motivated and as motivating.

7. Human needs arrange themselves in hierarchies of prepotency. That is to say, the appearance of one need usually rests on the prior satisfaction of another, more prepotent need. Man is a perpetually wanting animal. Also no need or drive can be treated as if it were isolated or discrete; every drive is related to the state of satisfaction or dissatisfaction of other drives.

8. Lists of drives will get us nowhere for various theoretical and practical reasons. Furthermore, any classification of motivations must deal with the problem of levels of specificity or generalization of the motives to be classified.

9. Classifications of motivation must be based upon goals rather than upon instigating drives or motivated behaviour.

10. Motivation theory should be human-centered rather than animal-centered.

11. The situation or the field in which the organism reacts must be taken into account, but the field itself must be interpreted in terms of the organism. Field theory cannot be a substitute for motivation theory.

12. Not only the integration of the organism must be taken into account, but also the possibility of isolated, specific, partial or segmental reactions.

    It has since become necessary to add to these another affirmation.

13. Motivation theory is not synonymous with behaviour theory. The motivations are only one class of determinants of behaviour. While behaviour is almost always motivated, it is also almost always biologically, culturally and situationally determined as well...

Summary

There are at least five set of goals, which we may call basic needs. These are briefly physiological, safety, love, esteem, and self-actualization various conditions upon which these basic satisfactions rest and by certain more intellectual desires.

These basic goals are related to each other, being arranged in a hierarchy of prepotency. This means that the most prepotent goal will monopolize consciousness and will tend of itself to organize the recruitment of the various capacities of the organism. The less prepotent needs are minimized, even forgotten or denied. But when a need is fairly well satisfied, the next prepotent ("higher") need emerges, in turn to dominate the conscious life and to serve as the center of organization of behaviour, since gratified needs are not active motivators.

Thus man is a perpetually wanting animal. Ordinarily the satisfaction of these wants is not altogether mutually exclusive, but only tends to be. The average member of our society is most often partially satisfied and partially unsatisfied in all of his wants. The hierarchy principle is usually empirically observed in terms of increasing percentages of non-satisfaction as we go up the hierarchy. Reversals often average order of the hierarchy are sometimes observed. Also it has been observed that an individual may permanently lose the higher wants in the hierarchy under special conditions. There are not only ordinarily multiple motivations for usual behaviour, but in addition many determinants other than motives.

Any thwarting or possibility of thwarting of these basic human goals, or danger to the defenses which protect them, or to the conditions upon which they rest, is considered to be a psychological thereat. With a few exceptions, all psychopathology may be partially traced to such threats. A basically thwarted man may actually be defined as a "sick" man, if we wish.

It is such basic threats which bring about the general emergency reactions.

Certain other basic problems have not been dealt with because of limitations of space. Among these are (a) the problem of values in any definitive motivation theory, (b) the relation between appetites, desires, needs and hat is "good" for the organism, (c) the etiology of the basic needs and their possible derivation in early childhood, (d) redefinition of motivational concepts, i.e., drive. desire, wish, need, goal, (e) implication of our theory for hedonistic theory. (f) the nature of the uncompleted act, of success and failure, and of aspiration-level , (g) the role of association, habit and conditioning, (h) relation to the theory of interpersonal relations, (i) implications for psychotherapy, (j) implication for theory of society, (k) the theory of selfishness (l) the relation between needs and cultural patterns, (m) the relation between this theory and All port's theory of functional autonomy. These as well as certain other less important questions must be considered as motivation theory attempts to become definitive.

Behavioural Models for Analyzing Buyers

Marketing decisions are based upon assumptions concerning consumer behaviour. A consumer's overt purchasing behaviour is a function of several factors, all processed by his psyche. Five "partial" behavioural models are presented, and their underlying theories are evaluated.

In times past, management could arrive at a fair understanding of its buyers through the daily experience of selling to them. But the growth is the size of firms and markets has removed many decision-makers from direct contact with buyers. Increasingly, decision-makers have had to turn to summary statistics and to behavioural theory, and are spending most money today than ever before to try to understand their buyers.

Who buys? How do they buy? And why? The first two questions relate to relatively overt aspects of buyer behaviour, and can be learned about through direct observation and interviewing.

But uncovering why people buy is a extremely difficult task. The answer will tend to vary with the investigator's behavioural frame of reference.

The buyer is subject to many influences which trace a complex country throughhis psyche and lead eventually to overt purchasing responses. This conception of the buying process is illustrated in Figure 1. Various influences and theirmodes of transmission are shown at the left. At the right are the buyer's responses in choiceof prodct, brand, dealer, quantities,and frequency. In the center stands the buyer and his mysterious psychological processes. The buyer's psyche is a "black box" who workings can be only partially deduced. The marketing strategist's challenge to the beavioural scientist is to construct a more specific model of the mechanism in the black box.

Unfortunately no generally accepted model of the mechanism exist. The human mind, the only entity in nature with deep powers of understanding, still remains the least understood. Scientists can explain planetary motion, genetic determination, and molecular behaviour. Yet they have only partial, and often partisan, models, of human behaviour.

Nevertheless, the marketing strategist should recognize the potential interpretative contributions of different partial models for explaining buyer behaviour. Depending upon the product, different variables and behavioural mechanisms may assume particular importance. A psychoanalytic behavioural model might throw much light on the factors operating in cigarette demand, while an economic behavioural model might be useful in explaining machine-tool purchasing. Sometimes alternative models may shed light on different demand aspects of the same product.

What are the most useful behavioural models for interpreting the transformation of buying influences into purchasing responses? Five different models of the buyer's "black box" are presented in the present article, along with their respective marketing applications: (1) the Marshallian model stressing economic motivations; (2) the Pavlovian model, learning; (3) the Freudian model, psychoanalytic motivations; (4) the Veblenian model, social-psychological factors; and (5) the Hobbesian model, organizational factors. These models represent radically different conceptions of the mainsprings of human behaviour.

The Marshallian Economic Model

Economists were the first professional group to construct a specific theory of buyer behaviour. The theory holds that purchasing decisions are the result of largely "rational" and conscious economic calculations. The individual buyer seeks to spend his income on those goods that will delivery the most utility (satisfaction) according to his tastes and relative prices.

The antecedents for this view trace back to the writings of Adam Smith and Jeremy Bentham. Smith set the tone by developing a doctrine of economic growth based on the principle that man is motivated by self-interest in all his actions. Bentham refined this view and saw man as finely calculating and weighting he expected pleasures and pains of every contemplated action.

Bentham's "felicific calculus" was not applied to consumer behaviour (as opposed to entrepreneurial behaviour) until the late 19th century. Then the "marginal-utility" theory of value was formulated independently and almost simultaneously by Jevons and Marshall in England, Menger in Austria, and Walras in Switzerland.

Alfred Marshal was the great consolidator of the classical and neoclassical tradition in economics; and his synthesis in the form of demand supply analysis constitutes the main source of modern micro-economic thought in the English-speaking world. His theoretical work aimed at realism, but his method was to start with simplifying assumptions and to examine the effect of a change in a single variable (say, price) when all other variables were held constant.

He would "reason out" the consequences of the provisional assumptions and in subsequent steps modify his assumptions in direction of more realism. He employed the "measuring rod of money" as an indicator of the intensity of human psychological desires. Over the years his methods and assumptions have been refined into what is now known as modern utility theory: economic man is bent on maximizing his utility, and does this by carefully calculating the "felicific" consequences of any purchase...

Marketing Applications of Marshallian Model

From one point of view the Marshallian model is tautological and therefore neither true nor false. The model holds that they buyer acts in the light of his best "interest." But this is not very informative.

A second view is that this is a normative rather than a descriptive model of behaviour. The model provides logical norms for buyers who want to be "rational". Although the consumer is not likely to employ economic analysis to decide between a box of Kleenex and Scotties, he may apply economic analysis in deciding whether to buy anew car. Industrial buyers even more clearly would want an economic calculus for making good decisions.

A third view is that economic factors operate to a greater or lesser extent in all markets, and, therefore, must be included in any comprehensive description of buyer behaviour.

Furthermore, the model suggests useful behavioural hypotheses such as: (a) The lower the price of the product, the higher the sales. (b) The lower the price of substitute products, the lower the sales of this product; and the lower the price of complementary products, the higher the sales of this product. (c) The higher the real income, the higher the sales of this product, provided that it is not an "unferior" good. (d) The higher the promotional expenditures, the higher the sales.

The validity of these hypotheses does not rest on whether all individuals act as economic calculating machines in making their purchasing decisions. For example, some individuals may buy less of a product when its price is reduced. They may think that the quality has gone down, or that ownership has less status value. If a majority of buyers view price reductions negatively, ten sales may fall, contrary to the first hypothesis.

But for most goods a price reduction increases the relative value of the goods in many buyers' minds and leads to increased sales. This and the other hypotheses are intended to describe average effects.

The impact of economic factors in actual buying situations is studied through experimental design or statistical analyses of past data. Demand equations have been fitted to a wide variety of products—including beer, refrigerators, and chemical fertilizers. More recently, the impact of economic variables on the fortunes of different brands has been pursued with significant results, particularly in the case of coffee, frozen orange juice, and margarine.

But economic factors alone cannot explain all the variations in sales. The Marshallian model ignores the fundamental question of how product and brand preferences are formed. It represents a useful frame of reference for analyzing only one small corner of the "black box."

The Pavlovian Learning Model

The designation of a Pavlovian learning model ha sits origin in the experiments of the Russian psycholoist Pavlov, who range a bell each time before feeding a god. Soon he was able to induce the dog to salivate by ringing the bell whether or not food was supplied. Pavlov conciuded that learning was largely an associative process and that a large component of behaviour was conditioned in this way...

The model has been refined over the year, and today is based on four central concepts—those of drive, cue, response, and reinforcement.

Drive. Also called needs or motives, drive refers to strong stimuli internal to the individual which impels action. Psychologists draw a distinction between primary physiological drives—such as hunger, thirst cold, pain, and sex—and learned drives which are derived socially—such as cooperation, fear, and acquisitiveness.

Cue. A drive is very general and impels a particular response only in relation to a particular configuration of cues. Cues are weaker stimuli in the environment and/or in the individual which determine when, where and how the subject responds...

Response. The response is he organism's reaction to the configuration of cues. Yet the same configuration of cues will not necessarily product the same response in the individual. This depends on the degree to which the experience was rewarding, that is, drive-reducing.

Reinforcement. If the experience is rewarding, a particular response is reinforced; that is, it is strengthened and there is a tendency for it to be repeated when the same configuration of cues appears again...

Forgetting, in contrast to extinction, is the tendency for learned associations to weaker, not because of the lack of reinforcement but because of nonuse.

Cue configurations are constantly changing. The housewife sees a new brand of coffee next to her habitual brand, or notes a special price deal on a rival brand. Experimental psychologists have found that the same learned response will be elicited similar patterns of cues; that is, leaned responses are generalized...

A counter-tendency to generalization is discrimination. When a housewife tries two similar brands and finds one more rewarding, her ability to discriminate between similar cue configurations improves. Discrimination increases the specificity of the cue-response connection, while generalization decrease the specificity.

The Freudian Psychoanalytic Model

The Freudian model of man is well known, so profound has benefits impact on 20th century thought. It is the latest of a series of philosophical "blows' to which man has been exposed in the last 500 years...

According to freud, the child enters the world driven by instinctual needs which he cannot gratify by himself. Very quickly and painfully he realizes his separateness from the rest of the world and yet his dependence on it.

He tries to get others to gratify his needs through a variety of blatant means, including intimidation and supplication. Continual frustration leads him to perfect more subtle mechanisms for gratifying his instincts.

As he grows, his psyche becomes increasingly complex. A part of his psyche—the id—remains the reservoir of his strong drives and urges. Another part—the ego—becomes his conscious planning center for finding outlets for his drives. And a third part—his super-ego—channels his instinctive drives into socially approved outlets to avoid the pain of guilt or shame.

The guilt or shame which man feels toward some of his urges—especially his sexual urges—causes him to repress them form his consciousness. Through such defense mechanisms as rationalisation and sublimation, these urges are denied or become transmuted into socially approved expressions. Yet these urges are never eliminated or under perfect control...

The individual's behaviour, therefore, is never simple. His motivational wellsprings are to obvious to a casual observer nor deeply understood by the individual himself. If he is asked why he purchased an expensive foreign sports-car, he may replay that he likes its maneuverability and its looks. At a deeper level he may have purchased the car to impress others or to feel young again. At a still deeper level, he may be purchasing the sports-car to achieve substitute gratification for unsatisfied sexual strivings.

Many refinement and changes in emphasis have occurred in this model since the time of Freud. This instinct concept has been replaced by a more careful delineation of basic drives; the three parts of the psyche are regarded now as theoretical concepts rather than actual entities; and the behavioural perspective has been extended to include cultural as well as biological mechanisms...

Marketing Applications of Freudian Model

Perhaps the most important marketing implication of this model is that buyers are motivated by symbolic as well as economic-functional product concerns. The change of a bar of soap from a square to a round shape may be more important in its sexual than its functional connotations. A cake mix that is advertised as involving practically no labour may alienate housewives because the easy life may evoke a sense of guilt.

Motivational research has produced some interesting and occasionally some bizarre hypotheses about what may been the buyer's mind regarding certain purchases. Thus, it has been suggested at one time or another that. Many businessman doesn't fly because of a fear of posthumous guilt—if he crashed, his wife would think of him as stupid for not taking a train.

Men want their cigars to be odoriferous, in order to prove that they (the men) are masculine.

A woman is very serious when she bakes a cake because unconsciously she is going through the symbolic act of given birth.

A man buys a convertible as a substitute "mistress."

Consumer prefer vegetable shortening because animal fats stimulate a sense of sin.

Men who wear suspenders are reacting to an unresolved castration complex.

There are admitted difficulties of providing these assertions Two prominent motivational researchers. Ernest Dichter and James Vicary, were employed independently b two separate groups in the prune industry to determine why so many people dislike prunes. Dichter found, among other things, that the prune aroused feelings of old age and insecurity in people, whereas Vicary's main finding was that Americans had an emotional block about prunes' laxative qualities. Which is the more valid interpretation? Or if they are both operative, which motive is found with greater statistical frequency in the population?

Unfortunately the usually survey techniques—direct observation and interviewing—can be used to establish the representatives of more superficial characteristics—age and family size, for example—but are not feasible for establishing the frequency of mental states which are presume dot be deeply "buried" within each individual.

Motivational researchers have to employ time-consuming projective techniques in the hope of throwing individual "egos" off guard, when carefully administered and interpreted techniques such as word association, sentence completion, picture interpretation, and role-playing can provide some insights into the minds of the small groups of examined individuals; but a "lea of faith" is sometimes necessary to generalize these findings to the population.

Nevertheless, motivation research can lead to useful insights and provide inspiration to creative men in he advertising and packaging world. Appeals aimed at the buyer's private world of hopes, dreams, and fears can often be as effective in stimulating purchase as more rationally-directed appeals.

The Veblenian Social-Psychological Model

While most economists have been content to interpret buyer behaviour is Marshallian terms, Thorstein Veblen struck out in different directions.

Veblen was trained as an ortfiodox economist, but evolved into a social thinker greatly influenced by the new science of social anthropology. He saw man as primarily a *social animal*—conforming to the general forms and norms of his larger culture and to the more specific standards of the subcultures and face-to-face groupings to which his life is bound. His wants and behaviour are largely molded by his present group-memberships and his aspired group-memberships.

Veblen's best-known example of this is in his description of the leisurt class. His hypothesis is that much of economic consumption is motivated not by intrinsic needs or satisfaction so much as by prestige-seeking. He emphasized the strong emulative factors operating in the choice of conspicuous goods like clothes, cars, and houses.

Some of his points, however, seem overstated by today's perspective. The leisure class does not serve as everyone's reference group; many persons aspire to the social patterns of the class immediately above it. And important segments of the affluent class practice conspicuous underconsumption rather than overconsumption. There are many people in all classes who are more anxious to "fit in" than to "stand out." As an example, William H. Whyte found that many families avoided buying air conditioners and other appliances before their neighbours did.

Marketing Applications of Veblenian Model

The various streams of thought crystallized into the modern social sciences of sociology, cultural anthropology and social psychology. Basic to them is the view that mans attitudes and behaviour are influenced by several levels of society—culture, subcultures, social classes, references groups, and face-to-face groups. The challenge to the marketer is to determine which of these social levels are the most important in influencing the demand for his product.

Culture

The most enduring influences are from culture. Man tends

to assimilies his culture's mores and folkways, and to believe in their absolute rightner until deviants appear within his culture or until he confronts members of another culture.

A culture tends to lose its homogeneity as its population increased. When people no longer are able to maintain face-to-face relationships another culture.

Subcultures

A culture tends to lose its homogeneity as its population increaser. When people no longer are able to maintain face-to-face relationship with more than a small proportion of other members of a culture, smaller units or subcultures develop, which help to satisfy the individual's needs for more specific identity.

The subcultures are often regional entities, because the people of a region, as a result of more frequent interactions, tend to think and act alike. But subcultures also take the form of religions, nationalities, fraternal orders, and other institutional complexes which provide a broad identification for people who may otherwise be strangers. The subcultures of a person play a large role in his attitude formulation and become another important predictor of certain values he is likely to hold.

Social Class

People become differentiated not only horizontally but also vertically through a division of labour. The society becomes stratified socially on the basis of wealth, skill, and power. Sometimes castes develop in which the members are reared for certain roles, or social classes develop in which the members feel empathy with others sharing similar values and economic circumstances.

Because social class involves different attitudinal configurations, it becomes a useful independent variable for segmenting markets and predicting reactions. Significant differences have been found among different social classes with respect to magazine readership, leisure activities, food imagery, fashion interests, and acceptance of innovations...

Reference Groups

There are groups in which the individual has no membership but with which he identifies and may aspire to—reference groups. Many young boys identify with big-league baseball players or astronauts, and many young girls identity with Hollywood starts. The activities of these popular heroes are carefully watched and frequently imitated. These reference figures become important transmitters of influences, although more along faces of taste and hobby than basic attitudes.

Face-to-face Groups

Groups that have the most immediate influence on a person's tastes and opinions are face-to-face groups. This includes all the small "societies" with which he comes into frequent contact: his family, close friends, neighbours, fellow workers, fraternal associates, and so forth. His informal group memberships are influenced largely by his occupation, residence, and stage in the life cycle.

The powerful influence of small groups on individual attitudes has been demonstrated in a number of social psychological experiments. Thee is also evidence that this influence may be growing. David Riesman and his coauthors have pointed to signs which indicate a growing amount of other-direction, that is, a tendency for individuals to be increasingly influenced by their peers in the definition of their values rather than by their parents and elders.

For the marketer, this means that brand choice may increasingly be influenced by one's peers. For such products as cigarettes and automobiles, the influence of peers is unmistakable.

The role of face-to-face groups has been recognized in recent industry campaigns attempting to change basic product attitudes. For years the milk industry has been trying to overcome the image of milk a s "satisfied" drink by portraying its use in social and active situations. The men's wear industry is trying increase male interest in clothes by advertisements indicating that business associates judge a man by how we he dresses.

Of all face-to-face groups, the person's family undoubtedly plays the largest and most enduring role in basic attitude formation. From them he acquires a mental set not only toward religion and politics, but also toward thrift, chastity, food, human relations, and so forth, Although he often rebels against parental values in his teens, he often accepts these values eventually Their formative influences on his eventual attitudes undeniably great.

Family members differ in the types of product messages they carry other family members. Most of what parents know about cereals, candy and toys comes from their children. The wife stimulates family consideration of household appliances, furniture, and vacations. The husband tends to stimulate the fewest purchase ideas, with the exception of the automobile and perhaps the home.

The marketer must be alert to what attitudinal configurations dominant indifferent types of families, and also to how these change over time, For example, the parent's conception of the child's rights and privileges undergone a radical shift in the last 30 years. The child has become the center of attention and orientation in a great number of households leading some writers to label the modern family a "filiarchy." This is important implications not only for how to market to today's family, be also on how to market to tomorrow's family when the indulged child today becomes the parent.

The Person

Social influences determine much but not all of the behavioural variations in people Two individuals subject to the same influences are not likely to have identical attitudes, although these attitudes will probably converge at more points than those of.two strangers selected at random. Attitudes are really the product of social forces interacting with the individual's unique temperament and abilities.

Furthermore, attitudes do not automatically guarantee certain types of behaviour. Attitudes are predispositions felt by buyers before they enter the buying process the buying process itself is a learning experience and can lead to a change in attitudes.

Alfred Politz noted t one time that women stated a clear preference for G.E refrigerators over Frigidaire, but that Frigidaire continued to outsell G.E. the answer to this paradox was that preference was only one factor entering into behavior. When the consumer preferring G.E. actually undertook to purchase a new refrigerator, her curiosity led her to examine the other brands. Her perception was sensitized to refrigerator advertisements, sales arguments, and different product features. This led to learning and a change in attitudes.

The Hobbesian Organisational-Factors Model

The foregoing models throw light mainly on the behaviour of family buyers.

But what of the large number of people who are organisational buyers? They are engaged in the purchase of goods not for the sake of consumption, but for further production or distribution. Their common denominator is the fact that they (1) are paid to make purchases for others and (2) operate within an organizational environment.

How do organizational buyers make their decisions? There seem to be two competing views. Many marketing writers have emphasized the predominance of rational motives in organizational buying. Organizational buyers are represented as being most impressed by cost, quality, dependability, and service factors. They are portrayed as dedicated servants of the organization, seeking to secure the best terms. This view has led to an emphasis on performance and use characteristics in much industrial advertising.

Other writers have emphasized personal motives in organizational buyer behaviour. The purchasing agent's interest to do the best for his company is tempered by his interest to do the best for himself. He may be tempted to choose among salesmen according to the extent they entertain or offer gifts. He may choose a particular vendor because this will ingratiate him with certain company officers. He may shortcut his study of alternative suppliers to make his work day easier.

In truth, the buyer is guided by both personal and group goals; and this is the essential point. The political model of Thomas Hobbes comes closest of any model to suggesting the relationship between the two goals. Hobbes held that man is "instinctively" oriented toward preserving ad enhancing his own well-being. But this would produce a 'war of every man against everyman." This fear leads men to unite with others in a corporate body. The corporate man tries to steer a careful course between satisfying his own needs and those of the organization.

Marketing Applications of Hobbesian Model

The import of the Hobbesian model is that organizational buyers can be appealed to on both personal and organization grounds. The buyer has his private aims, and yet he tries to do a satisfactory job for his corporation. He will respond to persuasive salesmen and he will respond to rational product arguments. However, the best "mix" of the two is not a fixed quantity; it varies with the nature of the product, the type of organization and the relative strength of the two drives in he particular buyer.

Where there is substantial similarity in what suppliers offer in the way of products, price, and service, the purchasing agent has less basis for rational choice. Since he can satisfy his organizational obligations with anyone of a number of suppliers, he can be swayed by personal motives. On the other hand, where there are pronounced differences among the competing vendors' products, the purchasing agent is held more accountable for his choice and probably pays ore attention to rations factors. Short-run personal gain becomes less motivating than the long-run gain which comes from serving the organisation with distinction.

The marketing strategist must appreciate these goal conflicts of the organizational buyer. Behind all the ferment of purchasing agents develop standards and employ value analysis lies their desire to a being thought of as order-clerks, and to develop better skills in recording personal and organizational objectives.

Summary

Think back over the five different behavioural models of how the buy translates buying influences into purchasing responses.

Marshallian man is concerned chiefly with economic cues—pries and income—and makes a fresh utility calculation before each purchase.

Pavlovian man behaves in a largely habitual rather than thoughtful way; certain configurations of cues will set off the same behaviour because of rewarded learning in the past.

Freudian man's choices are influenced strongly by motives and fantasies which take place deep within his private world.

Verblenian man acts in a way which is shaped largely by past and present social groups.

And finally, Hobbesian man seeks to reconcile individual gain with organizational gain.

Thus, it turns out that the "black box" of the buyer is not so black after all. Light is thrown in various corners by these models. Yet no one has succeeded in putting all these pieces of truth together into one coherent instrument for behavioural analysis. This, of course, is the goal of behavioural science.

The Importance of Convenience in Consumer Purchasing

Both product and convenience costs influence consumer purchasing behaviour. The increased importance consumers are attaching to convenience offers a key to understanding consumer shopping behaviour and is a major opportunity for markets. Consumer valuation of several forms of convenience is discussed, with special attention devoted to place convenience.

Two factor are of utmost importance in understanding consumer shopping behaviour. First, consumers making shopping decisions achieve an equilibrium between commodity costs and convenience costs. Second, convenience costs are assuming more importance as patronage determinants.

Commodity costs are defined as the monetary price paid the seller to obtain possession of goods and services. Convenience costs are incurred through the expenditure of time, physical and nervous energy, and money required to overcome the frictions of space and time, and to obtain succession of goods and services. For instance, a consumer shopping in the business district spends time, energy, and frequently carfare or working fees, in addition to commodity expenditures. Such costs have always been involved in trading decisions. The new emphasis on conscience does not necessarily mean that consumers are less price conscious formerly, rather, insistence on convenience cost minimization has been superimposed on the desire for economically favourable commodity transactions.

Shopping Costs

The question of consumer time expenditures for shopping is an interesting one. t has been estimated that there is a minimum of five billion adult leisure hours each week in the United States. This reflects is part a population consensus to accept a substantial share of the benefits of the production and marketing revolutions in increased leisure. Paradoxically, the increase in leisure time has been accompanied by a reaction against spending much of that leisure shopping. The modern family is confronted with too many more attractive possible uses of time.

Many forces favour higher consumer valuations of leisure and other convenience considerations. The suburban population movement with is living habit changes and broader family interests is one such force s urban areas also, fundamental social forces are operating which has resulted in families functioning more as a group than as individuals is certain activities, even to the extent of buying together. Such force favouring higher convenience cost valuations include the large numbers of working housewives, the age group imbalance within the population, and higher educational levels. Consumer estimates of purchasing costs are determined by the evaluations of alternative trading and social opportunities. Purchase decisions are made at the point whether total of commodity and convenience costs are considered minimal.

On the supply side sellers are operating in what seems to be a increasingly standardized production and legal matrix which is tending as limit price competition. The relatively narrow price spread among most retailers carrying identical nationally advertised merchandise suggests new importance for convenience costs in the strategy determination sellers. It appears reasonable to speculate that the range of competition advantage based on commodity costs will narrow. In this setting, it probable that convenience considerations will assume more importance determinants of purchase behaviour and seller strategy, and that more the competition of the future will focus on convenience considerations will assume more importance determinants of purchase behaviour and seller strategy, and that more the competition of the future will focus on convenience consideration.

Ten Convenience Forms

The importance of convenience as a determinant of consumer acceptance of products and services can be observed in an increasingly range of convenience features built into new products and in new convenience form appearing in the marketing system. Charles G. Mortine President of the General Foods Corporation, has described ten forms convenience which the American consumer now expects almost as a matter of course.

1. Form Convenience—cigarettes in various sizes and tips, and vet-pocket radios.
2. Time Convenience—typified by evening hours, and fresh fruits and vegetables out of season.
3. Place Convenience—file insurance in airline terminals, drive-it-yourself automobile rental services; and the planned shopping center.

4. Quantity or Unit convenience—aspirin in tins of 12, or bottles of 500; an small pianos for the smaller home.

5. Packaging convenience—disposable and utility packages; and the packaged vacation plan. The packaged home is already on the market.

6. Readiness convenience—instant coffee; pre-cooked foods; and The Reader's Digest.

7. Combination Convenience—do it yourself kits; and combination and matched sets.

8. Automatic Operations Convenience—automatic kitchen equipment; power steering and brakes on automobiles; and automation in many fields

9. Selection Convenience—the new variety of dairy products; and automobile color combinations.

10. Credit Convenience-cars; homes; vacation cruises; and education on credit.

Four Aspects of Place Convenience

Sellers should study all ten convenience forms to find areas in which consumer convenience costs may be reduced. This article is concerned specifically with place convenience. In maximizing place convenience advantages, sellers have related decisions at for levels to make about the capital positions that products ideally should occupy in the market.

(1) The geographic area or areas in which the goods or services are to be offered must be selected. In these areas or markets are found the consumers of the goods. This seller decision usually is not of concerned to the shopper who may choose from the offering of many sellers of substitute products.

The shopping mobility of consumers has tended to be limited to one metropolitan area, but this may not be the case in the future. Perhaps larger scale retailers may become concerned about competition between metropolitan areas as well as with competition within a metropolitan area. For instance, it may represent the same expenditure of convenience costs for a West Hartford resident to order by mail from Hartford, r even to make the trip to downtown Hartford. Conceivably, Hartford department store could become concerned about the drawing power of New York, Boston, and Providence department stores, as well as competition form suburban Hartford stores.

On the other hand, as metropolitan areas grow together to form urban regions, the primate cities of New York, Chicago, and Los Angeles are likely to lose some of their retail leadership to burgeoning regional and provincial metropolitan areas. This may occur in the same fashion, and for much the same reasons, that the central business district has lost ground to suburban elements in the retail structure.

(2) The most satisfactory positions within the market must be selected from those offered by distributors and retailers selling space in the market Channel-of-distribution decisions are involved. The one-stop shopping tendency of consumers has made channel selection more difficult for sellers in today's fluid market.

(3) Choices must be made among competing retail and wholesale institutions offering access to the customer. Should a full service hole sale be utilized, or would a limited function wholesaler represent a better channei choice? Are urban or suburban positions preferred? What is the role of the shopping centre?

The planned shopping centre movement can be rationalized with some justification in terms of consumer convenience. At the same time, planned centers are more than devices for convenient shopping or mechanisms for retail sales expansion in suburban areas. Planned shopping centers are a basic part of the restructuring of metropolitan communities. Their long-term importance to the economy is based on a continuing reassessment in consumers of shopping and social activities. Consumer convenience is still probably the basis of the shopping center movement. But the social economic, and architectural concepts underlying planned centers as geared to a new kind of social pattern and to what maybe an eruption into a new American social dimension in which consumer desires still require new patterns of marketing.

(4) Problems of positioning of goods within outlets must be settled Display and layout decisions are involved at this level. An experiment by Alfred Politiz Suggests the importance of convenience within the store studying the anatomy of the saie, he purchased and operated a large hardware store in Tampa, Florida. He found that if a product is sufficient well known to get consumer acceptance and is conveniently location the consumer will buy it in preference to a better known product. Why the customer will not select a product he has not heard about, "the little bit of inconvenience wipes out the impressiveness of even the known brands."

Conflicting Cost Considerations

A dominant characteristic of consumer goods marketing at present the state of flux of consumer valuations of commodity and conveniences costs. While such developments as the discount house reflect strong consumer interest in the reduction of commodity costs, it is quite possible that convenience costs will increase in importance as patronage determinants for more low dollar value items. This will pose anew one of the most challenging problems facing retailers in our complex distribution system: offering the right mix of convenience and economy to customers. Rich rewards may go to merchants able to do this successfully. A wedding of the shopping center concept and the discount house idea represents one promising approach.

Convenience cost pressures are likely to affect more marketing agencies in the future. Some of the possible impacts on planned shopping centers an established business districts are suggested below.

Convenience forces and the Retail Structure

Planned Center Increase

The shopping center movement is so new that currently two-thirds of existing centers are less than five years old. This fact, together with the predicted center expansion, indicated that the full impact of the movement has yet to be felt. A fundamental change in the retail structure of metropolitan communities seems certain, as a result of shopping center growth. Over 10,000 planned shopping centers are now in operation. Estimates have been made that by 1975, 17,500 of them will be operating. This means a planned shopping center for each 14,000 of a projectcd 1975 population of 245 million. This expansion is not expected to be uninterrupted. Many poorly planned intermediate centers are particularly velnerable to new competition.

Individual stores and shopping centers are tending to be larger. Department store branches of 300,000 square feet, and super markets of 50,000square feet have already appeared. A minimum site for regional centers seed to be considered fifty acres. Regional center developers are now thinking in terms of one hundred acres as a minimum site. Tracts of this extremely expensive, especially if they are in or near large cities. The increasing size of regional centers may mean that in the future such centers will be located farther from large population concentrations, and center the suburban periphery.

Consumer convenience considerations also set a limit to the growth of individual stores and centers. For instance, it is generally agreed that shoppers resist walking more than 600 feet from their parked cars to the latest center store. With planned centers, this suggests a limit for the maximum-parking distance that can be used before the planned center its advantages over unplanned shopping districts.

The Distance Concept and Convenience

The distance concept involves time-cost elements rather than a purely special one. High speed roads enabling consumers to travel farther from home on shopping trips are changing consumer views on distance. IN our society of automobile-borne suburbanites, distance between metropolitans point swill increasingly be judged on a time basis, not a mileage basis. The impact of this on established retail patterns is already evident. Downtown retailers have had to compete aggressively for suburban business is order to hold a satisfactory market position. Effective downtown competition for suburban trade is still possible. Indeed, a pattern for the rehabilitation of central business districts has developed. It includes improving access traffic, and parking conditions; modernizing physical facilities; conducting imaginative promotions; and strengthening mass transportation. In short, it means restoring some of the lost convenience aspects to center business district shopping.

Changing Functions in the Metropolitan Retail Structure

The central business district and suburban shopping center provide essential but different services to the community. Retail functions within the central business district and the other elements of the metropolitan retail structure are being modified. Store locations are shifting in the inner core, inner belt, and outer belt of the central business district and miss business thoroughfares. Similarly, retailers in planned an unplanned secondary commercial sub-districts, neighborhood business streets, small store clusters, and planned regional shopping centers are modifying functions to adapt to the needs of consumers living and shopping overall wide area. The downtown are may respond by becoming more of a business service, and recreational center and less of a mercantile one opinions as this vary widely. Frank Lloyd Wright visualizes the city of the future without a central shopping district. Others anticipate a downtown stimulated in part by shopping center competition, which will furthermore downtown property owners and merchants into rehabilitation and redesign programmes.

Other Dimensions of Convenience

In addition to spatial and temporal aspects, convenience has social and esthetic dimensions. This is one reason shopping center are likely to play an increasingly important role in community social life. All shopping centers are likely to benefit by following a policy of community identification although the benefits are particularly apparent with the large community and regional centers. Auditoriums, meeting rooms, restaurants, and other facilities making shopping more convenient are found in more planned centers. As more planned centers include such amenity shopping centers may come to resemble earlier market places, which served social as well as trading functions.

Consumers favour centers in which merchandise is presented conveniently, informally, and interestingly. Shopping-center planning, therefore, the excitement and pleasure to shopping. The modified bazaar concept of the center is likely to gain favour as weather-controlled centers without window displays and partitions come into being. For instance, Southdale, the new regional center outside Minneapolis, has a glass enclosed mall connecting the various stores in the center.

Convenience and New Retail Types

New store types are likely to appear in planned centers. Since shopping centers are located on choice, relatively low cost land compared to downtown stores, one floor retailing operations are possible to an extent not practical downtown. This may mean a reduction in handling costs and in the number of people needed to conduct and supervise operations. Some specialty store in planned centers should be in a position to offer more variety in prices and styles than down town specialty stores operating in less space.

Convenience pressures may provide a stimulus for other retailing developments offering lower convenience costs to consumers. Among these maybe increased direct-to-consumer selling, catalogue and telephone willing, perhaps a combination of television and telephone selling, and automatic vending machines. Improved vending equipment selling an increasing broad variety of merchandise could turn some planned centers and store clusters into round-the-clock merchandising machines.

Metropolitan for Decision Making

Understanding of the current state of the art requires acceptance of change itself as the dominant characteristic of marketing. If understanding of the process of market change, the forces producing change, and therefore, ability to develop policies under accelerated change condition is to be increased, more attention to the convenience aspects of marketing seems justified.

Measurement of convenience costs, while difficult, is not impossible Reillys Law represents one approach to quantifying some convenience dynamics, which beganin1927, that retail business gravitated from smaller cities and towns in accordance with a definite law. Reilly based has law of retail gravitation on two rules. The first is that, the larger the city the more outside trade it will draw. The second rule is that a city draw more trade from nearby towns than distant ones.

Reilly's contribution was in providing a quantitative measure of the rate that trade increases as the population of a city increases. His law of retail gravitation follows: Two cities attract retail trade from any intermediate city or town in the vicinity of the breaking point approximately in direct proportion to the population of the two cities and in inverse proportion to the square of the distances (via most direct in proved automobile highway) from these two cities to the intermediate town.

The law can be supplemented by discounts based on surveys, observations to obtain approximations of convenience cost consideration in trade areas. Factors such as time expenditures, distance (including distance to the store and with the store), and intervening shopping opportunities can be isolated in individual experiments. Development of consumer-distance concept to measure the costs of various locations possible. This could be based on the number of consumers within an multiples by driving time minutes from a location. But the core convenient analysis lies in the area of consumer psychology and sociology. This means that marketers will have to absorb more of what the and other disciplines, in addition to economics, have to contribute marketing theory.

Market Segmentation and Consumer Behaviour

In addition to the number of consumers and their incomes, the distribution of consumers over space is important to marketers. Changes in population distribution are producing important economic social, and marketing consequences. Interurbia is defined as "as agglomeration of cities and surrounding, densely populated, non farm counties," Marketers have a vital interests in the commercial impact of interurbia, and in the problems and opportunities created by this new population distribution pattern. Interurbian psychology and advertising media factors are discussed.

Interurbia: The Changing Face of America

Background

As a nation, we did not reckon with the pace of our growth. The quickened pace of our population growth has caused the Census Bureau to increase its forecast for 1965 by four million...its 1976 forecast by over 7 million.

The dimensions of the automobile boom were not foreseen either. In 1953, hard-boiled automotive economists forecast 50 million cars on the road by 1959. The fact is the 58,591,000 cars were registered in 1959. This forecasting error of approximately 8.6 million cars represents about half the passenger cars in Western Europe.

We failed to anticipate many factors that affect housing. By the late nineteen-forties, we did include playgrounds in city apartments built for young families. But we did not foresee the number of cars they would buy. And we did not reckon with the demand for television sets, automatic washing machines, and air conditioners that made these building electrically obsolete while they were still new. Most serious of almost city apartments do not have enough bedrooms for the baby crop. So the young families move out to the suburbs.

But they aren't much better off in the suburbs either. There are enough bedrooms of babies in the typical two-bedroom house built in this '40's. And many lack garages and carports. Young owners invest million trying to expand their little homes. Many give up and move out. Thanks to the automobile and the rise in real income, they can move still further from town, to find more space in the far suburbs in new homes they soon outgrow once again.

Business planers in the suburbs also failed to anticipate our growth. Many post-war shopping centers allowed only two square feet of parking space for every square foot of selling space. But today often ratio of firm square feet to one square foot is required.

As a result..

The 600-mile city arrives unherablded.

One of the main characteristics of this dynamic growth is the rapid evolution of the now-familiar phenomenon known as Suburbia into as infinitely more complex social pattern now known as INTERURBIA.

The most graphic demonstration of this evolution is in New York City. There, as elsewhere, it is no longer quite realistic to speak of a city and is suburbs. The New York metropolitan area has long been a conglomeration of many cities and many suburbs. Interms of population and physics plant, the "city" goes beyond the already obsolete limits of the New York metropolitan area. Indeed, it is no longer a Greater New York of a Greater Boston, Philadelphia, Baltimore or Washington. It is virtually about 600-mile city from Maine to Virginia. Actually, there are only two stretches in this 600-mile city—one of 2 miles, the other of 17 miles which are not part of metropolitan areas. And while this 600-mile "city" comprises less than 2 per cent of its nation's land area, it represents 24 per cent of its retail sales.

Interurbia, by definition, has these characteristics: it contains two more adjacent metropolitan areas with either two cities of 100,000 more, or one city of 100,000 and 3 cities of 25,000 or more, plus adjacent counties with less than 25 per cent farm population and more than 100 people per square mile.

There are now 14 of these Interurbias in the U.S. based on the last Census—plus two Interurbias in the making in the Southwest. They dot the landscape of the Eastern Seaboard, Midwest, Southwest and Pacific Coast. Together they account of or almost half of the country's population of 178 million and for more than half of its retail sales, yet they stand on less than 4 per cent of the country's total land. Within these fourteen interurbias, an average of 620 people live in every square mile—over 12 times as many people per square mile as there are in the rest of the country.

There are also some areas that did not at the last censure quite fit the definition of an Interurbia, but that almost certainly will fit it soon.

One of these is long the Florida coast and across the middle of the peninsula. North of Miami the coastal strips is already filled in for many miles. A big Interurbian growth is now under way south of Tampa and is beginning to touch the Fort Myers area. By 1965, this Interurbia will probably account for two thirds of the population of Florida.

Another potential Interurbia is to be found in the Piedmont area. So far this long chain of cities has reflected only the first stage of urbanization. Cities have grown faster than surrounding country. And there are long groups of open country between many of the cities. But the area is growing letter than the states it lies in and shows signs of becoming an Interurbia in the near future.

What has Caused Our Cities to Merge

The plantation is quite simple, although the results are incredibly complicated. What has happened is that homes and jobs, at one time closely tied to each other and firmly fixed in their places, have both been made movable—as tough at the end of increasingly long ropes.

The central fact which distinguishes Interurbia from suburbia is that that labour force does not move in a steady one-way stream, but more in a prices of cross currents. Westport, Connecticut, in Northeastern Interurbia serves as an example.

Most people commuting from West port move southwesterly to New York, but a significant percentage commute to Bridgeport, and New York. And Westport itself also receives part of its own labour force from Connecticut, nearby New York and the surrounding countryside.

The emergence of Interurbia from the now out-dated concept of city, and country has been stimulated more by the growth of satellite cities than it has from the big central city. The Interurbia in the Chicago and Milwaukee area or strip serves to illustrate this fact.

Between 1930 and 1959 the population in the suburban areas between Chicago and Milwaukee proper has increased 95 per cent while the cities themselves have increased 17 per cent. The same is true of the retail sales. In the areas between Chicago-Milwaukee, retail sales in 1959 were 460 per cent greater than in 1930, while in the two cities themselves, retail sales had increased 167 per cent.

What is true in the suburban areas in the Chicago-Milwaukee strip appears to be true of the entire country. In 1958, dollar sales per capita in the Interurbian suburbs were, on the average, 68 per cent higher than in the other suburbs of the country.

Interurbia in 1975

As we look to the future, we can with some confidence, predict the day is not too far distant when most of our people will be passed within Interurbia—as most of our sales now are. In 1975, it is estimated that Interurbia will represent 60 per cent of our population 70 per cent of retail sales.

Our 600-mile city in the Northeast may well grow toward the paramount. Its arm now creeping up the Hudson, will in all probability with Cleveland, Detroit, and Chicago, and stretch down Illionois to Louis. That would be an Interurbia about twice the length of the Atlantic strip—a city more than 1,200 miles long.

On the West Coast, the future holds the distinct possibility of an urban strip stretching northward from San Diego and connecting somewhere in the Caligornia Valley with the southward movement from San Francisco and the Bay area.

In the South, Dallas and Fort Worth extend in one direction down to Housston and Galveston, and in another, through Waco and Austin to San Antonio.

People will, as in the past, settle close to water ways, whether they be ocean, lake, river, or canal; but there will be other motivations, too—climate, the need for land and, as always, the desire for better living.

How Interurbia may affect Our Way of Living

Beneath the shell of uniform mass housing there most likely will be a series of different communities each catering to a different age and income group. The trend toward physical uniformity is rating a counter desire to be socially different. And this desire to be different is already apparent in some of the ostensibly homogeneous suburbs a such as the Levittowans in the East and in Park Forest, south of Chicago.

Families are on the move. More and more people are leaving the old home town—in a series of moves—from home won to college, from college to a great organization, and then from one provincial outpost to another, until finally comes the day when the man is summoned home to Rome.

The old home town may look pretty much the same. Yet if you check the leadership in the traditional town, you will find that the sons of the "early" families have more often than not left to join the transient life. Someone else, very much like them, is now sitting in the place they might have had in the Junior Chamber of commerce, the Community Chest, or the Greens Committee of the Country Club.

Then there is the more familiar kind of mobility—the great exodus from the city to the country. Familiar, yes, except that the exodus does not necessarily consist of just one jump—from city to suburbs.

To illustrate: since the war, there has been a tremendous growth in row-house developments in Northeast Philiadelphia. Socially, however, for many of these people there is still another transition to be made. For all their boasting about what a wonderful place the "5600" block is, the unspoken goal is to move out of the city. If the husband gets that raise, the "For Sale' sign goes up.

Mobility breeds more mobility. Once a person has learned to change environment it becomes easier to adapt to another. The good transient is professional about this.

Another aspect of this mobility is the tremendous upgrading urge it produces. One of the most characteristic complaints to be found in the new villages of Interurbia is about the quality of goods they have in the stores. The complaint usually takes the lines of 'who-do-they-thing-we-are-anyway?"

The most interesting thing about this upgrading urge is how very much it is conditioned by the immediate group in which a couple find themselves.

It is the group in Interurbia that determines when a luxury becomes a necessity. Take something like an automatic dryer. When only a few housewives in a block have one, other housewives can take it or leave it. As more and more housewives follow suit, it soon becomes an almost unsocial act not to own one. Finally only the most resolute can hold out. This use to improve one's own status has caused the developer of one of the new suburbs to suggest somewhat facetiously building a "life cycle suburb." You would live in one court as a child, a two bedroom apartment as a newlywed: then a ranch house; final, then you're old and gray, and your children are scattered to the four winds, you would move back to a court to serve out your term as a baby sitter.

Interurbian Psychology

Do the psychological needs of the people living in Interurbia difficult from those in the rest of the country? They do most decidedly. Here from a special study of several thousand people, are the principal derives of these Interurbian people and some idea a to how they may differ five the rest of the population.

The Interurbian man is significantly above the national average in his expressed desire for achievement—his desire to rival and surpass others—to do hi best—to achieve prestige and acclaim. He has an equally pronounced need to dominate other people. He wants to be a leader influence others. The Interurbian man is more willing to talk about and less strict in his attitudes.

Our Interurbian man likes also to be the center of attention—to have others notice him-to make an impression on others. In short, vanity and self-dramatizatiȯn are stronger needs in him than they are in the living elsewhere in our land. Change he doesn't mind. In fact, tour Interest bian man likes to do new and different things...to change his daily routine. He likes variety and novelty. Possibly this is a key as to why accepts the need for mobility with such calm.

It is a fact of great significance in the development of future advertising appeals that the characteristics which are most highly developed in the men and women of Interurbia are those on which so many great advertising success stories have been built and will be built. The people of Interurbia might be said to represent a preconditioned audience for the skillful advertising of many products and services to a greater degree than the people outside Interurbia.

How Interurbia Stimulates and Stabilizes our Economy Interurbia will push us toward a national economy that certainly will be bigger, and probably more stable. The stability will be due to the changing pattern of ownership and consumption interurbia imposes. Except for a little furniture and a closet full of clothes, most Interurbia city dwellers have no passions. New York city, for example, accounts for only three per cent of the nation's automobiles, but represents 15 per cent of the country's restaurant sales.

By contrast, the Interurbiate who has left the big city is forced to become a man of property. His ownership of a house creates a hunger for hard goods that inevitably drives him into hard work more relentlessly than the metropolitan dweller.

For example, one large builder found that the purchase of every new home automatically created 17 other purchases, such as furniture, appliances, curtains, garden tools, a new car-even a second car.

The stabilizing influence of Interurbia also arises from the huge spending programme on the part of businesses, utilities and public authorities that interurbia demands. And Interurbia's need for new highways alone is accelerating the need for housing in a brutally direct fashion. The present highway construction programme calls for the destruction or removal of about 90,000 houses a year—just to build roads!

Still another stabilizing influence lies in the increased opportunity for workers to maintain employment by being more mobile.

While the automobile has become the symbol of many Inerurbian problems, it fills a basic need. The phenomenon of Interurbia is based on the mobility supplied by the private car to drive miles to shopping center school, church and job. If anything, the need for this mobility will grow as business and homes spread further out.

But the growing use of the automobile is outstripping the ability of the central city to cope with it. In fact, the congestion has become so overpowering that some planners are persuaded that the means taken to open the choked downtown arteries are mere expedients. Some are bold enough to predict a not-too-distant day when the private car is barred altogether from the metropolitan city, as an improved intra-city barred altogether from the metropolitan city, as an improved intra-city transit system takes on the job of moving people about faster than they are now moving.

New Marketing Problems

The marketing problems created by Interurbia will be no less complex. With 31,000,000 changes of residence every year, the retailer worrying about new locations will have to keep a close watch on consumer movements.

The friendly neighbourhood dealer may lose some of his old sales punch as he sees new faces among his customers more often than before.

The manufacturer may find that the Central Cities in Interurbia are no longer the focus of marketing, but somewhere in between. Test marketing may be expanded to Interurbian strips, instead of individual markets. The same may be true do product research.

Sales organizations may grow smaller, as they concentrate more retail service. The two-thousand-man sales force may become a thing of the past.

Executives in charge of areas with traditional designations such as New England, Middle Atlantic, may be re-assigned to supervise a particular Interurbian strip.

New stores, service stations, and discount houses will expose customers to brands they've never seen before. As New York and Boston toward each other in the nation's largest Interurbia, they carry with these certain brands that New London, Connecticut, had never herd of. That same may apply to prices. Discount houses will introduce some cut price hitherto unknown to various communities along the way.

The Interurbian shopper for a refrigerator or other hard goods may soon be shopping in a retail store which carries no stock except the needed for demonstration or display. The retailer will simply phone in order to a warehouse, and the model ordered will be on the truck delivered to the customer's house within a matter of hours.

This new convenience for the retail shopper within Interurbia will made possible through a mammoth warehouse system handling may brands and a variety of product. It is conceivable, for example, that the hard-goods' needs of Northeast Interurbia alone could be efficiently supplied by four or five such warehouses.

The Interurbian influence can already be detected in the marketing procedures of many important good chains. The central city is no longer the sole location for their warehousing and buying. Rather their never centers have either moved out from eh metropolitan area, or they are being duplicated out in the growing Interurbian territory.

Even today, in major chains like Kroger and Colonial stores, we find some warehouse buying headquarters outside the central city with well developed "spokes" that are completely independent of any historic city or political boundaries.

As we change from the old concept of a metropolitan marketing area to a new Intrurbian marketing area, perhaps we should re-examine the traditional methods by which we separate and study our markets.

Perhaps it may not be too early for market research firms to break down their findings on the basis of interurbia versus non-Interurbia.

Advertising Media in Interurbia

Concentration of population has virtually always meant lower advertising costs. The bigger the mass of circulation an advertiser buyers, the lower the relative cost to him.

Today the space an advertiser buys in a country weekly can cost him ten times as much per unit of circulation as the space in a large daily. As interurbia develops, this discrepancy may be narrowed—with increased efficiency in advertising expenditure.

In the new Interurbia, the metropolitan daily may, of necessity, become less and less identified with the central city of Interurbia, and more with Interurbia as a whole. One ay of accomplishing this is to publish more zoned editions, as some large dailies are already doing.

The smaller dailies and weeklies may stand to benefit from the Interurbian development in two ways: first, they are in the happy position of serving their readers come to them; secondly, the pattern of marketing is changing so fast that major chain stores are becoming less and less identified with the central city, as they develop new spokes in their marketing wheel.

Interurbia also presents a challenge to Sunday supplements, whose substantial post-war growth has been based on their ability to provide coverage of the large metropolitan centers. More and more, the supplements may find it beneficial to buttress their circulation in the medium-size cities between their present major metropolitan markets. This would enable them to provide the same intensive coverage of the Interurbian areas that they now provide in central cities.

Today some 70 national magazines representing 71% of all audited magazine circulation accept advertising for circulation covering individual regions or markets. This trend of magazines toward regional adverting may gain further momentum as more advertisers begin to look at circulations for whole Interurbias, and not just their metropolitan segments. In so doing, they will find in many cases that the traditionally broad-base magazines can cover as many or more families within Interurbia as some of the individual local media that they have used traditionally.

TV set ownership throughout Interurbia will increase to something close to the 90 per cent that now exists in metropolitan areas. But TV network structures still lag behind the Interurbian development due to their historical tie to individual markets. Thus an advertiser seeking coverage of Northeastern Interurbia would have to supplement his ten network stations with several spot stations. Further network requirements for "must-buy" TV stations may be related more directly to Interurbias.

Radio's future welfare in Interurbia may rest in part on it becoming more and more a vehicle for news and music—an economical type of programming which could help keep costs competitive with TV. The degree to which smaller local stations within Interurbia are used will depend, as in the case of small dailies and weeklies, on the saturation required in the new areas which retailers are cultivating.

In closing...

We are at the foothills of a way of life which will require a more intensive study than we have ever given it before...a study of people's motivations and desires... of how they live and why they live as they do. And we must learn all this before it is too late.

Of one thing we are certain as we center this new way of life; that Interurbia will produce fundamental changes. And as it does, probably to one of us will be able to do business as we have been doing it. No one will find paradise in Interurbia. Paradise will always be just around the comes. And that for all of us may be our greatest opportunity.

CHAPTER 8

MARKETING MANAGEMENT AN OVERVIEW

The term market originates from the Latin word Marcatus which means a place where business is conducted. It is not simply a place of exchange but an arrangement that provides an opportunity for exchanging goods and services for money. We have to examine the following terms—needs, wants and demands, products, value and satisfaction, exchange, transactions and relationships and markets. The basic concept underlying marketing is that of human needs. Man has different types of needs such as physical needs for food and clothing, social needs for love and affection and individual needs for knowledge and self-expression. When a need is not satisfied, people will develop object that will satisfy their needs. People have unlimited wants but limited resources. They will choose the products that will provide the most satisfaction for their money. When backed up by purchasing power, wants become demands. People satisfy their needs and wants with products. A product is anything which can satisfy a want or need. Products include physical products as well as services. Consumers generally face a number of products that might satisfy a given need. Consumers make buying decisions. On the basis of their perceptions of a product's value, the consumer will choose the product that will give him the most benefit for his money.

Marketing occurs when people decide to satisfy needs and wants through exchange. Exchange is the act of getting a desired object from someone by offering something in return. Exchange is the core concept of marketing whereas a transaction is marketing's unit of measurement. Transaction consists of a trade value between two parties. Transactions may be monetary transaction or barter transaction. Transaction marketing is part of the larger idea of relationship marketing. Progressive marketers try to build long-term relationships with valued customers, distributors, dealers and suppliers. They build strong economic and socialities by promising maximum benefits. The concept of transactions leads to the concept of a market. A market is the set of actual and potential buyers of a product. A market can grow up around a product, a service or anything else of value. Hence there are labor market, money market or donor market. The concept of markets finally completes the circle of the concept of marketing. Marketing means working with markets to bring about exchanges for the purpose of satisfying human needs and wants.

Concepts of Market

Place Concept: A market is a convenient meeting place for buyers and sellers to come together to carry on buying and selling activities.

Area Concept: A Market develops in an area, the moment there are three preconditions for exchange: (a) Two or more individuals with unsatisfied wants (b) They have products or services to exchange and (c) They have some means of communications such as telephone, telex, e-mail correspondence, etc.

Demand Concept: The term market is also used to represent total customer demand. In this sense, market means people with needs to satisfy the money to spend and they will to spend money to satisfy their needs.

Marketing Management Functions

The achievement of predetermined marketing goals requires integrates and coordination of all market-related elements of the firm. Marketing management's task is to combine these elements into an effective creating system and to manage the system in its interaction with a dynamic environment. Marketing management functions that must be informed to plan and manage a corporate marketing system are assigning marketing opportunity, planning and programming marketing actively, actuating marketing organization and leadership, and evaluating and adjusting marketing effort.

Assessing of marketing opportunity involves the identification of company goals and the analysis of established and new profit opportunities be the firm. The significance of this function is that market opportunities continually changing, and marketing management must develop creates strategies to cultivate these market opportunities. A planned program innovation is essential for marketing effectiveness. The firm must be expand to the market and adopt a broad and dynamic view of marketing opportunity. Performance of the assessment function on a continuing basis the firm that it will be dynamic in its marketing and production sections, that identification of the set of challenges and problems facing the company is possible, and that changing marketing opportunities will set effectively by the firm.

Meaning is an integral component of the marketing management scope and is a vital element of he systems orientation. This function, when based on the assessment of market opportunity, is a key successful marketing management and performance. Market planning used to develop and define objectives and then derive programmes that enable the firm to achieve these objectives. The systems approach quires a concise statement of these goals and encourages a system analysis of the impact of the programs devised. Planning provides the best for an integrated and coordinated marketing strategy. Coordination of the firm's marketing programmes is a must if the planned objectives of the business are to be achieved. To make planning central to the marketing concept, both sort-and long-range planning are involved.

The innovistic and dynamic nature of marketing activity places demands on the marketing organization. The systems approach influence the firm's thinking about the marketing organization.

Viewing the organization as a goal-directed system can stimulate fundamental thinking about the firm's marketing operations and problems. The interaction process between the organization and the environment is a central concern of the marketing discipline. Application of the newer organizational theories have an impact on marketing operations. New product developments and the growing importance of international marketing are some of the marketing changes that have raised organizational problems for the firm Implementation of the marketing management concept will be direct reflected in the organizational changes that occur.

Diverse changes are influencing the patterns and styles of leader required for effective performance of marketing functions. Developments of newer patterns of leadership are testing traditional views of management methods and practices. For example, one organizational problem is raised by the tendency toward centralization of responsibility for integration the total marketing task. Balanced against this centralization tendency the need for greater participation in management and decision making people at subordinate levels. A solution requires analysis of management philosophy, communication patterns, the scope of responsibility authority, leadership abilities and staffing policies and practices, and development of appropriate policies in the setting of the individual section and firm.

In order to take advantage of profitable marketing opportunities marketing manager must continually evaluate and adjust the market effort. The firm must adjust to its ever-changing environment. An effective judgment, the marketing manager must have knowledge the entire marketing system so that the components of the system evaluated, controlled, and adjusted to bring the system in to line of the marketing opportunity. Essentially the major challenge confirmed marketing management is that of creative adaptation to change. This challenge, the firm should have a complete appraisal of its marketing operations through a marketing audit. The continuing problems of marketing management is to match marketing effort with marketing opportunity.

Nature and Dimension of Marketing

Marketing is the most important business activity because it links the two basic economic functions of production and consumption. Trade in the sense of exchange of goods and services is as old as civilization itself. But trade as such is different from marketing. Trade takes place after production but marketing precedes and pervades production and even follow up trade or exchange. Some definitions of marketing are given below with a view to highlighting its nature. The American Marketing Association defines marketing as the performance of business activities that direct the flow of goods and services from producer to consumer or users.

Marketing as the process which links producers and consumers by enabling transactions of exchange to take place to the mutual and continuing benefit of both parties—Robert Maxwell.

Edward Cundiff and Richard Still defines, marketing activities are those most directly concerned with the demand-stimulating and demand fulfilling efforts of the enterprise. These activities interlock and interact with one another as components of the total system—by which a company develops and makes its products available, distributes them through marketing channels—promotes them and prices them. In others words, marketing is concerned with product-market interrelationships and transfers of ownership.

Interrelationships

Product-market: Marketing is the business process by which products are matched with markets. Marketing and production activities are interlocked—we can market products that can be produced and we should only produce those that can be marketed.

Ownership Transfer: Ownership transfers occur repeatedly as products flow from producers to final buyers. A manufacturer may sell its output to wholesalers who, in turn resell to retailers who, again in turn, resell to consumers. In this case, every unit of the manufacturer's product that is finally purchased by a consumer has had its ownership transferred three times (from manufacturer to wholesaler, from whole seller to retailer and from retailer to consumer). There can be no marketing unless ownership transfers are effected.

Marketing as a Concept: By viewing a business through the eyes of the customers. The continued property of a firm can be ensured by providing the customers will 'value satisfaction' at a profit, satisfying their needs rather than simply selling what the firm has to offer. In other words, marketing is an organizational attitude which puts the customer at the centre of the decision-making process. The marketing concept recognizes the truth of Adam Smith's Dictum that Consumption is the sole purpose of all production. What this simple statement means in practices is that effective organizations must focus their attention externally upon customer needs and customer satisfaction and not simply internally upon products and production processions. This is because customers do not buy products or services. What they actually buy is utility—what the products and services purchased will do for them. So for marketers that key point of focus is not upon what is produced or delivered but rather upon the benefits and satisfactions that products and services can provide. The marketing concept calls upon organizations to recognize that it is the customer who determines what a business is. What the business thinks it produces is not of first importance. What the customer thinks he is buying or what he considers value, is decisive.

Marketing should be viewed as not merely a departmental function, but a guiding philosophy for the whole organization. The marketing concept calls for the whole organization to accept the truth of Drucker's assertion that 'there is only one valid definition of business purpose—to create a customer.'

The customer receives special attention because markets have two dynamics—competition and environmental change—which cannot be ignored. Most markets today are highly competitive. It means that the customer always has an alternative source of available supply. Unless the marketers understand the customers' needs and meet them effectively, then the customers will simply walk away. The customers should not be taken for granted. The other reason to be market-oriented is the fact of constant environmental change. This means that markets, customers and competition are constantly changing shape. Unless we are market-oriented, we have no way of keeping pace with change and our customers can slip from our group.

Marketing Functions

It is not enough to accept the marketing concept. It is also necessary to work out the definite ways in which customer satisfaction can be delivered. This is where the processor functions of marketing is critical. The marketing process is responsible for identifying, anticipating and satisfying customer, needs profitability. In practice, marketing process can be reduced to two crucial questions—who is our customer and how should we compete. The process of marketing begins with an attempt to understand the structure of the market place. It is not possible to attempt to appeal equally to all customers in all markets. Hence at the heart of the marketing process is the concept of market segmentation. The idea of a market as an economic obstruction of little practical use to the marketing. For this reason marketers seek to disaggregate overall markets into distinct and separate segments which can provide the basis for targeted marketing activity. The fist stage of the marketing process is the clear isolation of a clear target market. After the market has been satisfactorily segmented, the question is which segment should be selected as the organization's target market. The decision on where to compete is a key determinant of marketing success. We have to know who is our customer and what benefits does the customer seek.

The second question of our market offering concerns competition. Most industrial markets these days are highly competitive and what is needed for successful marketing is the development of a clear competitive advantage. Competitive advantage refers to a set of benefits which are superior to those of our major competitors.

In order to be competitive we need to know what our customers seek and what our competitors deliver. We can then build a sustainable competitive advantage. The sources of that competitive advantage are often described as the marketing mix. The marketing mix is a phrase used to describe the major operational variables which a marketing organization has under its control. These have traditionally been characterized as the product, price, promotion and place and people.

Marketing Techniques make the process possible. They include market research, pricing strategies, product development, distribution management and communication with the market and others.

Exchange is at the heart of marketing, without exchange marketing is redundant. The lowest form of economic organization is the subsistence economy. But this stage is devoid of a concept of marketing. Exchange first comes about where a producer creates a surplus in excess of the immediate needs of himself and his family, a surplus which he is willing to trade for some other goods. Any society which encourages specialization necessarily encourages exchange; Planned mixed and capitalist economies all share similar marketing problems. Each has physical distribution problems, each has mechanisms for determining what and how much should be produced; each has to make consumers aware of what is available an each has to set prices. Marketing techniques are applied irrespective of political structure. Marketing can be looked upon as an art, as a science and as a discipline. To define marketing a an art puts the emphasis on doing. To define marketing as a discipline stresses the academic side. To define marketing as a science is to see it as a body of knowledge with concepts, theories, principles and laws.

Evaluation and Adjustment of Marketing

Marketing must be treated as a total interacting system of business management, and the components of this system must be carefully evaluated and controlled. While a complete marketing audit may not be a feasible goal, much misplaced and misdirected marketing effort can be uncovered and corrected by a comprehensive analysis of sales volume and marketing costs.

The concept of an audit is not new to business management. Traditional it has carried the connotation of a review and evaluation of some sales activity. It has long been used in accounting and financial operation Management is also accustomed to manpower or personnel audits.

A complete marketing audit is something of an ideal or goal management to work toward. Rarely does a firm conduct an audit of the total components of its marketing mix and the interactions among the elements. The reason is that such an audit is too expensive and their consuming. Also, a total marketing-mix audit would be based to some extent upon data whose validity would be doubted by management.

Consequently it may be more reasonable first to conduct a complex analysis and investigation of the separate components of the marketing mix and to maximize the productivity and effectiveness of each of their elements before evaluating the interaction among them. With respect to field selling efforts, for example, such an approach to evaluation would involve an appraisal of the sales volume results, the related marketing expenses, and the performance of individual salesmen.

Oftcn in individual firms there is a considerable amount of misdirect or misplaced marketing effort. Marketing efforts and cost follow the number of territories, customers, products, or other selling units, than the actual or potential sales volume or profit in these units.

The social aspects of marketing acquire importance because markets directly involve either people or institutions in which decisions are made by people. The social structure of a market is influenced by interpersonal and intergroup relationships. The response of people to market stimuli is most properly analyzed in terms of demographic factors, psychological influences and the influences generated by society's culture and traditions. Thus when a market is said to have social influences, it means that the disciplines of sociology, psychology and cultural anthropology can be utilized to understand some of its phenomena. An examination of socio-psychological influences relevant to marketing affords insight into the consumer's behaviour in he market place.

Although the economic influences in marketing are many, the essential ones are (a) economic status of consumers, (b) kind of competition that permeates the market and (c) price determination.

Even though many influences in the market are not economic, the economic status of a society's people is the ingredient that turns desires into effective demand. Without income and money to spend, the socio-psychological aspects of an economy would be dormant. Money income remains the most fundamental basis for the functioning of the social variables and as such it gives impetus to other market influences.

Marketing is Political and Ethical Character: The political character of marketing lies in the legal nature of marketing activities which lead to exchange process. No business can operate very long without contact with the legal framework. Marketing functions within the framework of law. The legal dimension is one of the most highly formalized and complex influences on marketing behaviour. The ethical aspect of marketing has subtler impact than the legal framework. Law and ethics set boundaries of operation for marketing.

Modern technology has wrought many changes in man and has profound effects on an economic system. It is the basis for today's production and distribution methods. Though the state of technology and its impact on marketing have seldom been a concern of marketing, technology becomes an integral force along with the others.

Scope of Marketing

The cope of marketing include all functions inherent in the marketing process. Marketing functions are as follows:

Marketing Functions

(i) Functions of Exchange

(a) Buying (b) Assembling (c) Selling

(ii) Functions of Physical Distribution

(a) Transportation (b) Inventory (c) Warehousing (d) Material Handling

(iii) Functions of Facilities

(a) Financing (b) Risktaking (c) After-sales Services

Exchanges Functions

Buying Functions: Buying functions have to be performed at various levels. A manufacturer has to buy raw materials, chemicals, etc. for production purpose. A wholesaler has to buy goods from manufactures for the purpose of sale to the retailers. A retailer has to sell goods to consumers.

Assembling Function: In assembling the manufacturer assembled goods purchased from various sources with a view to satisfying the needs of buyers.

Selling Function: Selling is the most important function for any company. Selling involves the transfer of ownership from the seller to the buyer. Goods are produced for selling them.

Physical Distribution

Transportation: Physical distribution consists of those marketing activities related to the physical handling of goods. Goods have to be transported from the end of production line to the consumer. Decision has to be taken on the efficient mode of transport.

Warehousing: Finished goods should be kept in the warehouse properly. Finished goods are packed, stored and dispatched to field warehouses which act as distribution centers.

Material Handling: It is necessary to select proper equipment for material handling.

Functions of Facilities

Financing: The importance of finance at reasonable rate of interest cannot be over emphasized. Arrangement for securing finance is very important for a marketer. There are various sources of finance like Commercial Banks, Government Agencies Cooperative Banks, etc. The marketer must have a knowledge of the terms and conditions of credit facilities provided by different financial institutions.

Risk Taking: There are many risks which a marketer has to borne in the process of marketing goods and services. There are certain risks which can be insured against such as fire and accident risks. But there are other risks which cannot be insured, such as risks involved due to change in Government Policy or business cycle risks etc.

After Sales Service: These days the importance of after-sales facilities cannot be ignored by the marketer. The marketer has to plan for providing after-sale services, like repairs, replacements, etc.

Management Overview

Current assessment of interdisciplinary contributions to marketing is offered. Indications are that advances in mathematics, statistics, computer science, systems engineering, and some functional areas of business administration have helped accelerate the interdisciplinary process. Not only is this process making a positive contribution to the advancement of science in marketing, but it is also becoming a reciprocal exercise in which marketing is making its own contribution to allied disciplines. Some problems inherent in the interdisciplinary approach are presented.

The Interdisciplinary Concept

To discuss the interdisciplinary approach with clarity, several related concepts should be examined, particularly transdisciplinary, multidisciplinary, and interdisciplinary. Transdisciplinary is the broadest concept. It refers to the crossing of discipline boundaries. Both the multidisciplinary and interdisciplinary approaches, by definition, therefore, are transdisciplinary. There is, however, considerable difference between their respective approaches.

The multidisciplinary approach uses stores of knowledge and viewpoints from many disciplines. It borrows concepts and techniques. It solving capability. But it tends to leave the general discipline boundaries more or less intact.

The interdisciplinary approach integrates concepts and ideas, restructures fields, changes subject-matter boundaries, and bridges theoretical gaps. It tends to develop more coherent and logical structure, more adequate theories, and leads to new concepts, techniques, and even subjects. It synthesizes concepts, findings and ideas. Sometimes it even results in new disciplines. Often the interdisciplinary approach follows the multidisciplinary.

Since marketing problems have been studied by subject-matter specialists external to marketing—for example, psychologists and sociologists – marketing has long felt the impact of a multidisciplinary approach. Specialists, however, investigate marketing problems from the perspectives of their own particular disciplines. A useful overflow from one area to another often occurs, and disciplines are given new vitality, but they are not transmuted Yet this very transfer of knowledge can challenge old categories and strain discipline boundaries.

Marketing has borrowed from both the social and behavioural sciences. Initially, major contributions from the social sciences resulted in a heavy macroperspective. Later multidisciplinary contributions emphasized the behavioral sciences and a microemphasis. This is to be expected since "the twentieth century. Marks the coming-of-age of the behavioural sciences"

The interdisciplinary approach requires a true federation of disciplines. It is not just a matter of borrowing among disciplines. It is concerned with the combination and integration of the endeavor of several specialized fields of study for the purpose of gaining marketing knowledge and solving marketing problems. The interdisciplinary approach offers tentative concepts, findings, postulates, working hypotheses, an methodology for the direction and organization of inquiry in marketing. It abandons reified categories o disciplines and tends to unify scientific inquiry.

The interdisciplinary approach, however, is not one unified approach—rather it is many approaches. It is a loose coalition of perspectives, findings, and avenues. It can sometimes be a maze of conflicting hypotheses, findings, and ideas. This conflict, of course, can be challenging and desirable, and can lead to imaginative research.

In relating to other disciplines, marketing has drawn from four discipline groups.

1. Those that are directly allied to marketing. This includes microeconomics, management, organization theory, finance, and accounting. These disciplines investigate many marketing problems and subjects as part of their normal approach.

2. Those that study behaviour, particularly human behaviour such as psychology, sociology, and cultural anthropology.

3. Those that focus on broader societal issues and problems such as philosophy, political science, and macroeconomics.

4. Those that concentrate on tools and techniques. This includes mathematics, statistics, systems engineering, and computer science.

It is worth noting that an intradisciplinary approach has also been felt in marketing. It leads to the integration and blending of concepts, ideas, and findings within the marketing discipline itself. It is being spurred by the acceptance of a systems approach to marketing. For example, physical distribution, the result of a systems approach, integrates transportation, storing, warehousing, distribution, handling, sorting, and moving. Marketing intelligence results from an amalgamation of various subjects dealing with gathering, analyzing, interpreting, and using data. Marketing promotion refers to the coordination of all promotional aspects—advertising, personal selling, and publicity.

Kinds of Interdisciplinary Contributions

The interdisciplinary approach to marketing results in three kinds of contributions: those that are direct and immediate, those that are direct but potential, and the indirect and potential contributions.

Direct and immediate contributions refer to those concepts, ideas, and findings that can be applied directly by marketing. Included are various techniques of measurement, concepts such as life cycle, social stratification, and data including income and demographic data. They result in an immediate infusion of knowledge. We shall consider such contributions later.

Direct but potential contributions are those that seem to have direct tarry over but require further research, development, or refinement. They constitute the bulk of the interdiscipliary contributions. For example, research on farm product innovations reveals that innovators and early adopters are more means-oriented, tend to be more secure as individuals, and have greater ability to with abstractions. Is this true for other product categories? Similarly, the following changes in values have been ascribed to our society:

1. Less emphasis on personal values and more on group standards and welfare.
2. Increased positive evaluation of psychological criteria.
3. Receding of value on future success in favour of respectable and stable security.
4. Rise in value of aesthetic considerations.
5. Greater value placed on explicit values.

These changes seem to hold implications for marketing, but further research is required before the implications are those which are somewhat tangential but contain a glimmer of an idea, a concept, or suggest hypotheses that, with considerable work, may be useful. Resemblances, analogies, and identities often fall into this category. For instance, reasoning that marketing might be analyzed as a system, or seeking what correspondence the concepts of homeostasis, transaction, and transaction have in marketing while indirect, at least initially, and requiring development, often proves useful. Hart's two laws of social change: (1) that Law of Cultural Acceleration, which states that the means for accomplishing purposes have increased at an accelerating rate; and (2) the Law of Logistic Surges, which explains that the logistics curve describes specific instances of cultural accumulation, are examples of indirect potential contributions. They are suggestive in developing and understanding product innovation and acceptance. Similarly, diagrammatic representation of ten theories of the direction of change have been offered. They seem to hold potential for developing marketing thought.

Current Status

What is the present status of the use of other disciplines in marketing. Marketing's use of other disciplines to date may best be charactrised as multidisciplinary rather than interdisciplinary. Yet, marketing as an area of study is moving from the multidisciplinary to the interdisciplinary stage. This current multidisciplinary emphasis is the prelude to the adoption of a more integrated interdisciplinary orientation. As a result of the current stage of progress, throughout the rest of the paper I shall not distinguish the multidisciplinary from the interdisciplinary.

Cronbach's statement about the lack of integration of various psychological approaches is very appropriate for marketing. He states that if approaches are "kept independent, they can give only wrong answers or no answers at all regarding certain important problems." For example, we cannot argue that marketing will deal with market forces and consumer behaviour, while psychology will formulate the laws of motivation or change.

But the aim of the interdisciplinary approach should not be the cross-fertilization of ideas to unify the disciplines. Rather it should be the use of various tools and concepts to come to grips wit marketing problems. It should offer a joint attack on common problems in marketing, using the contributions of various disciplines, rather than promise unification of all disciplines.

The lines of disciplines are blurring, and an integration and federation of some of them is occurring. It is becoming more difficult to differentiate parts of psychology and sociology from marketing and vice versa. Will the disciplines be united into fewer and fewer subject-matter areas: Will the marketing boundaries vanish? The answer, I believe, is no. Several forces will hold the marketing discipline intact. Its problems, theories, and methods; its instructional involvement; its identification with functions that are most significant to business; and its meaning for competition and international development will insure that marketing will continue as a unit for teaching, research, and problem solving.

But the gaps among marketing and other areas will narrow. The tools will become similar. The concepts and ideas of many disciplines will continue to converge on marketing problems. More hybrid disciplines will emerge, and common concepts will evolve. Conceptual bridges between marketing and neighboring subject-matter areas will emerge. Marketing's relationship with other disciplines will change. It will become more reciprocal in nature.

Currently, there are shifts in environmental factors encouraging the convergence of the research effort from many disciplines on marketing factors. Psychology, for example, is now feeling the impact of automation and abundance, and the "area of psychological research interest tends to shift from the producer to the consumer...what is needed is an understanding of consumer behaviour." Such influences will buttress the interdisciplinary approach to marketing.

Interdisciplinary emphasis is affecting the development of marketing in yet another way. As the marketing discipline built on concepts from other disciplines, and as the field of marketing became established, specialization spread. Marketing as a discipline turned inward and became fractionalized. With the interdisciplinary approach, marketing has turned outward, and the result is more meaningful perspectives, new concepts and theories, improved techniques, and a more useful body of knowledge.

An investigation of marketing management practice and marketing thought reveals that a more rigorous and penetrating analysis of marketing and business has resulted from multidimensional approaches to the study of marketing. Consider the use of economic theory. Demand a core marketing concept, is now analyzed in terms of dimensions that extend well beyond those of the initial economic boundaries. It is viewed in terms of motivation, perception, status, imagery, symbolism, communications networks, conformity, resistance to change, levels of aspiration, life cycle, life style, mobility, search and expectations. New questions are asked and new answer sought. Realistic involvement of many disciplines results. "A vast body of material which is potentially useful to marketing management exists in other disciplines."

Kapp has noted that "the essential characteristics of society are those of structural interdependence. Social structure is primary, and from it all social inquiry must derive its basic scientific strategy." In fact, some disciplines have been referred to as integrating disciplines. "For example, both anthropology and sociology are claimed to be ;integrating sciences,' the one taking 'culture' as the basic and integrating idea, and the other, 'social group or society.' Viewed from this perspective, marketing is an integrating discipline. Markets are among the core institutions of our society. Marketing is characteristically American and exerts basic influences on our life style, culture, wealth, production, and values. Marketing provides a common conceptual framework for studying many problem that cross disciplinary lines. The very scope and dimension of marketing problems carry theorists and practitioners over discipline boundaries. Although the "point of departure and the focus of study differ among the disciplines...there are frequently great similarities between marketing and other disciplines in both methodology and content."

The interdisciplinary approach confronts the empirical findings of marketing with the conceptual an theoretical formulations of other disciplines and vice versa. The result is that all confronted disciplines benefit. Marketing's direct and significant ties with economics and sociology are examples.

It seems that the most rapid period of progressive change in marketing is associated not with discoveries within the field but wit the importation, borrowing, and diffusion of contributions outside marketing. In turn, however, these borrowed elements are changed in the assimilation process which results in new ideas and concepts.

In reality, marketing and its research are brought into existence to serve a purpose—a specific area of study. Yet as soon as marketing discovers ideas and information, it also serves other purposes and works with other subjects. As it does, it adds valuable dimensions and a wider purview to one's understanding of both marketing and relate areas. Marketing problems are seem in many dimensions.

Discipline Contributions Evaluated

It is difficult to evaluate contributions of other disciplines to marketing. First, it is often impossible to classify contributions by disciplines because of the cross-fertilization that has taken place. People trained in one discipline work in another, and there is a tendency to select concepts, tools, and techniques from any discipline and modify and adapt them to solve marketing problems. Second, it is impossible to develop a rating scheme to evaluate objectively the overall contributions of various disciplines to marketing.

Yet, Table 2.1 presents an assessment about the nature of discipline contributions.

Disciplines are rated on the basis of whether they seem to have very limited application or perhaps undeveloped potential; whether they are useful in suggesting general approaches, or as framework knowledge; whether they provide useful tools, theories, or concepts; or whether they are being actively applied and shape marketing. These categories are imprecise and are not mutually exclusive nor collectively exhaustive. Ratings are subjective and represent one opinion at this point in time, but the general meaning of the rating s will be clear. Other researchers will have different opinions, and an interchange of ideas should be useful.

Specific use of related Disciplines

Direct and specific use of various concepts of tocls from other disciplines in marketing. It lists various marketing sectors, the specific decision area in which interdisciplinary concepts are used, the related discipline, and the concept or tool. Each of these contributions is keyed to a literature reference. The table is designed to be illustrative rather than comprehensive or definitive.

Problems in Using the Interdisciplinary Approach

The interdisciplinary approach could result in the misguided direction of research and problem-solving activities in marketing. First, attempts to manipulate the concepts, ides, and findings of other disciplines to achieve verifying research results can lead to a neglect of marketing and its particular needs. Marketing activities may be shaped and structured to meet the dimensions, requirements, and constraints of other disciplines.

Second, although the problems, concepts, and findings of many disciplines have marketing relevance, the details, assumptions, and perspectives vary. Researchers from other disciplines bring a different point of view, different training, and experience to a problem. Researchers and discipline specialists often make marketing and marketing problems correspond to their own background and interests rather than the reverse. In reality, common concepts have different operational meanings to each specialist.

Third, controversies exist within and between the disciplines, and they are hard to resolve. Behavioural and social scientists are not unified in their approaches, concepts, and findings; and bewilderment and confusion result. "For example, consider the important marketing subject area of motivation... rather than anyone unified approach emerging, there are at least thee major directions followed by psychologists pursuing motivation studies." The integration of numerous conflicting explanations into practical solutions for marketing is a most perplexing task.

Fourth, marketers generally have tended to overstate the value of contributions of other areas. They have not evaluated situations realistically. The limitations of other areas are skirted or ignored. Consider for example, the early reactions to motivation research or operations research. Marketing failed to examine and adjust the theories, concepts, and findings of other disciplines, and modify them in light of its own knowledge and intellectual insights. Marketing has failed in its search to sort the contributions, to order the directly useful, adjust and adapt the relevant, and discard the irrelevant.

Fifth, it is possible for the interdisciplinary approach to delay and even deter marketing developments. For instance, the uncritical application of stimulus-response theory, psychoanalytic tools, findings of 'rat psychologists," or hypothetical economic models to marketing problems can lead to intellectual barrenness in various marketing area. The concept of equilibrium, for instance, with its analog in the mechanical concept of forces and counter forces that reach a point of stability, has severe limitations when applied to energy and matter, or to the dynamic aspects of marketing.

Sixth, the results of an interdisciplinary approach are often qualified and indecisive. Sometimes they tare theoretical and cannot stand up to the pragmatic demands of problem solving. The assumptions made by other disciplines are often unreal or tool limiting. Many times the kinds of problems that can be handled best are often those that are not critical or which can be dealt with adequately at present.

Seventh, discipline specialists can only make a great contribution to marketing to the extent that we are able to communicate with and question them, and evaluate what they offer. Despite contiguous borders among disciplines, adequate communications are lacking. Jargon and terminology vary, and attempts to relate findings, theories, and constructs are usually very frustrating and ineffective.

As specialization and compartmentalization increase and new hybrid discipline evolve, communication tends to decrease.

Eighth, there are also a number of problems associated with getting people from other disciplines to concentrate on marketing. Included are problems of loss of identification and stature in one's discipline and the loss of security inherent in tackling new concepts and idea.

The following are several statements about the interdisciplinary approach to marketing.

1. The development of marketing science is closely tied to the amenry of marketing to the methods and findings of other disciplines, particularly mathematics, statistics, and the behavioural sciences.

2. Marketing is now, and will continue to be, one of the major environmental factors influencing man in society. Since the consideration of man his environment is one of the tasks that pervades social and behavioural sciences, marketing is a natural area of interdisciplinary convergence for understanding human relationships, and its interdisciplinary role will became increasingly important. It will become one of he sciences of society.

3. The interdisciplinary approach has had a profound effect in shaping marketing thought, ideas, and research effort. As a result of the interdisciplinary approach, curricula have been restructured, courses revised, and new marketing subject-matter areas developed. It has had a score modest but still important impact on marketing action.

4. The greatest and most lasting contribution of the interdisciplinary approach may be its influence on ways of conceptualizing, formulating, and thinking about marketing problems rather than providing marketing information and solutions for problems. The systems approach and functionalism are examples.

5. Most of the concepts, theories, hypotheses, and facts of other disciplines have only limited relevance for marketing. Marketing has failed to fit and sort in a systematic fashion the findings and concepts from other disciplines and to identify those that have direct importance for marketing. The result is that the interdisciplinary approach has not made the impact it could.

6. The successful injection of subject-matter specialists from other areas into marketing requires a rather unique individual. Competence in a behavioural, social, or quantitative discipline is not enough. People rooted of the marketing discipline, rather than behaivoural or social scientists, or quantitative specialists, will contribute most to the future development of the marketing discipline.

7. It is easier to use the concepts and approaches of other discipline sin general way than it is to apply theories and findings to solve specific problems or to use specific data.

8. Much of the contribution of the interdisciplinary approach lies in data, concepts, and theories that have marketing overtones but which must be developed further. The direct transference of concepts of findings from other disciplines to marketing is often not practicable. Adaptation and adjustment is required to integrate them into marketing thought, Marketing faces the challenge of determining the concepts, models, and theories required to solve its problems, which are not available in other disciplines, and developing them itself. Such contributions can in turn shape the related disciplines.

9. Marketing is an integrative subject-matter area. Marketing problems may be viewed from social, behavioural, and measuremental perspectives. Marketing is a fundamental economic activity. The result is that marketing can contribute actively to the development of other disciplines.

10. Among the most direct and significant contributions to marketing thought are those from other business administration areas.

11. As an economy matures, the marketing problems come to the forefront and their sociological and psychological dimensions become more important. The tools of economics, then, must be bolstered by those of other behavioural and social disciplines. Theory, adequate to the demands of marketing tasks, must be concerned with the political, economic, sociological, cultural, and psychological dimensions. The multidisciplinary and interdisciplinary movement is a natural development.

12. As a direct result of transdisciplinary efforts, some of the findings and theories of a variety of disciplines will eventually be integrated into theories of market action that will parallel those of social action.

Marketing Organisation

The marketing concept must be translated into an organisational structure that provides an operating mechanism for systemic decision making and programmed marketing action. The objective of organizational design is the integration. The objective of organisational design is the integration and coordination of people, facilities, and functions in a manner consistent with the marketing concept. Organisation is often the weakest link in the marketing structure. Dynamic leadership is required to critically analyse the firm's need and overcome the barriers of tradition in developing an integrated marketing subsystem.

Organisational Implications of the Marketing Concept

Modern marketing is both a philosophical and an organizational concept. As a philosophy, the modern marketing concept recognizes that the customer is king; that a business entity's only purpose for existence is to service the customer; and that all commercial activity must begin with a determination of the customer's wants and desires and end with a fulfillment of them in most expeditious and efficient manner.

Inherent in this philosophy is existence of a truly customer-conscience organization embracing all personnel from the lowest operating level to the president. Indelibly imprinted on each employee's mind must be the dictum: "We are forever beholden to the customer."

But a company cannot become customer conscious by edict. Since the organizations tend to emulate their leader, it is most important that the head of the business be thoroughly customer conscious. There can only be one marketing head in any business and that must be the president. It can develop a mood, an atmosphere, and an esprit de corps reflecting the pre-eminence of the customer that permeates every nook and corner the company.

The best evidence of a truly customer-conscious company is that it in intimately acquainted with the customers' business. A market-oriented company acts anal thinks in terms of the final end use of its product, raw materials, parts, or sub-assemblies. For example, the fertilizer business not just concerned with selling fertilizers, it is involved in growing food. Therefore, it is necessary for fertilizer manufacturers to understand the farmer, in all of his requirements, to be in a better position to serve distributors who must ultimately appeal to farmers for the sale of fertilizer.

While this philosophical view is an essential prerequisite to success marketing it must be supplemented by a strong organizational approach. For in addition to being customer conscious and market oriented company must also organize and programme marketing activities to provide the customer with adequate products and services. This is probably the weakest link in the marketing activities of most companies. Company may have the will and the desire to serve the customer, but all too of they are inadequately organized to do so.

Proper organization must result in a total integration and coordination of all of the factors that can influence the final sale.

This is the every essence of the modern marketing concept. If advertising, direct selling merchandising, transportation, publicity, and the other ales influences treated as separate entities, and are autonomously executed, their respective contributions are fairly well vitiated. When they are integrated in the completely coordinated communications programme, the total impact greatly compounded.

Managers sped a very high proportion of their time not only with their subordinates, but also with their superiors and their equals and as well as with a great range of individuals outside the firm. No single definition discussed in the above paragraphs touches the entirety of the essence of management. But a very comprehensive definition was given by a team of academicians of the United States business schools in around 1940. the team aimed at deciding a definition that businessmen would accept and practice and that academician would teach. According to that team: "Management is guideline human and physical resources into dynamic organization units that attain their objective to the satisfaction of those served and with a high degree of morale and sense attainment on part of those rendering the service". According to this definition management consists the following five ingredients. Management involves guiding human and physical resources. A manager must balanced between these two resources. He can not put more emphasis on physical resources and ignore human resources or vice-versa. He should not neglect people over technology. There should be equal concern for human and as well as physical resources.

Nature of the Organisation

The environment in which organizations are existing is dynamic. The environment is subject to change which brings stress on organisations. For example changes in technology, market condition, competitive products and services, attitudes of customers demands the organization to adapt timely measures to achieve there determined goal. Managers must e competent to predict in advanced of these changes so as to make able the organization to readily adapt to such changes in the environment. Such organizations are said to be dynamic. Thus management make organization to become dynamic.

Attainment of predetermined objective will be the ultimate goal of the organization which should be accomplished by the management. The purpose of the organization should not be lost. Goat realization is the mission of the management. Goals may differ from organization to organisation but the takes of management is to reach such goals.

The performance in regard to attainment of objectives can be measured through the degree of satisfaction derived by those who are served. The public or the consumers are the people who are served by the organisations. Hence the consumer satisfaction should be he prime concern of the management. Management can become successful only through attaining consumer satisfaction.

This segment of the definition refers to members of employees of and organisation. It is the management's responsibility to see that all the employees are happy with the organisation. The level of their morale, and sense of belongingness to organisation strongly influence the success of the organisation. Because the kind of satisfaction derived from their work will have impact on the achievement of their individual goals ultimately the organization goal. Thus management tries to maintain high level of morale among the employees. In brief management is attainment of the objectives through harnessing the resources giving equal importance to human and physical resources where the satisfaction of the served and employees will be the prime concern.

Management, organisation, Administration are the three words most commonly used in he management literature. They attribute rather confusing meaning because of he failure t distinguish among fundamental concepts. It is not even uncommon to use these words indiscriminately. Some writers have used management as the most comprehensive term embracing within its scope the entire process of planning policy—making, coordination of activities, maintaining morale and discipline as well as controlling the operations.

Some other writers regard all the activities like direction, guidance and control as a part of administration. Certain other writers do not make any distinction between the two. Therefore, it is necessary to define those terms restricting their scope to the field of activity that they designate.

Organisation vs Management

Refers to the mechanism or structure that enables people to work effectively. In view of George R. Terry "Organisation is the management of functions deemed necessary for attainment of the objective and is an indication of the authority and the responsibility assigned to individuals charged with the execution of the respective functions. In a nut-shell organisation is a basic structure functions. In a nut—shell organisation is a basic structure having established relationships between various factors. It is the task of destinating the departments and the manpower that are to carry the work, defining their function and specifying relations that should exist between various departments and individuals. Organisation is in total a mechanism of management and where management is attainment of the objective through guiding human and physical resources at the utmost satisfaction of those served and those rendering service.

Administration vs. Management

According to Oliver Sheldon "Administration is the function in the industry concerned in the determination of corporate policy the coordination of finance, production and distribution, the settlement of the compass of organisation and the ultimate control of executives." On the other hand management is the execution of policy within the limits set up by the administration for the particular objects set before it.

Breach regards management as an all inclusive function involving responsibility for the effective planning and regulation or guidance of operation of an enterprise. According to Breech: "Management is the total process of executive control and administration is that part of management which is connected with the installation and carrying out of the procedures by which the progress of the activities is regulated and checked against plans".

Fayol and Newman do not make any distinction between the two terms – administration and management. But when the two words are used to indicate deferent functions and not the persons who perform those functions. The distinction assumes much importance.

Taking all these views into account, and on the basis of the generally accepted view e may say that administration means overall determination of policies and major objectives, whereas management is an executive function which is the active, direction human efforts. It is the work that a manager does as he seeks to get results through other people. It may be reiterated that administration as a function is largely determinative and management is essentially executive and organisation in the basic structure that is necessary to carryout these functions.

Management Thought

In the preceding guidelines we examined the writings and contributions of various management pioneers, and saw their ideas evolved through time into one or more aspects of management theory. Every one of them introduced a new fact to the totality of management. Since many of these individuals emphasized different aspects of management and gathered followers through the years, this state of management though following World War II was somewhat a maze. As such, at the present time, management theory is in the School Phase and any author who approaches the field without a basic understanding of these schools will be at a considerable disadvantage. The view points regarding what management is, how it should be studied. Nevertheless the background and training of management theories and practices is reflected in their beliefs about management and in most cases make them candidates for one of the schools of thought that we will be examining in this guideline.

The line of thought adopted here was by reviewing what was done in the past by managers under similar circumstances. By observing what the leading business managers are doing in circumstances similar to ours and applying the same techniques and actions in our managerial work, is what is considered to be traditional approach. Some time, the school is also called as the empirical school, because it contributes generalizations and masses of practical management information. Normally this is written descriptive or in narrative form with the experience gained earlier. This can also be done through a cases study approach or through the study of decision making. The management by customs traditional and also includes the studies of the biographies of outstanding managers and the studies of historians of phenomenal companies. The case study approach helps develop in skill in problem determination and in analytical amenity. It also suggest that if a manager is traced with an actual situation closely resembling the one described and discussed, his best recommendation and solution may well be the one developed for the case study. To this degree, it can be considered to promote use of the custom management.

Management - Science or Art?

Science may be described as a systematic body of knowledge pertaining to an area of study and contains some general truths, explaining past events or phenomena. It may be classified into two groups: (1) Positive science and (ii) Normative Science, the first deals with 'what is and the other with 'what ought to be.

Art refers to the way of doing a specific thing. It indicates how an objective is to be achieved. Art means the 'knowing how', the application. Whereas under science one normally understands the 'knowing why.'

If management is considered as an art, expertise in this field can only be gained by practice. Like any other art, mastering the profession of management requires practice. This practice gives an intuitive knowledge to solve various organizational and managerial problems. Only by experience and practice one gains such knowledge. If management is regarded as science, organisation and managerial problem-requires the knowledge and application of scientific methods and techniques.

Management fails to stand for the tests of either science or art, because management discipline contains both the characteristics of science and art. The science of management provides a body o f principles for law for guidance in the solution of specific management problems and objective evaluation of results. On the other hand, the art of management deals with application of kill and effort for producing desirable results on situations in specific cases.

Art and science of management complement each other and thus. Are not mutually exclusive. With every increase in the knowledge of science, the art is bound to be improved Management art and management science are inter-woven and overlapping in nature. Art of management is an old as human civilization but the science of management is an event of receipt past.

Recently considerable attention has been given to analytical approaches to management resulting in the emergence of mathematical formulate business games, operational research and scientific decision-marking.

Management science is not regarded as exact a science as physics or chemistry, Koontz O 'Donnel and Weihrich commented that management as an inexact science. It is a social science and hence it is subject to certain limitations. The dynamic nature of business situations and he nature of human behaviour are subject to produce uncertainties and to that extent the science or management functions less exactly.

Management as a Profession

A profession has been defined as an occupation in which one professes to have acquired specialized knowledge which is used either in instructing, guiding or advising others. A full-fledged profession usually has the following characteristics:

1. An organized and systematic body of knowledge.

2. A formal method of acquiring knowledge and skill through established institutions.

3. Establishment of professional associations.

4. Growth or professional consults.

5. Professional code and conduct.

6. Licensing to restrict the entry of others, not having the requisite qualifications.

Management profession has almost all the characteristics mentioned above except that it does not require licensing of managers nor it doe restrict the entry of people into this profession, who do not have specialized training. The systematic development or management associations and consultants prove that management is a developing profession. But it cannot be described as a full-fledged profession like medicine or low, unless there is a professional conduct and licensing of managers. Some academicians contend, that the master of business administration degrees should constitute the minimum pre-requisite for entering the profession of management. But per Drucer the father of modern management opposes this idea b stating that "no greater harm could be done to economy or to society than to professionalise management through licensing requirements or specifying special academic degrees as necessary training'. Beside he educational qualification several other factors which influence his performance must be taken into consideration.

Management functions are having he universal applicability. As stated earlier the functions of management viz. planning, organising, staffing directing and controlling are practiced similarly in the organisation irrespective of their basic structure, goals, environment an nature of business. This is known as university of management, it is clear from the fact that management continued its development as an increasingly sophisticated discipline. Today management is accepting the administration challenges of even not for-profit organizations in government, education, charitable, service and healthy-care environment.

In all forms of organisations either profit making or non-profit making the practice of functions of management is one and the same but the technique of performing these functions may differ from organisation to organisation having relation to its basic structure goals, environments and nature of business. Here a distinction should be made between function and technique function is the task that should be accomplished whereas technique is the way of performing that function. Management functions are quite similar in all organisations in the universe despite their diverse characteristics. Hence we can talk about the universality of management. The limitations that organization may select dissimilar techniques to perform these universally accepted functions.

In all forms of enterprises and at all levels of organisation s the environment of management can certainly differ. However, management itself is essentially the same process. The functions apply equally to all the managers., whatever be their level in the organisation or the task they perform.

Management Theory and the Marketing Concept

The relationship between McGregor's Theory Y, concerned with human resources management, and the marketing concept are explored, and some implications of the relationships are examined. The underlying theme of both the marketing and Theory Y concepts is dependence upon participation and cooperation by subordinate units. Both theories need to be extended before widespread endorsement occurs.

One of the most important problems faced by men in all professions is that of "keeping up." For the executive, this means reading in a multiple of areas. Wendell Willkie's One World concept has descended upon business. As interrelationships and interdependencies appear, the scope of the businessman's "specially" broadens. To keep up in his reading, the executive must not only read but also develop the criteria for sifting through the volume of materials.

The acquisition of an up-to-date posture is difficult at best.

So time-assuming can this be that the most important questions rarely. How does this report relate to the one read last week? What applications do the new empirical research findings pose for the future? How valid are the assumptions underlying the newer theories?

This article represents an attempt to gain this broader vision. In and first to approach current business topics in such a manner, this writer discusses upon two recent major developments in business-the newer management and marketing theories. The following paragraphs contain a discussion of these theories origanised around four basic questions. What the management and marketing theories that are receiving attention in current literature? What are the similarities of thee theories that suggest more basic trend or characteristic? How is this basic trend identified. What are the implications of this trend for marketing and management operations and therefore for society? Starting with the first question then, the following discussion will attempt to relate these theories and it present possible implications.

The Contemporary Theories

The New Management Theory

In 1960, Douglas McGregor of the Massachusetts Institute of Technology presented in book form some ideas that represented the more advanced management thought of the time. In particular, Profession McGregor emphasized the management thought that related to the managing of the human resources of the firm—a topic appearing in more and more academic and professional journals and one which gains international attention daily. In McGregor's words.

This volume is an attempt to substantiate the thesis that the human side enterprise is "all of piece"—that the theoretical assumptions management holds abut controlling its human resources determine the whole character of the enterprise. They determine also the quality of its successive generate of management.

In his book McGregor stated that every managerial act rests

on these and that theory and practice are inseparable; thus, he suggested that the assumptions about human nature and human behaviour (and so also the statements underlying managerial decisions and thus theory) should be clearly delineated and expressed. In short, McGregor contended that the traditional management practice (Theory X) should give way to a contemporary Theory Y. He built his case by analyzing the basis assumptions of both the traditional and the "called for." A brief summary of the major points will provide a common reference point.

Theory X Assumptions

The assumptions about human behaviour are

(1) The average human being has an inherent dislike of work and avoid it if he can.

(2) Because of this human characteristic of dislike of work, most people must be coerced, controlled, directed, threatened with punishment to get them to put forth adequate effort toward the achievement of organizational objectives.

(3) The average human being prefers to be directed, wishes to avoid responsibility, has relatively little ambition, wants security above all.

With these assumptions as a base, McGregor held that traditional methods actually stress direction and control of subordinates since the section and control of operations includes people as well as things. Although this pattern seems to have expressed the management practice of the years, McGregor contended that these practices should change because the basic assumptions of Theory X are in error and also are lacking a validity.

This is a brief summary of some of the characteristics of the traditional theory of management; a review of what McGregor hoped would replace it will follow.

Theory Y Assumptions and Practice

The more appropriate assumptions about man should be

(1) The expenditure of physical and mental effort in work is as natural they or rest.

(2) External control and the threat of punishment are not the only means the being about effort toward organizational objectives. Man will exercise self-direction and self-control in the service of objectives to which he is submitted.

(3) Commitment to objectives is a function of the rewards associated and their achievement.

(4) The average human being learns, under proper conditions not only to except but to seek responsibility.

(5) The capacity to exercise a relatively high degree of imagination, liquidity, and creativity in the solution of organisational problems is likely, not narrowly, distributed in the population.

(6) Under the conditions of modern industrial life, the intellectual potentials of the average human being are only partially utilized.

The central principle which derives from these assumption sis that conditions should be created to encourage subordinates to achieve their goals best by working for the success of the enterprise.

This summary, McGregor believed that the traditional management practice is based upon assumptions about human nature which are consences of a management practice using organizational concepts derived early military and church organisations—authority through direct and control. If management were to change its practices, the proponents of Theory Y say, the truer nature of man would be revealed. This position, of course, gains support from psychology and sociology research. The manager under Theory Y would create positive conditions in a climate wherein the subordinate would see that fulfilling the needs the organization would in turn enable him to fulfill his own personal needs. The subordinate, therefore, would become much more involved in the matters that affect his work behaviour. He would plan, organize direct and maintain self-control overwork that was his responsibility.

This review presents only the highlights of the newer management theory presented by Douglas McGregor—a theory finding widespread acclaim, acceptance, and expression in other articles, in executive development courses, and in graduate and undergraduate curricula.

Now, let us turn to the development of another new theory representing changing thought in the marketing field. At the moment there should be no attempt by the reader to compare the new marketing concept with Theory Y; this discussion will occur later in the article.

The New Marketing Concept

This new theory sounds almost arrive in its simplicity; that is marketing activity should start with the consumer. While the consumer has always been important, he has not always been the key figure in the design and manufacture of the product. In past years, the problem of reducing cost and increasing efficiency have required the major effort of the corporation; however, a new focal point is being discussed. No long can the engineer demand the most attention. The important man on the emerging scene is now the consumer.

In some instances, men have expressed the newer concept as part of the evolutionary process.

Te function of marketing is still growing within the corporate organized and it will continue to grow for some time to come. Business has comes way since the day when most corporations were production-oriented manufacturing companies. The swing to the customer-minded philosophy brought the marketing-oriented manufacturing company into full bloom.

But not all the experts hold the newer marketing theory to be a evolutionary outgrowth. Much more urgency and change is expressed such persons as Robert . Keith. In his article, "The Marketing Returns Mr. Keith likens the relationship between the new marketing concept and the traditional one to the revolution in science created by Copernicus. "The market is the center of the economic universe in the sun is the center of our universe." A similar picture is expressed by J. Borch, new president of the General Electric Company. "Under marketing, the customer becomes the fulcrum, the pivot point about which the business moves in operating for the balanced best interests of all concerned."

Problems and Criticisms

Not everyone agrees that the benefits just described are the natural extension of participation. The first charge thrown at the participation proponents is that of manipulation. The social scientists, particularly the newer group of behavioural scientists who have worked in industry, have been labeled by Loren Baritz as the "servants of power." The behavioural servants respond to the wishes of their masters, the corporation executives, who have hired them at a salaries far above their meager university earnings to conduct "research studies" that will "uncover the truth Baritz maintain that most of these "findings" are really post facts findings: a company needs data to support some point and data are found. The Harwood studies, for example, which are purposed to exemplify the benefits to be derived from participation, are seen by Baritz as ingenious methods for having the employees "participate" in a management-planning situation so that the goals of the corporation would be better achieved.

Baritz' criticism has been used here to exemplify some thinking an uneasiness about the use of social findings. Actually, one of two possible assumptions must be made before carrying the discussion further. Our assumes that subordinate units can help set objectives in the best interest of the firm or one assumes that they cannot. If the latter position is held then efforts to guide behaviour in the direction of predetermined patterns must be vulnerable to the charge of manipulation. The control of individual behaviour is beset with many problems of ethics. The reader can survey extend his thinking along these lines to see how involved this charge of manipulation can become.

But the other assumption may also hold. Perhaps the majority of the proponents of the newer management and marketing theories sincerely believe that goals and methods advocated by subordinate units will in fact work for the greatest good of the organisation. What then?

If subordinate units in fact were encouraged to make corporate plans and decisions, the mind would immediately turn to difficulties emerging in many direction. How could responsible leadership be encouraged? How could such units handle complex commodities such as defense mechanisms or drugs? Does the consumer know what he wants? These are only some of the pertinent questions. Even though such reflections ensure up multitude of problems, the discussion here will center about a broader area. Perhaps the most serious and far-reaching implication of the participation movement is the subtle impact it would have upon the standards of society.

The Social System

It has been suggested that the pursuit and questioning of implications is important because so many forces in society (management and marketing, in this case) are striving toward the goal of participation. True, not all locations of the business society may completely achieve this end but because of the striving, the question of direction is critical.

If a corporation actually becomes consumer oriented. This transformation does not come overnight but is the day-to-day attempts to have "the customer's wants become the criteria for corporate decision-making." What will happen to society when participation encourages the acceptance of mass values? Can society's goals be achieved when mass values may delay the process of innovation and individual creativity? And as Irvin Kristol suggests, if segments of our nation resists taking on the values of the masses, the government may become the protector or guardian of these segments—consulting in increased bureaucratic organization.

The point is that the very process of placing participation as the goal may erode the forces within this nation that have been balanced basically by our Constitution (the doctrine of checks and balances). The individual's values can be lost to those of the mass. Can minority or individual rights continue to be respected with this greater emphasis upon mass values?

In the same way that followership should be viewed as the countervailing force to leadership, participation should be viewed as the countervailing force to autocratic decision-making, and cooperation the countervailing force to conflict. In more specific terms, the two new theories being discussed contain an emphasis upon participation by subordinate units. In effect, this movement would invest new power in these groups. If the pendulum swings radically to one side, then it would be possible for the new power groups to overbalance the power of the executive organization. To provide an effective and constructive change, then, the new theories must include more specific corollaries relating to limitations extent, and scope.

Summary

Two concepts, one in marketing and one in management, were reviewed with special attention given to the relationship of each to a more fundamental movement of the times. Stress upon participation by subordinate units in management and marketing and the resulting aim of cooperation among the forces appeared as primary goals. The implications of such goals suggested that he newer theories in marketing and management—indeed, in all areas—need to be extended to their broader ramification before widespread endorsement occurs.

CHAPTER 9

CONSUMER IN THE NEW MILLENNIUM MARKETS

The growth of service industries can be traced to the economic development of society and the socio-cultural changes that have accompained it. The growth of a specific service industry is the result of increasing affluence coupled with the desire to utilize leisure time for leisure rather than for doing odd jobs. Services occupy a place of significant importance in the Indian economy. The service trade accounts for almost 46% of GDP in India. It is expected that its share would increase to 58% by the end of the century. It employs nearly a fourth more than the people employed in the manufacturing sector in India.

Teaching is an intangible service. When one travels by plane, the benefit which one is deriving is a service (transportation) but it has some tangible aspects such as the particular plane in which one flies. In this case the service has both a tangible and intantible aspects as compared to teaching which has no tangible aspect at all. A service is provided by a person who possesses a particular skill which is in direct contrast to products which can be produced in factory.

The human element is very much involved in providing and rendering services and this makes standardization a very difficult task to achieve. The physician who gave you his complete attention in our last visit may behave a little differently the next time. An unsold seat in a cinema hall represents a service capacity which is lost for ever. Apart from the fact that a service not fully utilised represents a total loss, the other dimension of this pershability aspect is that most services may face a fluctuating demand. In the case of a service one may pay for its use but never own it. By buying a ticket one can see the film show in the cinema hall; by paying wages one can hire the services of a driver who will drive his car. In case of a service, the payment is not for purchase but for use of facilities. A service is purchased for the benefits it provides.

Marketing Mix in Service

Product is the most important issue in the service product is understanding what benefits and satisfaction the consumer is seeking from the service. The marketing of services will be successful only if there is a match between the service product from the consumer's viewpoint and the supplier's viewpoint. Price is used for all kinds of goods but in the case of services, different terms are used for different services. The higher the intangibility, the more difficult it is to calculate cost and greater the tendency towards non-uniform services, such as fees of doctors and layers. On the other hand, in services where the tangible component (as in dry cleaning) is higher hand the services provided is homogeneous, it is easy to calculate the cost on a unit basis and have a uniform pricing policy. Usually the more unique a service the greater the freedom to fix the price at any level. Another characteristic of services is that prices are subject to regulations either by the government or by trade associations. Bank charges, electricity and water rates, rail fare are controlled by the government of India. In other cases, the trade association may regulate prices in order to avoid undercutting. International air fares are regulated by international agreement of airlines, sea freight fares may be regulated by shipping conferences. In all such cases, the producer has no freedom to determine his own price.

In the former, the price may be regulated by the government or industry association on the basis of the cost incurred by he most efficient unit. Such a pricing strategy is effective in restricting entry and aiming at minimum profit targets. The market-oriented pricing may either be a result of the competition or customer-oriented. In case of competition-oriented pricing, the price may be fixed at the level which the competitor is charging or fixed lower to increase market share. Customer-oriented pricing varies according to the customer's ability to pay.

The promotion strategy for services, it should be kept in mind that the customer relies more on subjective impressions rather than concreate evidence. This is the cause of the inherent intangible nature of services. Secondly, the customer is likely to judge the quality of service on the basis of performer rather than the actual service. Thirdly, sine it is difficult to sample the service before paying for it, the customer finds it difficult to evaluate its quality and value. Thus, buying a service is a more risky proposition than buying a product. Fourthly, methods used for promotion services—advertising, personal selling, publicity and sales promotion, are the same a used in the promotion of products. Advertising is any kind of paid, non-personal method of promotion by an identified organization or individual. Certain services such as entertainment, passenger and freight transport, hotel, tourism and insurance are advertised heavily in newspaper, magazines, radio. TV to promote greater usage and attract more customers. But certain service professionals such as doctors and lawyers rarely use advertising as a means of increasing their clientele. These groups have traditionally relied on word-of-mouth for attracting new customers. But this situation is changing and we see advertisement in the daily newspaper giving information about the location and timings that a particular doctor is available for consultation.

The problem with using personal selling to promote services is that in certain types of services, the service cannot be separated from the performer. Moreover, it is not a homogeneous service in which exact standards of performance can be specified. In such situations, personal selling implies using an actual professional rather than a salesman to sell the service. Personal selling is effective no doubt, but very expensive. Publicity is unpaid for exposure which is derived by getting coverage as a news item. It is possible to get publicity when the service offered is unique by holding a press conference in which the service offered is associated with some issues of greater social relevance. The sales promotion techniques in the case of services are various in number. A doctor may charge lesser amounts as fee on subsequent visits to encourage the patient's loyalty or a chartered account may offer his services free for the first two visits to allow the customer to evaluate his work.

The distribution strategy relates to the issue of location of the service so as to attract the maximum number of consumers. The inseparability characteristic of services poses a distribution constraint since they are able to serve only a limited, local market. The other characteristic of services which affects the distribution strategy is the fixed location of services which necessitates the customer to go to the service location rather than vice-versa. The first, decision variable in planning the distribution strategy relates to the location of the service. The second decision variable in the distribution strategy is whether to sell directly to the customers or through intermediaries. In case of services which are inseparable from the performer, direct sale is the only possible way of reaching the consumer. In case of other services, such as hotels, or airlines o life insurance, they may operate through middlemen. The third decision variable in the distribution strategy is how to provide the service to a maximum number of customers in the most cost-effective manner. People constitute an important dimension in the management of services in their role both as performers of services and as customers.

People as performers of services are important because a customer sees a company through its employees. The employees represent the first line of contact with the customer. The firm must recognize that each employee is a salesman for the company's service. Service personnel are important in all organizations but more so in an organization involved in providing services. The behaviour of the personnel providing the service is an important influence on the customer's overall perception of the service.

Customers are important because they are a source of influencing other customers. In the case of, say, doctors, one satisfied customer will lead to a chain reaction, bringing in his wake a number of other customers.

Marketing and Tourism

Tourism industry is identified by the products which are needed to satisfy the demand for travel accommodation, food and beverage away from home. Demand for accommodation is a function of travel and tourism. Tourism as a service industry comprises of several allied activities which together produce the tourist product. In the tourism product development there are three major sub-industries. They are (i0 tour operators and travel agents; (ii) accommodation sector, and (iii) passenger transportation. According to international estimates, a tourist spends 355 of his total expenditure on transportation, about 40% on food and lodging and the balance 25% on entertainment and shopping.

The highest growth rate in tourism in recent years has been in the third world. The product in this case is not confined to travel and accommodation but includes a large array of luxury services ranging from insurance and entertainment and shopping. Demand generation, in addition to the consumer motivation, is also heavily dependent upon powerful persuasive communication both at the macro and micro-level. As service industry tourism results in a complex series of economic, environmental and social impacts in the societies managing and marketing it. Lack of complete local control over the industry and valid criteria for measurement complicate the assessment of costs and benefits of tourism as an industry.

Tourism product, is an amalgam of the physical characteristics of a destination and the infrastructural as well as managerial efforts of the promoter, the determinants of tourism demand emanate from both individual tourist motivations and the economic, social and technological factors. The economic, social and technical determinants of tourism demand include high and rising incomes, increased leisure time, good education, cheaper and faster modes of transport.

The money and the mobility to travel, tourism will not occur unless people have the motivation to take a trip. Motivation to travel may spring form a variety of needs.

Some reasons for travel:

- Tourists look for discovery and involve with local people.
- People who favour special, individually tailore trips to exotic places.
- Visitors who are looking forward to trips with peculiar objectives such as physical danger or isolation.
- Travelling alone or in small organized groups using some shared services.
- The general packaged tour market, leading to tourist enclaves abroad.
- Mass travel to relaxation destinations which incorporate as many standardized, developed world facilities as possible. Each of these categories has a corresponding range of impacts on the host society and destination.

Psychographically all tourists can be viewed as being spread along a continuum. At one end of the centre are allocentric tourists who ant an independent vacation experience and at the other end are psychocentrics who become part of the mass tourism market. Different types of tourists are attracted to different tourist destinations depending upon their position between the two extremes of the continuum. The new destinations generally appeal to the small number of allocentric adventurous tourists who prefer to fit in the local culture and consequently make few demands. As the destination gains popularity, it loses its charm for the allocentric who moves away to untouched locales. The destination draws most of its tourists from the midcentric section now. As the destination gives way to larger and larger number of arrivals, it goes through another change and becomes dependent upon foreign investment and manpower. The psychocentrics now feel at home in such a place, as offers a range of facilities and services, "just like back home," which incidentally change its identity from the natural geographic and social locales which intiallylured the alloentrics. Generalisation like these help tourism marketers to view tourism from the perspectives of both the tourists' personal motivation and the host society.

Hospitality products are an output of the hotel and catering industry and can be defined as the set of satisfactions and dissatisfactions that a customer receives from a hospitality experience. These satisfactions could be physiological, economical, social or psychological.

Defines the geographical placement of a hotel in a particular village or town. Within a given area specific location defines access and convenience, freedom from noise and other disturbances, attractiveness of surroundings. Include the infrastructural and recreational facilities—bedrooms, restaurants, bars, conference rooms, swimming pools, tennis courts etc.

The core product in case of an hospitality service is a fundamental benefit that the consumer receives. Hospital products channel different core benefits to the consumers. The core product in case of an hospitality service is a fundamental benefit that the consumer receives. Augmented product is the complete product offering including the atmospherics, behaviour of the staff, décor and the accessory service like transportation to and communication and secretarial assistance.

Hotels are classified in different ways. The most widely used classifications is the RAC classification which classifies hotels by type and awards a star rating. Hotels are classified as simple in furnishing or menu or service. May be managed well by the proprietor personally.

Formal reception arrangements and more employed staff. More accommodation of a higher standard. Small luxury hotels offering a high degree of comfort. Telephones in bedrooms. Bedrooms with private bathrooms. Full meal facilities.

Large luxury hotels offering the highest standard of accommodation, service and comfort.

Strategies for the Tourism Market

Tourism strategy are to match the firm's strength with market opportunities. The basis steps in the tourism marketing strategy are –(i) definition of the needs of he potential tourists and their possible destinations; (ii) segmenting the market according to the type of need the firms wants to satisfy; (iii) defining environmental constraints and competitive scene; (iv) formulating marketing objectives and allocating marketing resources in terms of designing the tourism product.

Market penetration strategy entails building a foothold in the market through creating a differential advantage in pricing or promotion or both. Market Extension strategy entails reaching new types of tourists through modification of existing tourist products, by planning advances launch of a new product, managing the lifecycle stages of a tourist product. The tourist firm here seeks new classes of tourists for products or would add salient product characteristics to the existing offer. The objective is to widen the appeal to cater to tourist segments which the firm has not been catering to earlier. The strategy may be either to add the new segments to the existing ones or to replace the present segments with more profitable growth segments by revamping the basis appeals used. Product differentiation and product reformulation strategies are also being utilized in the tourism market. The former is achieved by offering different combinations of product features to different market segments.

Economic Development

Tourism is a catalyst for stimulating economic, social and cultural activities. The money spent by tourists tends to percolate through many levels and has a multiplier effect. The development of a tourist circuit results in the development of the hinterland too, from which the entire community benefits. Tourism carries great potential for generating direct employment and offers opportunities for self-employment. Tourism acts as a positive force to stimulate economic development to foster national integration and to bring people and culture of different nations closer.

An infrastructure based service product. Effective marketing of tourism needs constant gearing up of the infrastructure to international standards and presupposes its coordination with the tourism suppliers. It calls for the adoption of an integrated approach to management and marketing tourism.

The government initiated efforts in its development in the mid-50s, it is only in the last 15 years that sustained efforts have been put in to strengthen this industry. The year 1986 was the first year when the international tourist arrival crossed the one million mark in India. Between 1986 and 1990, the average annual growth rate has been around 11 p.c. The foreign exchange earnings during 1987-88 were Rs. 1,890 crore, making tourism the highest net foreign exchange earner in the country for the year. Western Europe, North America and West Asia are the major contributors to tourist arrivals in India. The market share of tourists from USA to India has gone down from 20% in 1970 to 11.6% in 1987. The average per capita expense of the West Asian tourists far exceeded the rest. The Japanese tourist stayed for a shorter duration but spent much more for everyday of stay in the country. Sight-seeing, business or official trips and visiting friends and relatives constitute the main purpose of visit to India by as many as 75% of the tourists. Pilgrimage, archaeology, hill and beach resorts and cultural events were yet to attract sizable tourists. The total employment in tourism during 1984-85 was estimated to be over 4 million and it is likely to be 10 million by 2000.

The political and communal situation in 1990 hit the tourist arrivals in India. To make matters worse for 1991, the Gulf crisis and the kidnapping and maltreatment of foreign tourists has pushed our image further down. Tourism thrives s good word is spread, and can easily collapse also if a wrong impression goes around. A tourist is a difficult person to woo but can ran away easily at the smallest pretext. A view to study the perceptions of inbound tourists about India, foreign tourists were surveyed in March, 1991.

More than 40% of the tourists come to India with the image of a poor heavily populated country while 30% thought that they were coming to a beautiful country There seems to be a very diverse perception of India abroad. The opportunity of experiencing Indian festivals. The transport sector (Indian Airlines, Indian Railways and Roadways) lacked adequate availability and courtesy to tourists.

We must correct India's image of a nation in permanent crisis; of the socially based on a rigid caste system; a land of snake charmers, sadhus and gurus; and a nation trapped in red-tapism. The festivals of India programmes may have bolstered India's conventional exotic and mystic image but has failed to project its technological achievements. In fact, India has not as yet aggressively marketed itself abroad so far.

On-line Marketing

The information technology has had a revolutionary impact on all spheres of human life all over the world. The idea of doing business electronically over networks is nothing new. We think of ordering products we have seen advertised on television over the phone or fax and ATMs are always within the reach for quick, easy and automatic banking. Particularly through the Internet, forward-looking businessmen will be able to make their products available to a global market, the largest possible market without having to create and maintain their own private network for sales delivery and customer support. E-commerce will take over the present ways of trade and commerce.

E-commerce means, it is the sophisticated computer technology which allows the commerce through the electronic media. It is a marketplace where business is using the information technology and network to securely transform their business relationship and selling and buying the goods and services. People all around the world can sit in the houses and can accomplish what they desire through a few mouse clicks and taps on the keyboard. The system of e-commerce is very interesting because here no question of money transformation takes place. The companies will keep their catalog and order form on the net, and the customers have to send that. Hence, the mere transformation of the information and order forms are exchanged. The total system can be called the Electronic Data Interchange (EDI) is the globally accepted method of fast and efficient business transaction.

Hence EDI eliminates the need for the paper-based system by providing the electronic link between companies and companies and companies and customers. It is the blend of a number of internets and intranets. The technology involved in the EDI can be explained with an example. Suppose a customer wants to buy a Maruti car, he will find the order form by imprinting his credit card number and sends it to the respective company in an encrypted format. On receipt of the form they will again decrypt it and depending upon the quantity or the value of the order they will confirm the account of the said customer through the respective bank. And the bank people will furnish the information to the customer. Then the customer will send it to the company through the pockets. On receiving of that information the company will send the said commodity to the customer through the courier. And all of this work will be done in a few seconds only. In this way the selling and buying of foods and services will be done.

Business to consumers does mean performing any commerce activities by utilizing open networks such as internet, i.e., a system to provide consumers with infrastructure for purchasing and distributing products and services. This includes the exchange of goods and services for which the payment is done through Internet Technology (Cyber Payment). It can be presumed that it is equal to the retailer business. The transactions will not be dallied and the sales are done immediately. No question of middlemen will be involved in this sort of business as the gap between the company an the consumer is abridged. It involves both wholesale purchasing and electronic data in the change will be done in between the businessmen and business partners. This takes place among the companies to companies. As per their consent and understandings, they can mutually do the business. This is especially for the companies. It is the internet transactions.

E-commerce in Marketing

Development of Business-Relationship. The business development can be done through the e-commerce being the primary and the basic object. As their direct contact in between the company and the consumer, their business relationship will be enhanced. Hence the area of the market can be increased.

Customer service is done round the clock, the customer will always have online help regarding the products. As all the information is furnished to the customer, it becomes easy to him to choose the best product among all other alternatives. As even the service can also be done through the net immediately, the customer service will be ballooned. By highlighting the customer service, the companies are trying to subjugate a lion-share in the market.

Direct marketing are electronic channels. E-commerce describes a wide variety of electronic platforms, such as the sending of purchase orders to suppliers via electronic data interchange (EDI); the use of fax and e-mail to conduct transactions; the use of ATMS, and smart cards to facilitate payment and obtain digital cash and the use of the Internet and on-line services. All these involve doing business in a 'markets pace' as compared to a physical 'marketplace.' Electronic business involves two phenomena—digitalization and connectivity. Digitalization consists of converting text, data, sound and image into a stream of 'bits' that can be dispatched at incredible speed from one location to another. Connectivity involves building networks and expresses the fact that much of the world's business is carried over networks connecting people and companies. These networks are called intranets when they connect people within a company; extranets when connect a company with its suppliers and customers and the Internet when they connect users to an amazingly large 'information highway". The most popular consumer purchases over the Internet have been in computer software, airline tickets, books electronics.

Commercial channels

Various companies have set up on-line information and marketing services that can be accessed by those who have signed up for the service and pay a monthly fee. These channels provide information, shopping services and e-mail.

The Internet is a global web of computer networks that has made instaneous and decentralized global communication possible. Internet usage has surged with the recent development of the user-friendly World Wide Web and Web browser software. Users can surf the Internet and experience fully integrated text, graphics, images and sound. Users can send e-mail, exchange views, shop for products and access news, recipes, art and business information.

The benefits of e-commerce are money, beginning with the ability to broaden the reach of the firm and offer a large potential customer base. Geographic boundaries no longer exist and the e-commerce site, depending upon the software and hardware behind the website can operate 24 hours day, 365 days per years. The Web opens a new channel to service current customers and build sales with new customers. Business to business marketers should be natural users of –e-commerce, as they have a customer base that has computes and are likely to be connected to the Web. Payment systems and delivery systems are in place and management control can be established through control of who is authorized to buy and where the product may be shipped. E-commerce makes in possible to reduce the costs associated with holding large physical inventories as the time gained in order processing reduces the need for holding inventories in branch locations. The value network can be connected electronically improving the responsiveness of the system and reducing inventory. The cost of serving a customer who specifies his needs and places an order over the web are significantly less than making a sales call or using a telephone sales system. Faster customer response is accomplished with 24 hour access. Customers with questions are able to access directly centrally maintained current information. Customers can seen the status of their orders and shipment information.

Since e-commerce may offer the buyes a choice of how to connect with the company—either through a sales person, over the web or a combination—customers will be able to build the type of relationship that they prefer. A customer profile can be developed for each customer by running a data collection programme in the background. These data can be used as input for new product development, target marketing and gaining better understanding of the customer. A data base marketing system is the heart of Web marketing. The data warehouse is built up on operational data such as customer descriptions, sales histories, billing and accounting records, responses to promotions and a myriad of other internal records. External overlays are purchased such as credit ratings, usage f the product category and other relevant data that describe the customer. Data marts of specialized data are extracted from the warehouse to be used by marketing analysts to create new products or marketing programmes. E-commerce will be a potent force in redefining value networks. Channel members such as distributors, may be the firms most at risk, as their functions may be eroded as firms go direct to their customers. The term 'dis-intermediated' was coined to explain the removal of middlemen in the world of e-commerce. Looking into the future it is possible to visualize a web-based customer system that would elicit customer needs from a technology buyer and then create a product to meet those needs. The buyer would then be able to manipulate the product and make a trade-off between different levels of engineering performance and price.

- Internet 'search engines' give consumers access to varied information sources making them better informed shoppers. Buyers have gained the following capabilities in the new information-rich regime.

- They can get objective information for multiple brands including costs, pries, features and quality without relying on the manufactures or retailers.

- They can initiate requests for advertising and information from manufacturers.

- They can design the offerings they want.

- They can use software agents to a search for and invite offers from multiple sellers.

These new buyer capabilities mean that the exchange process in the age of information has become customer initiated and customer controlled. Markers an their representatives are held at by till customers invite them to participate in the exchange. Even after markets enter the exchange process, customers define the rules of engagement and insulate themselves with the help of agents an intermediaries. Customers defines what information they need, what offerings they are interested in and what prices they are willing to pay. In many ways, this customer-initiated and customer-controlled marketing completely reverses time-honoured marketing practices.

* On-line marketing has become so popular because they provide three major benefits to potential buyers.

* Customers can order products 24 hours a day wherever they are.

* Customers can find heaps of comparative information about companies, products, competitors and prices without leaving their home.

* Customers do not have to face salespeople or expose themselves to persuation and emotional factors; they also do not have to wait in line.

Marketing Benefits

Firms can quickly add products to their offering and charge

pries and descriptions.

On-line markers avoid the expense of maintaining a store and the costs of rent, insurance and utilities. They can produce digital catalogs at a lesser cost of printing.

On-line markets can dialogue with consumers and learn from them. Marketers can download useful reports or a free sample of their news setter.

Marketers can learn how many people visited their on-line site and how many stopped at particular places on the site. This information will improve offers and ads.

It is quite clear that markets are adding on-line channels to find, reach, communicate and sell. On-line marketing has the following advantages.

Both small and large firms can afford it.

There is real limit on advertising space, in contrast to print and broadcast media. Information access and retrieval are fast, compared to overnight mail and even fax. The site can be visited by anyone anyplace in the world at any time. Shopping can be done privately and swiftly.

But on-line marketing is neither for every company nor for every product. The Internet is useful for products and services where the shopper seeks greater ordering convenience or lower cost. The Internet is also useful where buyer need information about feature and value differences (e.g., automobiles). The internet is less useful for products that must be touched or examined in advance.

Performing on-line Marketing. Marketers can do on-line marketing by creating an electronic presence on the Internet; placing ads on-line, participating in forums, newsgroups and Web Communities and using e-mail and Webcasting. Thousands of businesses have established a presence on the Internet. Many of the Websites offer users a wide variety of services.

A company can establish an electronic presence on the Web in two ways: It can buy space on a commercial on-line service or it can open its own website. Buying a location on a commercial service involves renting storage space on the on-line service's computer or establishing a link from the company's own computer to the on-line service's shopping mail. The on-line services design the storefront for which the company pays the on-line service an annual fee plus a small percentage of the company's on-line sales.

A company provides basic information about its history, philosophy, objectives, products, services and locations. It might also provide current events, financial performance data and job opportunities. These sites are set up to answer customer questions by e-mail, build closer customer relationships and generate excitement about the company. They are designed to handle interactive communication initiated by the consumer.

This kind of website is designed to bring prospects and customers closer to a purchase or other marketing outcome. The site might include a catalog, shopping tips, and promotional features such as coupons, sales events or contents. In order to attract visitors, the company promotes its website in print and broadcast advertising and through banner ads that pop up on other websites.

On-line advertising companies can place on-line ads in three ways: They can place classified ads in special sections offered by the major commercial on-line services.

Ads can also be placed in certain Internet newsgroups that are set up for commercial purposes.

Lastly, the company can pay for on-line ads that pop up while subscribers are surfing on-line services or web sites. These include banner ads, pop up windows and "Roadblocks" (full-screen ads) that users must click through to get to other screens.

Companies may participate in or sponsor Internet forums, newsgroups and bulletin boards which appeal to special internet groups. Forums are discussion groups located on commercial on-line services. A forum may operate a library, a "chat room" for message exchanges and even a classified ad directory. Newsgroups are the Internet version of forums. However, these groups are limited to people posting and reading messages on a specified topic. Internet users can participate in newsgroups without subscribing.

Bulletin board systems are specialized on-line services that centre on a specific topic or group. BBSs deal with tops such as health, vacations, real estate etc., marketers can participate in newsgroups and BBSs.

Web Communities are commercially sponsored Websites where members congregate on-line and exchange views on issues of common interest. On such community is Agriculture On-line where farmers and others can find commodity prices, recent farm news and chat rooms of all tapes.

Companies can also sign on with any of a number of webcasting services such as Point cast and fusion which automatically download customized information to recipients PCs. For a monthly fee, subscribers can specify the channels and topics they want to receive. Then they can sit back while the webcaster automatically delivers information of interest to their screens. Called "push" programming on-line marketers see this as an opportunity to delivery information and ads to subscribers without the subscriber having to make a request. A company may encourage customers to send questions, suggestions and even complaints to the company via e-mail. Customer service representatives can respond these messages. The company may also develop Internet based electronic mailing lists. On-line marketing will bring far-reaching changes to various sectors of the economy. Consumers' ability to order direct will seriously affect certain groups, such as travel agents, car-dealers, stock-brokers and insurance salespersons. These middlemen will be dis-intermediated by on-line services. At the same time some reintermediation will take place in the form of new on-line intermediaries, called informediaries who help consumers shop more easily and obtain lower prices. On-line marketing will change world commerce. The on-line marketer can reach a global market.

CHAPTER 10

MANAGEMENT OF INTERNATIONAL MARKETS

Comparative Marketing

Comparative marketing is one of a number of contemporary developments in the practice and study of marketing which has broadened its type far beyond the basic processes of buying, selling, pricing, sales portion, channel selections, and facilitating services. In addition to economics and the quantitative disciplines—long recognized as marketing major foundations—useful insights into marketing structure and nations have also been gained in recent years from geography, and politics, philosophy, sociology, anthropology, social psychology, history, and other social sciences. Comparative marketing involves the marketing systems, operations, and practices in various parts of world, and its therefore natural that it should avail itself of all needed tools, and concepts to analyze and to relate common factors and differences. Without the aid of the affiliated disciplines, comparative marketing is likely to remain more descriptive than analytical, since marketing in various regions must be related in terms of such basic factors as social, economic and political systems if one if to understand the reasons for the likenesses and differences.

Because of he embryonic nature of comparative marketing, any generalizations must necessarily be tentative, especially since they are frequently based upon data from economics, the quantitative disciplines, and the social sciences which themselves have a high degree of uncertainty. While this magnifies the tenuous nature of these generalizations, it should stimulate comparative marketing to keep in close touch with these basic disciplines so that comparative marketing will develop along with these affiliated fields, and its tentative generalizations acquire a surer footing.

A Concept of a National Marketing System

Just a the major inputs of an individual firm may be considered as a trinity of physical assets, financial assets, and people, soothe most significant inputs of a national marketing system may be conceived of as geographic factors, economic elements, and human factors. The human factors are the sum total of the nation's characteristics with reference to vital statistics, education, cultural patterns, social structure and relation ships, ethnic configurations, psychological viewpoints, religious precepts political beliefs and governmental systems, etc. Naturally there is a large degree of mutual interaction among the geographic, economic, and human factors. This analysis of inputs to the national marketing system will, nevertheless, focus on these three categories since they are fairy well defined entities.

Geographic Factors

Geographic features which exert a major influence on an area's marketing system included land topography, the availability and location of water surfaces, soil fertility, climate, and mineral resources. Nations with large undeveloped areas of land tend to have highly concentrated marketing centers, such as Iran. The growth of long-range transportation and communications enables a country's marketing system to become more highly integrated, as currently observed in the Soviet Union and in Australia. The United States, with its complex network for transferring goods information, has largely overcome the physical barriers posed by mountain ranges and deserts. Great Britain, on the other hand, has hill rather closely integrated marketing system for several centuries, due to the small size, it high population density relatively well dispersed throughout the nation, and an absence of formidable geographic barriers.

Agricultural industrialization, often going hand in hand with traditional social patterns in rural areas, frequently drives multi-trades of people from the hinterlands to the urban centres, sometimes selling the population of the cities to enormous proportions within actively short periods. While industrial development has enabled metropolitan areas to absorb many newcomers in an adequate manner at certain periods, more frequently these recent arrivals have been crowded into deteriorating neighborhoods or into newly constructed slums, greatly directing the geographic patterns of marketing activities. Cities with a basic Latin culture have tended to reinforce the nuclear characteristics of their city centers, often because of the strategic locations of cathedrals and other major churches, of principal governmental buildings, and of residences of the elite. Newer industries and the mass of immigrants are likely to be dispersed to the cities' peripheries.

In addition to population growth, mobility of people among and within sets up pressures to which marketing systems, must respond. For trades the dispersion of Canada's population was considered a deterrent large-scale methods of distribution, but recent developments, along the modern tier have altered this situation, and Canada's marketing system is landing accordingly. Powerful centripetal economic and cultural facts are focusing many marketing operations (and even more of the decisions) on large business and political capitals, within individual nations as well as on a world-wide scale. Spread effects serve as a countervailing pressure reminding marketers of the necessity of catering to unique characteristics of each region, or even neighbourhood. On balance, though, areal differences in merchandise preferences within nations appear to be leveling off, even as they are among nations.

Economic Factors

Foreign trade and other aspects of international business are major forces shaping nations' marketing systems, sometimes directly by causing product standardization and more efficient means of assembly and/or distribution, and at other times more indirectly by the introduction of new ideas and methods. Since international business as a rule is concentrated in the hands of a more limited number of enterprises than domestic trade, each individual enterprise tends to wield considerable influence on the import and export of marketing ideas by means of foreign trade, and also through finance (including banking), and through direct foreign investments in manufacturing, in the distributive trades, and in service companies such as advertising agencies.

Shortages of goods, of skilled services, and of funds tend to restrict competition, and thus to dampen experimentation and innovation of marketing institutions and operations. The increased availability of merchandise experienced by a number of Western European countries since the end of the Second World War has spared the large-scale introductions of new marketing methods and institutions which, judging from earlier records, might have been repressed. National economic planning increasingly evident throughout the world, has also strongly shaped domestic marketing systems and operations.

The sparse settlement of many areas, their low levels of economic demand, and th scarcity of transportaton caused the introduction of market rings centuries ago in many pars of the world, and they are still functonign in mnay less highl yindustrialisedregions of Africa, Asia, and Latin America. The increased availability of goods, and consumers, ability to purchase them, resulted in the establishment of permanent sales outlets initially as stalls and workshops in market places and in bazaars and at a later period, in stores, display rooms, auction houses, and other facilities. Occasionally older forms of market organization have been adapted in more recent requirements, a most notable example being the developed of the contemporary shopping center essentially based upon the traditional market place and the bazaar.

Few elements of the economic infrastructure affect marketing as a recently as transportation, with the effects ranging from the shipment of agricultural products to points of processing and of consumption, to the transfer of goods from places of production to those of use, to the movement of sales personnel and of potential customers in order to expedite the sales transaction. Less highly industrialized regions frequently suffer from lack of a modern transportation system to support their marketing efforts, while many of the most highly industrialized regions—especially metropolitan areas—experience inadequacies because their transportation systems are unbalanced in terms of rolling stocks, permanent facilities (e.g., roads, airports, railroad package, distribution points), and time of use. The clogged industrial and commercial cores of some of the major cities of the world are prime examples Another element of the economic infrastructure of import to marketing is communication, which runs the gamut from sporadic messenger services in some remote corners of the earth, to the teletype systems tied into electronic data-processing systems in the most highly industrialized nations.

Of all the economic factors basic to marketing, none is so point as production; whether of raw materials, of finished products, or of other goods. Unquestionably marketing under certain circumstances has stimulated production, as was true after the entrance of Sears, Roebuck & Company into Mexico following the Second World War. But by and large marketing systems appear to take their major cues from a nation's production, and adjust to it accordingly, Small-scale agricultural units producing minute quantities of perishables at sporadic intervals must sell their output at high costs. Even when national productivity in agriculture, manufacturing, another industrial segments increases appreciably, it say be difficult to adjust marketing practices to the new conditions.

Poorer nations, that high ratio of individuals existing partially or wholly in a subsistence economy and otherwise not involved with a monetary economy (e.g., India), have little need for a highly developed, hyperactive marketing system. A nation's pattern of income distribution is the primary indicated inmost low-income nations; that is, a tiny elite group at the top, and myriads of very poor at the base. Even so, social, ethnic, psychological, and other cultural variations also play a role in these countries, although it is in the most affluent nations with a square-type pattern of income distribution that non income factors are much more significant as determinants of market segmentation.

Human Factors

A wide array of explanations has been offered for the origins of trade, managing from the ceremonial exchange of prestige goods (often of religious significance) to payment for services rendered. Ina number of civilizations widely separated geographically and in time, trade in prestige merchandise and over long distances and in large quantities has been considered a high-status occupation, whereas person-to-person dealings on small scale have been viewed as demeaning, perhaps because of a lack of understanding of the expenses needed to perform marketing functions and the fact that "huckstering" in the market place does require the seller to forego some personal dignity.

Trade has historically been a major vehicle for cultural transmissions from one area to another, but in recent decades the prevalence and the dispersion of this process have been greater than ever. Frequently specific ethic groups have played major roles in spreading trade concepts and practices to other regions, with notable contemporary examples including the Chinese in Southeast Asia, Levantines in West Africa and parts of Latin America, and East Indians in South Africa and East Africa. Although traders have often arrived in the wake of military conquest, in recent times merchants were more likely to be migrants in search of opportunities to earn better living. The pace with which larger manufacturers and retailers in the more highly industrialized nations, anxious to expand their potential markets, have been tempted to cross borders into other countries has been stepped up considerably since the end of World War II. And major retailers, no longer content merely to expose their customers to sporadic assortments of imported merchandise, have conducted major promotions of the wares of a single country or region, with many of these events exposing he clientele to more than the produce of foreign nations. Not all countries have welcomed foreign entries of people, produce, or idea can do some have actively opposed them.

Closed societies, best illustrated by the vanishing caste system of India, have long regulated distribution in accordance with traditional status levels in many lands, but essentially Western concepts of the open society are now making themselves felt throughout the world. As a result merchandise and services once limited to particular classes have become available on a broader social basis, and social restrictions and taboos are being lifted. The predisposition of people to accept change apparently is not necessarily related to their socio-political framework, however, since marked evidences of traditional-directed choices have been observed in the freest nations of the West (e.g., France, Great Britain, and Italy) While Iran, Until recently steeped in feudalism, has for centuries been noted for its willingness to accept new modes.

Religion has been intertwined with trade since the dawn of history, and has frequently been the dominant factor in the regulation of marketing transactions. Although it is rare for religion to function so prominently today, it still forms an important ethical base to guide buyer-seller relations, and it is at the root of many market customs. Colors associated with religious occasions may be used in various societies to pure sales or, on the other hand, their employment may be taboo. Other societal customs pertinent to marketing may once have had religious foundations, but the derivations have been lost. Nevertheless an acquaintance with them the often vital for the modern marketer.

An individual's age I an important factor not only as an influence on his purchases, but also on the readiness with which a marketing entrepreneur or executive accepts and applies new ideas. A nation's educational system molds future customers by helping develop their value judgments, their interests, and their general cultural and technological knowledge. In addition, the educational system is largely responsible for supplying personnel to the marketing system. Illiteracy poses many obstacles in the way of marketers, sometimes, causing them to substitute nonliterary means for more common forms of advertising and sales promotion. As distribution of many products becomes more international, pressures are created for advertising to serve many nations. Despite difficulties in the efforts to internationalize advertising, considerable progress has already been made. A society's achievement syndrome affects both will of consumers to work to acquire possessions and the wish of marketers to build and maintain successful enterprises. Value judgments concerning income rates, social status, and socio security may discourage individual enterprise, as may less rational factors—e.g., the Cargo Cultists of New Guinea. A group's ethical viewpoints may assist marketing practices, as was the case with the Chinese in Indonesia; or they may hinder them, as was true in the United States in the late 1950's and early 1960's following the revelation of several scandals implicating certain marketing organizations. Except in societies where women by tradition are sheltered in the home, they frequently form a considerable part of the work force in marketing, especially at the retail level. As a rule, however, as the marketing system becomes more complex, men assume more important roles, specially in raw materials and manufacturing, and particularly as entrepreneurs and at higher organizational echelons. Countering this move in the more highly developed economies is the growing power of women as purchase decision-makers within the family.

The pressures which political governments bring to bear on marketing systems and practices vary from tacit approval or disapproval, to outright support or rejection. Today most of the more highly industrialized, democratically oriented Capitalist nations attempt to balance individual property rights and the public welfare, while at the same time seeking to increase the overall standard of living. Government direction of and distance to marketing concentrates on legislation involving taxation, both personal and business; foreign trade; antitrust; pricing; advertising and sales promotion; and business hours. In addition, governments may offer a vide array of services to marketing, ranging from the standardization of services, to the sponsorship of trade fairs both at home and abroad.

Although overt political colonialism fostered by Western powers has considerably since the end of the Second World War, close economic ties are still widely maintained between the former ruling powers and their erstwhile colonies, France and its former colonies in West Africa being an instance. Moreover, a new kind of relationship with the semblance to colonialism has sprung up between the Communist nations. The socialization of economic activities—including marketing—has also become more pronounced during this period, not only in the Communist states but also in many "new" socialist-type states in Asia and Africa. Consumer cooperative have often been encouraged as a means (and sometimes as a guise) of expediting the socialization of marketing in the Communist and new socialist-type nations. The formation of common economic markets in several regions of the world has progressed at diverse rates, with political differences frequently forming the major barriers to closer integration. The continued growth of common markets would speed the transfer of concepts of marketing institutions and practices, and act as a strong propellant for the further internationalization of marketing.

The International Consumer

After many millions of years the number of international consumers on the earth reached one billion by about 1820. Then, 110 years later 1930), there were two billion of them. But, only 35 years later (1965), there wer ethree billion. Only 11 years from now (1977) theywill exceed four billion. I 1990 there will be over five billion. This century will close with the unbelievably vast population of six billion international consumers, with all the accompanying dangers, problems tragedies—and opportunities, too. Mankind's ability to and the way to make the benefit of the civilization we have so laboriously developed over millions of years available to these hordes will be the measure of these opportunities.

These projections are based on the medium population series of the United Nations. High and low projections were also made by the U.N. certain differing assumptions. The implications of these facts should be as challenging and as shocking to business leaders as to the U.N. and national leaders. They are the basis for the world's greatest problem—assuring peace and assuaging hunger and hopelessness. The revolution of expectations and the dreams of simple, easy solutions are outrunning the possibilities of satisfying hem. The high birth rate bestowed on humanity assure its survival has now become its greatest problem.

At mid-year 1963 the population of the world was estimated to be proximately 3,160,000,000 and is projected to the year 2000 as approximately 6,000,000,000. The distribution by continents of regions of these populations are shown below.

Comparative Populations 1963 and 2000 by Continents or Regions (In millions)

Continent or region	*Population 1963*	*Percent of Total*	*Population 2000*	*Percent of Total*
World Population	3,160	100	6,267	100
Africa	294	9.3	421	6.7
North America (excluding Mexico)	208	6.6	312	5.0
Latin America	231	7.3	592	9.4
Asia	1,748	55.3	3,966	63.3
Europe (including U.S.S.R.)	662	20.9	947	15.1
Australia, New Zealand, Melanesia, Polynesia and Micronesia)	16.8	0.5	2.9	0.5

Source: Provisional Report on World Population PROSPECTS As Assessed in 1963. Department of Economic and Social Affairs, United Nations.

Based on data from Statistical Yearbook 1964, United Nations and Provisional set on World Population prospects as Assessed in 1963. Department of Economic Social Affairs, United Nations.

Inmost cases the United Nations includes the U.S.S.R. in Europe but the comparative purposes the 1963 (mid year) estimate of Russian population was 225,000,00 and for U.S. population 189,375,000. At the time of this chapter U.S. population was approximately 195,000,000. Approximately 450,000000, or about 14% of present world population, in 20 countries with a relatively high standard of living. Thee are at present 120 countries. The U.S., with by far the highest standard of living, accounts for about 6.0% of world population and 7.0% of world area. However, it accounts for roughly 11.0% of world imports and 23% world exports; over 25.0% of steel production; about 55.0% of nor vehicles in use; a gross national product almost twice that of the European Common Market (Belgium, France, West Germany, Italy, Luxembourg and the Netherlands) and more than twice the per capita grass national product of the Common Market; and total consumer expenditures two and a half times those of the Common Market. Our per capita annual steel consumption is 1,190 pounds and is in sharp contrast to India (35lbs.; Indonesia (5 lbs.); Communist China (35 lbs.); Pakistan (17 Lbs.) Brazil (97 lbs.); Philippines (44 lbs.); South Vietnam (10 lbs.); U.S.S.R. (758 lbs.); Mexico (123 lbs.); and United Kingdom (811 lbs.)/

Of the present 120 countries those having populations of approximately 100 million or more are according to the most recent estimates available (in millions):

China	700
India	480
U.S.S.R. (Russia)	229
United States	195
Indonesia	105
Pakistan	103
Japan	98
Total for all countries	1,910

Of these countries, which account for almost two-thirds of the worlds population, China, India, Indonesia and Pakistan are technologically simple peasant societies with largely illiterate agrarian populations living mostly in scattered rural villages.

Approximately 80% of the population in rural and agricultural practices are so primitive that all these countries have chronic food deficiencies of ten reaching the famine stage in large areas. The Far East has slightly more than half the world's population produces little more than a fourth of the world's food. Maldistribution of available food is as chronic as the shortage. The 20% urban population and these countries is largely concentrated in a few very large cities.

Japan and the United states are highly developed, industrial nations. The U.S. has large agricultural surpluses and adequate sources of new raw materials. Russia (in Europe particularly) is developing her industrial economy rapidly, but erratically, and her agricultural problems have been yet been solved. At great social costs and through ruthless methods the steel output has been increased to the point where her tonnage output to actually exceeded ours for short periods of time. Consumer goods are inadequate in quantity, quality, variety, and distribution.

The only large areas of food surpluses left in the world are the United States, Canada and Australia. Even Latin America, with about 75% of world population, produces only about 6.5% of the world's food, coffee, largely exported, is about the only item in surplus.

The greatest need for the future I painfully and threateningly of "production explosion" in agriculture and industry greatly exceeding the scale of the "population explosion." If this and drastic population controls do not come soon, the Malthusian remedies—war, pestilence and famine—will operate on a vast scale to reduce the number of international consumers before they become even potential customers for anytime.

Misery and Markets

Markets are people with at least some disposable income. Good markets people with both disposable and discretionary purchasing power—and the desire to use them. Mot of the world's consumers have very little disposable purchasing power. With the exception of some 20 countries with relatively high standards of living there is precious little discretionary purchasing power. What there is in most other countries is restricted to a top layer or "class market." What we think of usually as the middle-classes, on which we place so much stress in our marketing, are very small in numbers and in proportion to the population. The mass-market, as e use that term, is nonexistent except for the most inexpensive based indispensable items. The American with his frame of reference and experience restricted to the economy of plenty of North American must turn an entire new scale of values in judging the international consumer and the markets of the world outside of Western Europe where his own standards partly apply.

About half the world's people already suffer from hunger and malnutrition and only about one sixth are well fed according to a study by the Food and Agriculture Organization (F.A.O.) of the United Nations. In most of the world, population growth continues to exceed production growth in both agriculture and industry. This is true of nearly all the underdeveloped countries, where, unfortunately, population is increasing the highest rates and in the largest numbers.

Approximately 255% of our North American diet is made up of animal products but only 17% in Europe and 3% in Asia. Our urban consumer about 5 pounds of food per day. The Indian consumer eats 1.23 pounds per day and about 85% of it is rice, deficient in proteins, fats and vitamins. The effects of diet are well illustrated in Japan—with a very high standard of living as compared to the rest of Asia. Changes in diet are World War II are said to have increased the height of Japanese sons almost two inches over that of their fathers.

Hungry and malnourished people do not make good markets. They can not work well, learn readily, resist disease or think of much beyond the next inadequate meal and the fuel, grass, sticks or cow dung, which to cook it. And, all radical ideologies use hunger, hopelessness against as their most effective weapons.

No country attains a dynamic and rapidly growing economy until approximately half its labour force has moved from agriculture to industry and business, thus providing a reasonable minimum of construction, communication, transportation and goods other than agricultural. Most countries have far to go before reaching even this limited stage of development necessary to provide the basic necessities beyond a subsistence level of existence. The industrial equivalent of present day China with its 700 million people for instance, is probably that of little Belgium or little Holland.

A few indications of comparative purchasing power and living standards should be of interest to the marketing man and convince him of the need for the best marketing research that can be done, usually under very trying circumstances.

From India with its 480 million consumers, the following is quoted from a report of the Perspective Planning Division of the Planning Commission:

"Poverty is. not confined to groups of unfortunates or to backward areas. It engulfs almost the entire population. The average per capita product is barely $80,000 per year. The consumption of the poorest 10% is as low as five cents a day and, notwithstanding the conspicuous consumption and the riches of the tiny minority at the top, the consumption of the richest 5% aggregates to no more than fifty cents a day."

Thee are only 10 to 12 million in India who constitute a market for American products, except those selling for a few cents.

India is threatened with widespread famine at the time this is written. To prevent this, or at least give substantial relief, the United states scheduled shipment for 1966 of the following: 10million tons of when 200 thousands tons of corn; 150 million pounds of vegetable oils million pounds of powered milk; and up to 700 thousand bales of cotton These are being sent under out P.L. 480 surplus disposal programme Canada is providing another million ton of wheat. France is the only other surplus country. Undoubtedly another two million tons of wheat will be needed to give adequate relief. The 1966 wheat crop of India is expect to be 12 million tons short of last year's crop.

In South Africa (the country) the urban "African" (Negro) buying power is relatively high. About 10% of these "Africans" are classed skilled and their earnings range roughly from $125 and $225 per month. The 255 who are classed as semi-skilled earn approximately $60 to $100 per month. The other 65%, classed as labourers and domestics usually less than $60 per month. With a family subsistence level estimate at about $75 per month there is considerable discretionary spending power for upper 35% particularly if more than one member of the family words.

In Yugoslavia in 1947 the per capital income was only $180 and 80% of the population were peasants. Now industry accounts for a over half the national income compared to 9% in 1939. The income is about four times that of 1947. Yugoslavia has already becomes semi-industrialized economy with 19,500,000 consumers, is still development rapidly, and is now attracting a surprising number of tourists.

Canada with a population approaching 20 million has a per capita income exceeding $2,200 (In constant 1957 Candian dollars). Its farm population has shrunk to 11% and is still decreasing rapidly, Its major industrial development has taken place since 1939. An as indication of the standard of living it has already attained—and in a surprisingly short time it reached the "take-off point"—the in a surprisingly short time it reached the "take-off point". Africa accounts for 20% of the world's land area; about 11% of world population; about 4% o the world's trade; and less than 2% of the Gross National;" Product of the world.

These three countries and an entire continent give a good idea of the large of potentialities afforded by international consumers in various parts of the world. Any comparison with our American market, excepting Canada, is disappointing.

This is all the more tragic because the industrial and agricultural techniques and machines aggressively developed over the last century and a half in Europe and the United states are available to them now. Capital from those and other industrialized countries is available to them now if only there were trained management to made effective use of its and narrow nationalism were not so rampant. Know-how, developed in our businesses and our universities, is available to them now and tomorrow, not a decade or a century in the future. An unbelievable wealth of potential electric power now runs wasted and unused into the oceans bordering these undeveloped and poverty stricken countries while millions yearn for the light, factories and goods which this water power could bring them if utilize. Each American workmen has more than 10 horsepower at his elbow to multiply his output of goods. Even adequate capital cannot quickly eliminate the handicaps of status quo and unstable government, traditional social attitudes, maldistribution of income, physical and regional isolation, cultural deprivation, lack of education, communal and religious tensions, class and caste differences and language and ethnic variations.

The world-wide craving for a better and more abundant way of life more and better food, better health, more education, has for the first time in history become a major and dominant force in international affairs, in relations between nations and in the United Nations, in vast intergovernmental aid and relief programmes, in newspapers, magazines, television and public discussion. The difficulty is: can we solve the problem before the world-wide craving and envy grow into aggressive impatience, then deteriorate into widespread violence?

In the meantime the world is the marketing man's oyster and the countries his oysters, but the number of oysters containing being pearls and few. Even the small peals are not plentiful and it takes good research to find any of them.

Exporting is not Enough

When you merely export goods to international consumer

you are only taking advantage of the markets others have built. That is not enough today with a world grown small for its teeming consumers and dangerous impatient of better living. Businessmen must help but markets as well as sell in them.

When sears, Roebuck and company established its store in Mexico city, and revolution in distribution and small industries resulted. The semiquated and moribund French department stores suffered shock commissions over Sears' aggressive methods—then found out they could do the same with better profits. Sears encouraged and assisted in the establishment of several relatively small manufacturers to supply Sears and other with goods. This was intended to cut imports to a minimum income employment and raise more consumers into the middle class.

Exporting is the process of selling domestic goods to foreign consumers. Exporting is the easiest way to enter global markets with little cost and risk. Exporting is particularly attractive to entrepreneurs who do not have capital for foreign investment or the expertise to set up international ventures. Entrepreneurs can choose to become direct exporters or indirect exporters. Direct exporters sell directly to overseas buyers. Direct exporting requires taking responsibility for selecting overseas markets, making contacts with foreign customers, arranging shipments and payments and handling necessary documents required to export.

Direct Exporting entering the international arena via indirect exporting has one primary difference from direct exporting i.e., exporter deals directly with the buyer in the foreign market. This difference is significant because it substantially increases the risk to the producer while providing the firm's management with complete control over the product until it reaches its ultimate destination. Direct exporting is much like selling in the domestic market in regard to channels of distribution. Essentially the same channels are used except that the transportation involves shipping abroad. If direct exporting is chosen, the entrepreneur has additional tasks to complete. In this case, arrangements must be made for proper packaging, shipping the product to the coast, getting if off the ship in the destination port and getting it to the ultimate customers.

Many products are not exportable Products which would not be exportable are those that are already produced in the target countries, those that are produced more cheaply abroad and those that encounter significant trade barriers. The nature of the products themselves determine the extent to which exporting could be successful. A small toy or a ball pen would require little training instructions or warranties. Little adaptation would be required. Small electrical gadgets could be readily exported to countries tat use the same electrical current that the originating country does. Specialty equipment may require extensive training of operators by the producing firm's personnel. Thus exporting becomes more complex.

Some questions must be addressed in determining whether a product is readily exportable or not. This needs considerable research. For example, determining whether the product really satisfy needs in foreign markets may require extensive market research. Attempting to export a product that will not operate to its fullest capacity in the foreign market is futile.

Nature of the countries should be gathered from Export Directories, Chambers of Commerce and government's Foreign Trade Department. A common mistake especially for the relatively new exporters, is to choose orders from a number of unrelated areas of the world, each of which may have different customs, cultures and uses for the product. The firm becomes so entangled to deal with various customers that none are dealt with well. It is better to being exporting to a particular region. One the product is successfully marketed in that region, then the firm should move to the next selected region.

It is proper that new exporters should start with countries that are as close as possible to the culture and language of the venture's home country. For Indian ventures, the first target should be Bangladesh, Nepal, Sri Lanka and Singapore. For US Ventures, the first target should be Canada. Direct exporting has the advantage of personal control by entrepreneurs, but they must understand foreign markets and have experience negotiating with foreign customers. The most important task is to select a distribution channel to reach the target customers. An entrepreneur's primary responsibility is to identify the best channel and then negotiate sales to foreign customers with that channel. There are three channels for direct exports, in addition, companies sell directly to end-users.

Foreign Agents: A foreign agent is any person or company legally entitled to import goods to an overseas location. Most foreign agents are foreign in the sense that they are citizens of the nation to which goods will be exported.

Distributors: A foreign distributor is a merchant or wholesaler who buys directly from the domestic exporters and resell products while providing all necessary support services overseas. The distributor is the customers, unlike an agent he is not representing someone else. Sales are made through direct contracts and the distributor is carefully selected by the exporter to handle sales exclusively in a distinct market. For example, Toyota maximizes its world distribution of automobiles through a system of distributors.

Foreign Retailers: An exporter can also sell directly to foreign retailers who resell through stores or direct marketing promotions. This approach will be attractive to entrepreneurs with unusually products. For selling directly to foreign retailers, exporters have to negotiating contracts, transporting products and arranging financial transactions.

Direct Sales to End Users: A sizable export business exists between domestic companies in USA such as Boeing sell aircraft directly to foreign-owned airlines. In the medical field, 200 US and Canadian companies well medical instruments and pharmaceuticals directly to independent foreign clinics. Doctors, hospitals and Government agencies.

Indirect Exporting: Entrepreneurs can simplify the export

process by indirect marketing through an expert intermediary. Entrepreneurs' responsibility will be minimized if someone else handle foreign negotiations and legal transactions. Several types of intermediaries are described below.

Commission Agents: Foreign trades are commission agents who act simply as middlemen to find outlets for exporters' products or to find products to meet import demands for their clients. They receive commission from one or both parties to be transaction. Commission agents must be registered traders licensed to transact business and they act as wholesale brokers. They find buyers and sellers, negotiate terms, handle transactions. In some countries agents are government departments.

Export management Companies: An export management company is a private business that contacts as manufacturer' representative for exporting. Most EMCs develop a reputation in a particular industry and do business in many different markets. The EMCs often present many companies at one. This practice is potentially dangerous to the exporter because the EMC could represent several competitors at the same time.

Export Trading Companies are private companies organized to facilitate trade and represent clients within a specialized field. Export trading companies are the major marketing channels for nearly 60% of all Japanese goods. Virtually every major Japanese and European company maintains ETCs. For example, Mitsi, Mitsubishi, Itoh are Japanese trading companies.

Export Decision: Deciding to become an exporter is similar to the pre-start-up planning process The process of business planning is the same. Aspiring exporters must determine the commercial feasibility of the product, do thorough market research, and obtain the necessary resources.

Importing: Entrepreneurs seeking to expand their businesses, can provide goods to customers in the home market by importing goods from foreign countries. Faced with a trade deficit the India Government is not eager to encourage import, but import is an inevitable fact of economic life.

Importing is the reverse of exporting with similar choices for distribution. Entrepreneurs can import directly from foreign companies, buy from agents or products or contract through trade commissions. Similar planning considerations also exist such as market research and organizing for the import market. There are legal restrictions, quotas and foreign exchange regulation affect these exporting.

One activity of importing that differs from exporting is sourcing products. Sourcing is the processes of finding products and contracting for their importation. This can be done in the following ways:

Direct sourcing is a purchasing process in which entrepreneurs contract, directly with foreign manufacturers. There are no intermediaries and goods are transported directly from the foreign company to the domestic point of sale.

Subcontracting: Many domestic importers contract overseas production, specifying the product to be made.

Indirect Sourcing: using intermediaries to source products or arrange for manufacturing is the most common practice. Indirect sourcing is accomplished through the same channels as indirect exporting; however, agents work on behalf of their import clients. Consequently they are commissioned to locate products and arranges contracts and for their efforts they receive a commission.

Other Methods of Sourcing: The most reliable method to source products is directly and the easiest method is to contract through broker. But there are other methods. One method is to attend trade shows. Most industry and professional associations hold regular trade shows. Another option is to advertise in trade journals and foreign newspapers.

International Ventures

Importing and exporting activities do not require overseas

investments: both activities can be conducted domestically. However, most companies involved in global business have some international presence. This may take the form of having an overseas branch office or may create a wholly owned foreign subsidiary. Let us see how entrepreneurs establish international ventures.

Licensing: Licensing is the process of contracting with foreign firms, granting them proprietary rights to use technology, copyrights, trademarks or specific products owned by domestic companies. Licensing is a simple way to expand business overseas because the foreign licensee assumes the risk and investment of ding business; the domestic licensor grants access to proprietary knowledge or technology in exchange for royalties.

Licensing arrangements include contracts to manufacture and market products, to conduct research and to provide services. Manufacturing is the most common form of licensing whereby an established product or technology gained a foothold overseas through a foreign company with necessary production and marketing capabilities.

Franchising: Franchising is a method of doing business by which a franchisee is granted the right to offer, sell or distribute goods or services under a system created by the franchisor. Basically franshising is a special form of licensing that involves rights to a business concept.

Joint Ventures: Entrepreneurs can pursue joint ventures with foreign companies. A joint venture is a shared ownership by two or more organizations in which the investors have an equity investment in a separate enterprise. Unlike a license or fanchise that seldom requires direct investments, the joint venture requires specific equity investments by all parts. The organizations are responsible for operational control and for profits and losses. They are separate legal entities of at least two organizations. Joint Ventures may be between two or more private companies or between companies and state-owned firms.

Joint Ventures have become the primary vehicle for foreign

investment in developing countries like India or China. In most cases, the foreign Government mandates a joint venture with at least 51% ownership held by one of its own organizations. This requirement gives the foreign power control and a majority voice in any dispute. The majority control will protect national interests.

There are many advantages of joint ventures. Labour costs in developing countries are extremely low and joint venture can take advantage of these low costs. Domestic material prices may be far lower than in the high-cost Western markets. Shipping is often subsidized by state agencies. Joint ventures my also enjoy 'tax-holidays'.

The combination of these factors can result in very low cost products. This is the method by which Korea and Taiwan expanded their economies by more than 300 p.c. in less than two decades and become cash-rich exporting nations.

Wholly Owned Foreign Operations: A joint venture I an enterprise that limit ownership and operational control but a wholly owned foreign operation is entirely owned and controlled by the parent company. There are two ways of setting up a wholly owned foreign operations. An Indian company can set up an oversea branch or it can acquire an existing overseas company as a subsidiary.

An overseas branch is a part of the parent company and simply an extension of domestic operations. A branch of Bombay-owned company located in New York is essentially the same as a branch located in Calcutta. Branch assets and liabilities are part of the domestic corporation. Profits or losses are part of the parent's finances and taxes are paid in the parent's country on total company profit. This arrangement will be advantageous if home-country taxes are lower than those overseas. Branch profits can be transferred home subject to certain terms and conditions.

Secondly, branch operations may start from scratch. They must be staffed, financed and managed like most new ventures. They must develop markets and often face competitive environments without a local track record. Unless the parent has an established reputation branch has to fight for a competitive position along with other local companies.

Foreign Subsidiary: A foreign subsidiary is a separate company organized under a foreign nation's legal code wit accountability district from the parent company. The subsidary has independent assets and liabilities and it is taxed by the host nation. This will be advantageous if the foreign tax rate isles than at home. Since the subsidiary is a separate legal entity, liability extends only to its operations not to the parent. A subsidary's earnings cannot be transferred home without paying home country taxes.

Establishing a subsidiary can also be expensive and complicated because a parent company either creates a subsidiary from scratch acquires an existing overseas company. In both cases, the parent must comply wit all existing host country laws. These will be advantageous in a country where the host Government is anxious to help new ventures by offering tax and financial incentives. However, there can be disadvantages in well-developed economies where Government. Discourage foreign investment.

Transactional Services: Services are less tangible than products, but most services can be taken overseas through similar methods as product based companies. The problem is how to define international services; they are called transactional services. This includes commercial banks, insurance companies or accounting services. Domestic bans do not export services in the sense of transporting tangible products but they set up branches or wholly owned operations.

Obeying legal consideration, services can go international following similar methods open manufacturers. The difference is that service enterprises must rely on skilled employees who are familiar about local conditions. Again, service marketing requires customized client assistance because clients have unique requirements influenced by cultures, social values, political and legal systems in each country. For an entrepreneur, thee differences mean that overseas services must be tailor-made for specific foreign markets.

Apart from this limitation, there are many opportunities for entrepreneurial services in foreign markets. Specifically, teachers are needed in African countries, engineers, medical doctors are needed in the Middle East, computer client its are needed in Singapore and Malayasia.

Environment of Business

Major environmental factors which the entrepreneur must consider before transplanting a domestic business into a foreign environment. These factors are:

Culture: Culture consists of values, beliefs, and attitudes shared by members of a society that collectively influence their behaviour. or example, in Japan women are seldom given promotion to important managerial posts, entrepreneurs in Japan will find that doing business is generally reserved for men. Hence a British or American women may find it difficult to do business in Japan. In Nigeria, payoffs are normal in business transactions, but such practices are illegal in India.

Political System: Political systems differ between countries. In India foreign trade is controlled by the Government. Most countries have trade quotas for both imports and exports. Changes in government can dramatically change policies.

Legal System: Legal systems affect taxation, licensing, bank lending, hiring practices etc. Contracting for sales, resource, distribution or investments is unique in every country. Foreign subsidiaries must be set up under domestic laws of foreign host nations.

Economic System: Economic differences influence all overseas decisions. In a foreign affluent country, foreign customers may be more affluent than domestic ones, product quality, packaging and methods of distribution will be different.

Before entering a trade agreement or establishing an overseas distribution office, the following critical questions must be answered.

There are many legal considerations that entrepreneurs must satisfy before going international. The entrepreneur has to take license, permit from the government otherwise he will not be allowed to enter into foreign trade.

Entrepreneurs must make sure that they can deliver cost-effective products or services in the overseas market. In most cases, there will be additional costs to exporting. Initially export prices are pushed up by higher costs, but when markets are opened in new high-volume areas, costs will spread over more item thereby reducing individual prices.

In underdeveloped countries, many people are willing to work at low wages but they lack education and skills, but qualified labour is not so cheap. Workers have to be trained extensively. Even then they may be unable to handle sophisticated machinery. Also local managers may be required, but it is difficult to get people with leadership skills.

Technical and Organizational Changes are needed. Products have to be redesigned to meet foreign customers' expectations. Technical changes are usually necessary to conform to skill levels of local employees. Sophisticated computers are difficult to use in developing countries where local language is not adaptable to standard software. Other organizing problems include reporting procedures that are unfamiliar, local prejudices among employees with different ethnic or religious backgrounds and work habits which conflict with modern Western nations of motivation and productivity.

There are many different channels of distribution ranging fro direct exporting to overseas brokerage. In addition to different channels, promotion methods (e.g., advertising or personal selling) must agree with local customs. Pricing will be controlled by law in some countries, and in others it may be unpredictable. In a country like Brazil where inflation has plagued the economy, prices can change every few hours thereby making market forecasts impossible.

Marketing is often complicated overseas through informal network of business contracts. Such habits can be frustrating to entrepreneurs who enter new markets expecting to complete as they do at home only to find that business do not occur. In countries where payoffs and bribes are common, a new venture may be boycotted until its managers offer payoffs to petty politicians.

Domestic lenders are unlikely to finance overseas assets or to risk money on foreign ventures. Hence overseas financing is essential. We see man us banks in India have offices here to serve their venture in India.

The constructive roles of capital and management and the inadequate indigenous supply of both are beginning to be recognized. Indian are getting a better look at how our capitalistic system operates, the opportunities it creates, and the resulting increase in the standard of living for all. It is quite obvious that everything businessmen say or do abroad has a favourable or unfavourable influence on employees, business associates and competitors, government officials and politicians, opinion leaders and rabble rousers, and all the rest of international consumers. Many times the reaction is neither the expected nor the rational one. Anti-foreignism or xenophobia—nationalism turned bitter—is widespread and unreasoned in most of the underdeveloped countries, and a grave handicap to cooperation in development. It is a form of militant traditionalism which resists change. As always the leading nation draws most of the criticism. Being the "good neighbour in every country where American businesses operate is the best way to slay the bogeyman of "capitalist Imperialism."

Heterogeneity is a Hex

Indonesia is 3,000 islands with about half its 105 million people living zone—Java. It is a very complex society in three layers:

1. Europeans, with their own social and economic organizations.
2. Foreign Orientals—mostly Chinese, Indians and Arabs—

each group retaining its own customers and social organization.

3. Javanese, mostly farmers, small traders and cottage industry workers with a very thin layer of the elite.

The Europeans formerly dominated heavy industries and plantations but recently they have been diverted of much of their property and power, The foreign Orientals dominate small industry, wholesaling and larger scale retailing.

Only about 8% of the country's gross domestic income is from manufacturing.

The Philippines are a country of 7,000 islands with only 4,000 of them armed and about 400 permanently inhabited by about 40 million consumers. About 19% of this country's gross domestic income is from manufacturing.

Yugoslavia, with a population of 19.5 million, is made up of six republics, five nationalities with three different languages written in two different scripts. It is three major religions, several national minorities and a wide range of regional cultures, customs and levels of economic development.

India, with its 480 million consumers, has 16 states, 14 basic languages, 102 distinct dialects and, until abolished or "ruthlessly integrated" in 1950 thee were 500 "princely states." Its rural population lives in approximately 550 thousand farm villages. It is a land of minorities with the following given official recognition:

Muslims	150,000,000
Christians	11,000,000
Sikhs	8,000,000
Parsees.	250,000
Anglo-Indians	50,000

Within the Hindu majority there also are the scheduled Castes and the Scheduled Tribes.

Fred J. Borch, "The Marketing Philosophy as a Way of Business Life," *Marketing Series* No. 99, American Management Association, 1957.

Ferrer, Robert, And Wales, Hugh, G. (eds). *Motvation and Market Behavoiur*, Homewood, Illinoois: Richard D. (rwin, Inc., 1958.

Festinger, L. A Theory of Cognitive Dissonaance, Stanford, Calif.: Stanford University Press, 1957.

George Katona, *Michigan Business Review*, July 161, pp. 17-20.

G. Charres Y. and Nicosia, Francesco M. "Uses of Sociology instudying ConsmptionBehaviour,*Journal of Marketing*, Vol. 28, No. 3 (July, 1964), pp. 51-54.

Gottman, J. "Megalopolis: The Urbanized Northeastern Seaboard of he U.S., "*Twentieth Century Fund Report*, New York: Macmillan Co., 1961.

Herman E. Koenig, "Theory of Modeling Socio-Economic Systems," mimeographed paper. Department of electrical Engineering, Michigan State University, p. 12.

James G. Drury, "Is Your Problem Overproduction—or Underproduction of Markets?" Printers' Ink, July 5, 1957, pp.19-22, 58.

J.L. Henderson, *The Order of Nature* (Cambridge, Mass: Harvard University Press, 1917), p. 172.

Jay W. Forrester, "Industrial Dynamics," Harvard Business Review, Vol. XXXVI, No. 4 (July-August, 1958), p. 52.

J.M. Clark, "Competition: Static Models and Dynamic Aspects," *American Economic Review*, Vol. XLV, No. 2, May 1955, p. 462.

Katona, George, "Rational Behaviour and Economic Behaviour," *Psychological Reveiw*, Vol. LX, No. 5 (September, 1953), pp. 307-18.

Katona, George, *The Powerful Consumer*. New York: McGraw-Hill Book Co., Inc., 1960.

Kelley, Eugene, J. *Marketing: Strategy and Functions*. Englewood Cliffs, N.J.: Prntice-Hall, Inc., 1965.

Kelley, Eugene J.: Lazo,Hector: Corbin, Arold:and Kahn, Edward. *Marketing Management: An Annotated Biblioraphy*, Chicago: american Mrketing Associiton, 1963.

Konrad Lorenz, *On Aggression* (New York: Harcourt, Brace & World, Inc., 1966), p. xi.

Krcoman, H.e., andHartley, E.L. "The Learning of Tastes," *Public Opinion Quarterly*, Vol XXIV, No. 4 (Winter, 1960), pp. 621-31.

Louis Finkelstein in Conference On The American Character, *Bulletin, Center For The Study of Democratic Institutions*, October, 1861, p. 6.

Malineau, Pierre, "Social Class and Spending Behaviour," *Journal of Marketing*, Vol. 23, No. 2 (October, 1958), pp. 121-30.

Michael Kraus, "The United States to 1865," The University of Michigan Press, Ann Harbor, Michigan, 1959.

M. Francesco, Consumer Decision Processes: Marketign and Advertising Implicaitons, Englewood Cliffs, New Jersey:Prentie-Hall, Inc., 1966.

M. George, L.F., "The Socio-Economic Status of cities and Suburbs," *American Sociological Review*, Vol. XXVIII, No. 1 (February, 1963),pp. 14-85.

Neal, James U. *Dimension of Consumer Behaviour*. New York: Appleton-Century-Crofts, 1965.

Nelson Foote, "he Anatomy of the Consumer," in Lincoln H. Clark, ed. *Consumer Behaviour, The Dynamics of Consumer Reaction*, New York University Press, pp. 21.24.

Nelson N. Foote, "The Image of the Consumer in the Year 2000," Proceedings, Thirty-Fifth Annual Boston Conference on distribution, 1963, pp. 13-18.

O.R. Young, "A Survey of General Systems Theory," *General Systems*, Vol. IX (1984), pp. 6-62.

Pitirim A. Sorokin, *The Crisis of Our Age*, New York, E.P. Dutton & Co., Inc., 1946, especially Chapter III.

Roger Girod, "Comment on Consumer Reaction to Innovation," In Lincoln H. Clark, ed. *Consumer Behavior, Research on Consumer Reactions*, Harper & Brothers, New York, 1958, p. 10.

Simonds, Rollin H.: Ball, Richard E.; and Kelley, Eugene J. Business Administration: PROBLEMS And Functions. Boston: Allyn and Bacon, Inc., 1962.

Stafford Beer, "What Has Cybernetics To Do With Operational Research?" *Operational Research Quarterly*, Vol. X, No. 1 (March, 1959), p. 3.

Tarpley, Lawrence X. "Marketign Resarch and the Behavioural Sciences," Business Topics, Vol. XIII, No. 1 (Winter, 1965), pp. 6-67.

Toynbee vs. Bernbach: As Advertising Morally Defensible?" *Yale Daily News*, Special Issue, 1963, p. 2.

Young, O.R. "A Survey of General Systems Theory," *General Systems* Vol. IX (1964, pp. 61-80.

William Lazer & Eugene . Kelley, "Editorial Postscript," *Managerial Marketing: Perspectives & Viewpoints* (rev. ed.; Hotnewood, III.: Richard D. Irwin, Inc., 1963), p. 683.

Wroe Alderson, *Dynamic Marketing Behavior* (Homewood, III.: Richard D. Irwin, Inc., 1965), chap.1.

W. Fckwardy, "The Challenge of Megalopolis," *Twentieth Century Fund Report*. New York: Macmillan Co., 1964.